THE
PRIVATE
ADAM

THE PRIVATE ADAM

⚬

BECOMING
A HERO
IN A
SELFISH AGE

SHMULEY BOTEACH

ReganBooks
An Imprint of HarperCollins*Publishers*

HarperCollins books may be purchased for educational, business, or sales promotional use. For information please write: Special Markets Department, HarperCollins Publishers Inc., 10 East 53rd Street, New York, NY 10022.

FIRST EDITION

Designed by Nancy Singer Olaguera

Printed on acid-free paper

Library of Congress Cataloging-in-Publication Data

Boteach, Shmuley.
    The private Adam : becoming a hero in a selfish age / Shmuley Boteach.
        p. cm.
    ISBN 0-06-039347-5
    1. Courage—Religious aspects—Judaism. 2. Bible. O. T. Pentateuch—Critism, interpretation, etc. I.Title

BJ1533.C8B58   2003
179'.6—dc21   2003041336

03 04 05 06 07 ❖/QW 10 9 8 7 6 5 4 3 2 1

To three biblical heroes who have made a great impact
on my life and shown me and my family
the utmost love and devotion

Ron Feiner
A father figure, counselor, and all 'round wise man

Cyril Stein
One of Anglo Jewry's most distinguished sons and
a man who inspired me to soldier on always
for the many years that I was Rabbi at Oxford

Nathan Gelber
A most refined gentleman, son of Holocaust survivors,
and one of my dearest confidants and soul-friends

☙❧

CONTENTS

❧

PART I

❧

The Princes Are in Peril

PART II

⤮

The Path to Biblical Heroism

I

❧

THE
PRINCES ARE
IN PERIL

1

୶ଈୢ

INTRODUCTION: WHAT'S WRONG WITH US?

America is in an unparalleled state of prosperity, but you can't tell by looking at her inhabitants.

We're living longer, healthier lives in the richest country in the world, and yet we're depressed, medicated, and divorced. It doesn't make sense. For all our material abundance and social progress, we don't seem to be very happy.

Something is clearly missing from our lives. What is it that we need but cannot get? What is this essential itch we just can't seem to scratch? What is the key that will finally unlock the secret to our happiness, since everything we have isn't enough?

It's clear that our needs go beyond the purely functional. Humans certainly do need shelter and food, but if a daily meal and a warm bed were all we needed, we'd be happier than we are. The German philosopher Georg Hegel was the first to point out that while animals will risk their lives for food, humans will risk their food and lives for recognition. For Hegel it was the thymotic urge, or the need to be recognized, that lies at the heart of human nature.

Everybody wants to be a somebody, Hegel said, and life consists of trying to attain that "somebody" status.

Victor Frankl, the Holocaust survivor who fathered the psychiatric school of logotherapy, put this urge in slightly different terms: he called it "the will to purpose." For Frankl, the most deep-seated human need is to find meaning and purpose in life. Depression and unhappiness, the bane of a healthy existence, result directly from a feeling of misdirection and purposelessness. My friend and colleague Rabbi Harold Kushner has simplified this idea further, writing in his recent book *Living a Life That Matters* that the most important thing to us in life is simply "to matter."

While I agree with all of this, I wish to take it further. These pages are written in the belief that every human's greatest wish is *to be a hero*. Every man, woman, and child's greatest desire is to end up a champion. Not just to have a bed and three squares a day, not just to be recognized, not just to have a purpose or to matter—but rather, all those things and more. And furthermore, I believe it can be every person's destiny to live a life of heroic greatness: to win glory by living courageously and with dignity, and by inspiring others to do the same. This, I believe, is our greatest ambition, and the key to discovering the joy we've lost.

Sadly, I believe that our ability to fulfill that ambition is blunted by our inability to grasp the true meaning of heroism. For many of us, aspiring to be a hero feels like an impossible dream. Heroism seems like something unattainable: a hero is a great general on a battlefield, a billionaire captain of industry, an NBA all-star shooting the winning basket in the closing seconds of the game, or a powerful politician with a fifty-car motorcade. We work hard at our ordinary jobs and go home to our ordinary families, all the while feeling unable to measure up to the heroic standard. So we have two choices: either we get depressed and settle for that life of ordinariness, or we dedicate our lives to accumulating the trappings of success in an attempt to make ourselves feel better. We find ourselves in a constant state of anxiety about our inadequacy, so we work frantically to earn the spoils of the victor, desperate to win approval and recognition and money—anything that will tell us that we're somebody.

So is it any wonder we're depressed? We're driven by insecurity, and so we place financial prosperity, recognition, and accomplishments at the top of our spiritual pantheon. But these things don't actually convince us that we're living valuable lives. There will always be someone richer and more famous than we are, and the chase only intensifies our insecurities. So we dedicate our off-hours to getting away from the terrible feeling that our lives are without meaning and medicate ourselves—with drugs and alcohol, television, frivolous sexual encounters, and pharmaceuticals like Prozac—to quash the pain.

We can't be happy living this way, with no peace at our center. To be sure, it's not easy to envision the alternative. I'm not advocating that we all retire to the mountaintops to contemplate our navels. We are absolutely meant to work toward success in our lives and to be passionately engaged by our chosen activities. But we must achieve a better balance between doing and being. A human being is meant to be like a hurricane, with turbulent winds on the outside but calm at the center. You can yell, you can build, you can conquer, but at your center you need to have peace. Today we live as inverted hurricanes. We are turbulent at our centers, always grating against ourselves, feeling inadequate, wanting to do more, and living with perpetual disappointment as a result. But on the periphery we're totally, scarily, numb.

What do we do with our own deep desire to be heroes? We live vicariously through our imagined heroes—our movie stars, pop icons, and presidents. We find the cable channel that gives us the best view of our chosen escape fantasy, and we give ourselves over to it, dropping out of the game. And because we have denied ourselves our deepest impulse, our desire to be a hero, we are miserably unhappy. We've misunderstood our destiny, so even if we're wildly successful, we never really fulfill our true inner potential, and we're tortured by regret.

Little do we realize that real heroism lies in a totally different realm, one that is completely within our reach and beckoning us to its threshold. We have to get back in touch with the real attributes of heroism. True heroism isn't about kicking ass and dropping names:

the one who dies with the biggest SUV isn't necessarily the winner. True heroism is a much greater challenge than that, and it delivers much greater rewards. True heroism is being good. It's living with dignity and doing everything within our power to help others live that way as well. It's doing the right thing just because it's the right thing to do. It's about the struggle to control, rather than be controlled by, our minds, our emotions, and our passions, and about the joy that comes when we conquer ourselves. Heroism is being respected and loved by the people in our lives who really matter—as opposed to the madding crowds who don't. It's about leaving our insecurities behind, rather than feeding them.

Throughout this book I turn often to the Bible and to the teachings of Judaism through the ages in exploring this question of heroism—not just because I'm a rabbi (though of course that comes in handy), but because I believe the Bible gives us the best model of true heroism. As we'll see, it is there in the stories of great biblical figures, from Abraham and Moses to less-celebrated heroes like Jacob and Joseph. It is there in the wisdom of the great Jewish thinkers, from the ancient rabbis to their modern-day descendants. And if there's one place where this vision of heroism is crystallized, it may be in the Bible's very first pages, in the twin visions of the creation of Adam that have fascinated me for years: the Public Adam, whom God commands to take dominion over the earth, and the Private Adam, whom he charges with cultivating and nurturing it. We live, I would venture, in the world of the Public Adam, a world that has elevated traits like ambition, self-promotion, competition, and aggression to the most hallowed place in our value system. What I would call upon us all to do is to take a step back, to revisit those values, and to bring them back into balance with the more selfless and generous spirit embodied by the Private Adam—the first biblical hero.

❧

I consider myself especially well suited to write this book, but in truth it isn't my rabbinical training, or the counseling work I've done, that best qualifies me for the job.

In fact, my real inspiration comes from something that might be considered one of my flaws: I have lived my entire life with a phenomenal fear of mediocrity. To combat this feeling, I have borrowed thousands of hours from my family to sit in front of a keyboard writing books. I have traveled around the globe to meet with world leaders and other people of influence in an effort to bring their diverse voices to a wider audience by arranging lectures and promoting vigorous debate.

I realize now that all those efforts were overwhelmingly directed to one purpose: to rise and become a hero. Like everyone, I wanted to feel that I had value and would be recognized for it. To be sure, an altruistic desire to do good was a big part of the equation. But so was my ego. Though I have undergone a soul-searching journey in recent years, my dream has not changed. I still want to be special. What has changed, however, is that I have begun to understand what real heroism is—and how we might begin to create it within our own lives.

2

❦

CLASSICAL SHMULEY
VERSUS
BIBLICAL SHMULEY

The real hero is always a hero by mistake; he dreams of being an honest coward like everybody else.

— Umberto Eco, *Travels in Hyper Reality*

The story of the making of this book is in itself a lesson about two different kinds of heroism.

I have always dreamed of making Judaism more of a mainstream religion. I wanted Jewish ideas about God to be as commonplace as Christian ones, Jewish spirituality and mysticism to be as well known as New Age spirituality and Buddhism, and Jewish institutions like the Sabbath to be as widespread as Christmas.

So when the *Times* of London and the College of Preachers opened their "Preacher of the Year" competition to non-Christian clergy for the first time in 1998, I jumped at the opportunity to participate. After moving forward in the written submission category and then preaching a live sermon in front of judges, I found myself the first-ever Jewish finalist in the competition's history. The six finalists, whittled down from an original four hundred applicants, were to meet in a live "Preach-Off" at Methodist Central Hall in

London. The accompanying ceremony was heavily laden with Christian content, and I was going to be the odd man out. If I was to win, I had to make a big splash—not only with great oratory, but with memorable content as well.

I thought long and hard about what the subject matter should be, eventually writing and discarding about ten sermons. It wasn't until late one night in my Oxford study that I was hit with the proverbial lightning bolt of inspiration. It came from pondering the inherent contradiction of my participation in these "religious Olympics." There could be no question: I was entering the competition because I wanted to be a hero. I wanted to be recognized as an outstanding preacher of religious ideas. I was seeking greatness. I wanted to tower head and shoulders above my Jewish colleagues *and* my Christian ones. But I felt conflicted—wasn't that aspiration the very antithesis of the religious message, a message I have devoted my life to exploring and promoting? That you should be humble and meek before God? That God is *el numero uno,* and that humans can only, *at best,* be secondary to Him? Wasn't my ambition, not to mention the competition itself, an abomination before God?

But I have never believed that ambition is a bad thing. Without the ambition to be a great orator, I would have watched my congregants drift into a deep coma, and my message would have been lost. So was there anything really wrong with my ambition to serve God to the best of my abilities?

I realized that I had struggled with versions of this question my entire life. So I looked back into the Bible for answers, with this idea of the place where ambition and heroism intersect as a starting point.

I have long felt that the Bible—which is read as a book of law, a book of ancient history, a chronicle of early man's relationship with God, or the inspiration behind prophecy—is first and foremost a book about heroes. It is the religious counterpart to the *Iliad* and the *Odyssey.* Moses is the counterpart to Homer; Abraham and David are the heroic equivalents of Achilles and Odysseus. The Bible inspires all of us to emulate their behavior; in other words, it is a primer for greatness.

It is a book filled with heroic gestures, but they are not ordinary acts of heroism. Unlike Achilles and Odysseus, the biblical hero is a reluctant hero, one whose primary purpose is righteousness rather than recognition, virtue rather than victory, moral courage rather than mortal conquest. The heroes I find in the Bible aren't men in armor wielding big swords, vanquishing enemies and collecting tribute. The Bible is not an accounting of the battles the Children of Israel fought, or the commonwealth they established in a land flowing with milk and honey, or the wealth they attained.

The Israelites were a nomadic people, wandering through the desert eating manna wafers, traveling from one nondescript location in the desert to another. Our forefathers were simple shepherds living in tents; their lot was one of torment and suffering rather than triumph and riches. Abraham watched his wife being abducted by Pharaoh. Isaac escaped sacrifice. Jacob was pursued by his own brother and watched his sons try to kill his favorite among them. As a people, the Israelites were enslaved to an Egyptian tyrant, whose paranoia about an uprising led him to cast all the male babies into the Nile. Read in a modern light, the Bible could be dismissed as the story of a few poor refugees and some escaped slaves who were traveling to a distant land they knew nothing about.

And yet there is much joy in this book; these downtrodden nomads are surrounded by glory. Their acts of heroism are small gestures of loving-kindness, a readiness to sacrifice without recognition, and a desire to serve God, even when such acts made them deeply unpopular. The biblical heroes consistently choose influence over power, exhibit forgiveness rather than ferocity, and show gratitude and indebtedness rather than a fear of dependence. All their actions are characterized by deep humility. They never hesitate to choose a relationship over material gain, or recognition, or even wounded pride. They dedicate their lives to conferring dignity on others and move out of the spotlight in order to shine light on those around them and the causes they serve. They withdraw from battle, shedding blood only when it is necessary. They practice restraint and passivity and maintain their authenticity. Most of all, they battle the very same demons—jealousy, envy, egotism, greed—that we battle with, and they win. They are ambitious, but their ambition is to be good, and that is the key to their heroism.

I discovered the biblical hero for the first time when I was preparing for my Bar Mitzvah, the celebration of maturity for a boy of thirteen. Like every young man since the dawn of time, I wished to distinguish myself. I was eager to make my mark, eager to achieve greatness. Subjected to television and movies, like any American youth, I had visions of grandeur. I wanted to be one of those special people the world remembers. I wanted to be like the great heroic figures of history: Caesar crossing the Rubicon, Hannibal atop an elephant traversing the icy Alps, Alexander the Great on a fiery steed cutting swathes through Darius's hordes.

But when I began to study the Bible, I discovered radically different heroes in its pages. I read of Abraham, the great knight of faith, whose heroism lay in discovering an unseeable God in the starlit heavens of Mesopotamia. Instead of rejoicing at the fall of the evil inhabitants of Sodom and Gomorrah, Abraham had the audacity to spar with God to save them. He is the Bible's first great hero. And yet he is depicted as a man who sits at the crossroads, looking to find a wayfarer to whom he can offer food and water. At thirteen, I was confused. What kind of heroism was this? Abraham, praised for being a water carrier? It seemed so lackluster compared to the great warriors of history. Was this not weakness rather than heroism? The Gentiles had great generals to inspire them, and what did the Jews have? Caterers!

The Bible passage I read at my Bar Mitzvah was about Jacob, my namesake. And what kind of hero was he, fleeing the wrath of his brother Esau? Of course, the key to understanding his heroism lies in the prayer he offered as he fled his brother's vengeance. He prayed for neither wealth nor glory. Rather, he prayed that God would accompany him, like an intimate friend, throughout the ordeal he was about to encounter. "If God shall be with me and keep me blameless on the path which I now embark upon, then I will make the Lord my God." Jacob prayed not for gold or silver, but for righteousness before God. He prayed not for gold-trimmed togas or the purple garb of imperial rule, but for the nakedness of innocence.

As I prepared for this rite of passage into manhood, I recognized that this brand of heroism, which was completely unlike anything I had found at the movies or in comics, was the real thing. These acts of heroism, I noticed immediately, were relational. This was a heroism based not on attention-grabbing but on soul-searching, not on victory but on values. The biblical heroes who were emerging from the pages of the Bible lived by a higher code: service, humility, forgiveness, morality, and spirituality. The classical heroes, in contrast, were straw men. Propped up by their desperate attempts to be noticed, they achieved ephemeral greatness. What I found in the biblical heroes were men anchored in the eternity of a spiritual foundation, rather than mired in the quicksand of material goals. Even at a young age, I intuitively realized that these people were heroic in areas that had real significance for me. I believed, as I do today, that the victories of the biblical heroes are the ones of real importance.

As I sat in my study at Oxford, remembering my first reaction to these stories as a child, I realized that in any duel with swords or spears, these biblical heroes would probably have been easily defeated by the superheroes of the classical literature. And yet, in the battle of history, they have somehow won out. The influence of the Bible, with its stories of more wholesome heroes, by far outweighs that of any other heroic literature. The classical heroes of old, the conquerors, and the generals are today dismissed as common thugs and bullies. Their names are Julius Caesar, Genghis Khan, Napoleon, Josef Stalin, Adolf Hitler, and Saddam Hussein. Their visions of greatness depends on the subjugation of their fellow man and the forceful incorporation of other countries into their own dominions. Their definitions of greatness are based on strength, their strength on power, and their power on ruthlessness. But these men have not had lasting success. Their empires have crumbled: many of them were killed or exiled by their trusted associates, and many are now considered among the most despicable men who ever walked the earth.

On the other hand, men of peace and perseverance like Nelson Mandela, Mahatma Gandhi, and Elie Wiesel have won the Nobel Peace Prize and continue to guide and inspire us. They are our heroes, even though they had no empires, no subjects, no riches. How did these "weaklings" triumph?

Devoting my Preach-Off sermon to exploring that question, I titled it: "The Classical and the Biblical Hero."

I didn't know how soon my theory would be tested. In the contest, the sermon easily won on content. But in delivery I lost ten points for speaking too fast and ended up the first runner-up, losing by two points. I won't lie. I was devastated to lose the competition. But in many ways, coming in second was truly in keeping with the content of my speech. As my friend Dan Williams, who was covering the competition for a newspaper, told me, "Today you became a biblical hero. You were gracious in defeat, you saluted the victor as deserving, and you focused on a godly message even if you received no recognition for doing so." That day I had the opportunity to put my own words into action—to be granted a taste of biblical heroism. And though I came back the following year and actually won the competition, I still see the previous year as a greater victory.

That day I also realized that I had been engaged in the wrong struggle all along. Like many of us, I am often consumed by a nagging fear of valuelessness—and almost everything I do is targeted toward assuaging the pain of that fear, by working toward the kind of achievements that will force the world to take me seriously. I am constantly striving just to prove myself worthy of love! It's a feeling that many of us struggle with every day.

Although I had dedicated much of my personal and professional life to the biblical goal of helping others, I knew I had also craved recognition for these efforts—a more classical goal. Yes, I had often done good deeds, but because I wanted to be recognized for them. Yes, I had tried to do the right thing, but often because I was looking for a reward. I was pursuing heroism, but the wrong kind. And the spoils of classical heroism hadn't alleviated the pain of my insecurity the way I'd thought they would—they'd made it worse!

Real, lasting change comes only with self-awareness. Before we can regain our connection with the heroism the Bible describes for us, it is important that we come to grips with the qualities—good and bad, attractive and destructive—of the classical hero.

3

⤷⧓⤶

THE WRONG KIND
OF HERO

I particularly like your American ones, where the hero is invariably amorous, alcoholic, and practically indestructible.
—Richard Leofric Jackson, president of Interpol, 1961

A little girl dreams of growing up to walk down a red carpet
toward a limousine, while flashbulbs pop in her eyes. A little boy
dreams of growing up to play guitar in front of a million screaming
fans who will throw their underwear at him onstage.

It's clear that we're wasting our time chasing the wrong model of
heroism. But where did this model come from?

Sometime around the eighth century B.C., in the Greek settle-
ment of Ionia in Asia Minor, a blind storyteller named Homer
invented the myth of the classical hero. Homer thought long and
hard about the men and women who surrounded him. He saw their
vulnerability, their mortality, their insignificance. They had brittle
bodies and even more brittle egos. Look around your own world, at
people bickering and assaulting one another over a few coins. Think
of the petty gossip about a neighbor that gets us through the grind
of the everyday, the jealousy and envy we feel upon hearing of
another's good fortune. Whenever we hear of another health scare,

another tragedy, another terminal diagnosis, we're reminded that we're ultimately nothing but fodder for worms. Where's the dignity in that? You don't have to be Homer to imagine the pathetic state of humanity that led to the invention of the classical hero.

Homer's ingenious response to our ordinariness was to dream up a superhero, a man who was extraordinary—the classical hero. Finally, here was someone who leads a life of epic proportions and cosmic-level struggles, and who is immortalized by his compatriots, living on in their memories, triumphing over death itself! His stories, the *Iliad* and the *Odyssey*, are epics filled with warfare and long, arduous journeys, beautiful women and impossible tasks.

All the classical heroes who have followed the Homeric heroes, from Hercules in ancient times down to Michael Jordan in our own, have five characteristics:

1. The strength of the classical hero is a physical strength; his heroic actions are physical actions. He's not a thinker, he's a doer. He takes what he wants, by force if he has to. Force can mean his hands, or his force of personality.

2. The classical hero subdues and triumphs over his fellow man. He is a champion in the field of battle, whether that battle is a military campaign, a sporting competition, a beauty pageant, or the markets of Wall Street. He must be number one and will not tolerate humiliation or subordination of any kind.

3. He receives the adulation of the adoring masses and lives entirely in the public eye, always playing to the crowds.

4. He receives great material rewards, usually in the form of riches and women. The quality and quantity of his possessions—the size and splendor of his houses, the endless variety of the beautiful women he's photographed with, the number of zeroes in his bonus checks—are essential to his demonstration of supremacy.

5. His memory is immortalized in some great tale. His heroics are never discreet, private gestures but must be broadcast, not only to his peers but in a historical document that will outlast him.

Sounds very impressive, right? But look closer and you'll see that each of the characteristics of the classical hero is born of insecurity. The classical hero's strength is physical, not an inner emotional or spiritual strength. He's insatiably competitive because he relies on his ability to dominate others to determine his own self-worth. He spends his lifetime in search of glory, and without the constant reassurance of an adoring public, he ceases to exist. He's out to collect rewards—he's not strong enough or sure enough to do the right thing simply because it is right. And he always ensures that his memory is immortalized—he needs to know that his reach will extend beyond the grave, which is another way of saying that even while alive, he's consumed with death.

The classical hero believes that he was born without any intrinsic value, and so he spends his entire life working to prove that the opposite is true. Unable to live with his own sense of worthlessness, he spends a lifetime in search of glory, playing to the crowds, hoping to earn their respect and homage. In so doing, he compounds his wretchedness and becomes a prisoner to the crowds—the mob holds the keys to his sense of accomplishment. He serves at their beck and call, and he will do anything to make them happy.

This is why so many of these "heroes" end up sad and pathetic at the end of their lives. A woman may go into film in the hope of becoming a respected actress, like Meryl Streep, but the moment the producers tell her that her movie's gross will increase if she meets the public's hunger for bared flesh, she will betray her conscience, indulge her insecurities, and take off her top. A man may go into politics because he wants to make a difference, but the moment he realizes that a vicious attack campaign against his opponent will boost his poll numbers, he'll sell out in an effort to get more votes. In their bid for what they believe to be heroism, people will betray everything they hold dear for the opportunity of the moment. But attention spans are short, and when the public has lost interest in them, they'll be discarded with nothing to show for their efforts.

Far from achieving glory, the classical hero is actually a mediocrity. For all his conquests, Napoleon remained a permanent prisoner of the European people. In his mind, unless they became his vassals, he was a worthless nonentity. This belief gave them a tremendous power over him—in a way, he was literally nothing without them. The same was true of Hitler's obsession with the Jews, which would have been pathetic had it not also been so terribly tragic. His obsession demonstrated the power the Jews held over him.

The classical hero is born and lives in darkness, a darkness so thick that no amount of illumination—no klieg lights, no flashbulbs—can ever penetrate it. Rather than rescue us from our pathetic state, Homer reinforced it by inventing the classical hero. Rather than pulling us out of the grave, Homer sealed the coffin. And he condemned us to a life of loneliness as well.

By definition, the classical hero is isolated and alienated. He can think only in terms of winning and losing. He sees the world as a pie, and since there is only so much glory, so much money, and so much happiness to go around, he will do whatever he has to do in order to secure the biggest piece. By cutting his fellow man out, by defeating him in business or on the battlefield, he thinks he will have all that much more for himself. In a broader sense, of course, this competitive mindset is at the very heart of Western capitalism. While I am not making an argument in favor of communism or socialism, it is important to note that nothing seems to motivate us like the desire to be at the top of the heap. How dysfunctional is that? Everything in our culture—from the Olympics to political "races" to the selection of a valedictorian to sibling rivalry—is predicated on the idea that people perform best when they are in a struggle against one another.

The classical hero must defeat his opponent; otherwise, how will he know that he has won? But nothing can completely satisfy the hero's insatiable appetite. He has a black hole at the center of his being, and no amount of money or women or accolades will fill that hole. He uses external objects to offset his own internal feelings of worthlessness. He drops names at parties because his own name is insignificant. He wears designer labels because he feels himself to be anonymous. Since his accomplishments only exacerbate his insecurity, it's impossible for him to find peace. And yet this type of heroism has remained our model from classical Greece until this very day.

When we strive for heroism in our own lives by viciously under-

cutting our opponents, backstabbing the competition, and sacrificing time with our families and friends in order to accrue the most
stuff, we're working toward the wrong thing—the wrong kind of
heroism. We can never be happy if we continue to dedicate our lives
to classical heroism. Contrary to Homer's intention, the idea of the
classical hero has not brought us comfort. It has given us a series of
impossible standards and empty goals to chase. It nips at our heels
with every hurdle we jump, pushing us harder and faster toward the
vanishing point, when real life is happening in the stands. Why do
you think that the most famous and the wealthiest among us always
seem to be the most unhappy and dysfunctional? Is it not an axiom
of modern living that our most illustrious celebrities are invariably
the ones miserably addicted to drugs, incapable of sustaining relationships, and suffering from deep depression?

We know, in our heart of hearts, that something is badly askew.
Ask anyone who their heroes are, and chances are good that they'll
spout something predictable about Martin Luther King Jr. and
Gandhi. That's all well and good, but what are they doing in their
own lives to emulate such people? In fact, it's hard to find an American who can tell you much about either King or Gandhi, past
hunger strikes and the "I have a dream" speech. Unfortunately, most
Americans seem to know a lot more about Robert De Niro's films
and Kobe Bryant's career stats than about the Salt March.

We know we should aspire to something greater. We have a fantasy of ourselves as better people. But the people we're emulating in
our lives are celebrities. They're our models of greatness. We want to
be powerful; we want to be better than the next guy, and we want
him to know it. We want recognition for our achievements and the
financial and material rewards—money, enormous apartments, trophy wives, sports cars—that inevitably accompany that recognition.
We want to be popular and famous, to get the prettiest girl or the
most popular guy. And our children are learning to want this too.
Even my daughters, raised in an Orthodox Jewish home with limited access to popular culture, often say they want to be actresses
when they grow up (to which I respond, "Over my dead body"—
unless they cut me in as their managers).

That the world today turns to the Hollywood celebrity as the archetypal hero is a tragedy of epic proportions. The world's obsession with celebrity culture has gone from a casual pastime to a form of worship. Gone are the days when humans would bend their knees to stone or prostrate themselves before the celestial host. No, our modern idols have moved from the carved totems of the ancient world to the perfectly sculpted bodies of actors and rock idols. Rather than pray to the heavenly stars, we bow before our movie stars. Rather than talk of the beauty of God's creation, we talk about the magnificence of Hollywood's creations. Rather than talk about how we can connect with God, we talk about who Julia Roberts is connecting with. Rather than contemplate the mysteries of the universe, we seek to uncover the enigma of Marlon Brando.

That people today are more interested in talking about J. Lo than God is a given. God's popularity has seriously declined in modern times. But what's truly astonishing is that most people have a greater interest in the lives of their favorite celebrities than in their *own* lives. A wife would rather read about what Madonna wore at her concert than hear how her husband fared at the office. Teenagers would rather ponder a boy band's new album than their own academic record. Celebrity culture is all-consuming and has become a dangerous and unhealthy obsession. Go to the home pages of any of the leading news websites, and the first thing you'll see posted, well before the update on the most recent violence in the Middle East, are updates on the warring record labels out to sign the diva of the minute and the latest on the celeb divorce de jour.

Like many of you reading this, I had always prided myself on being above celebrity gossip. While those around me read *Us Weekly* and *People,* I read *Time* and *Newsweek.* I tried to study the Bible, read history and biographies, write essays on relationships, and generally keep my TV-watching, moviegoing, and magazine-reading to a minimum. But I eventually learned that for all my supposed aloofness I could become just as obsessed with celebrity idolatry as anyone else. It started with an idea I had: that working with celebrities might be a beneficial way to go about advancing a wholesome message to the world. After all, they have the microphone. They are the heroes of the youth, not the rabbis or philosophers. If you can't beat 'em, join 'em. What harm could be done by floating these ideas through the mouthpieces of the superstars who found them exciting?

And so, in the year 2000, I joined with Michael Jackson to launch Heal the Kids, a one-year initiative designed to reprioritize neglected children in the lives of their parents. From the moment Jackson's involvement became known, the interviews I did about the organization would nearly all revolve around questions about what Michael's Neverland Valley ranch looked like, or what brand of clothing he bought for his kids. Taken off guard, I tried to preserve the hope that in time we would be able to focus on more substantive inquiries, but I have since learned that you cannot promote God through individuals who in the popular imagination have come, wittingly or unwittingly, to *supplant* God. You cannot inspire people to act heroically through an inherently self-interested medium.

The message will always be less important than, and subordinated to, the cult of the celebrity. The light of the idea will always be drowned out in the glow of the star. After a while, I realized that it's the personality that becomes the message. Elie Wiesel, long a true hero of mine, once told me in a discussion of the popular culture: "Shmuley, you don't want to believe in an us-and-them mentality. You want to believe that God's message can be channeled through any medium. But in time you will discover that the celebrity culture is antithetical to that message." He was right.

Celebrity isn't the same thing as heroism. Humankind's highest mission is to return God to the epicenter of human life, rather than allowing Him to be supplanted by the human personality. It's our highest duty to acknowledge God as the ultimate hero—to personify, to the best of our ability, His own heroic actions. We do this by preserving our own dignity and using our light to illuminate the dignity of others, by being responsible members of a spiritual community, devoted spouses and parents, and good citizens of our world. That message will always be subverted as long as we allow ourselves to live vicariously through our favorite celebs.

Let me make one point: I'm not at all arguing against the principle of worshiping heroes. I have spent my life looking up to, and being inspired by, great men and women. Indeed, this entire book is a call to us all to rise and become heroes, following the path of men and women in the Bible and outside of those pages. But only with time have I come to see that a true hero is someone animated by an inner light, not by a pathetic search for the spotlight. True heroes are the men and women who have subordinated their egos to a higher ideal, who have placed God and humanity at their core, and who seek to highlight a spiritual message rather than just boost their ratings. It is fine to follow in the footsteps of the Lubavitcher Rebbe, Eleanor Roosevelt, the Pope, Billy Graham, Nelson Mandela, or Martin Luther King Jr., because the lives of these people are not arrows pointing to themselves, but vectors pointing to the heavens and to their fellow man.

I've spent time with a handful of celebrities, and I can't deny that I enjoyed the limelight. But having realized that all false gods are formed of tin rather than gold, I now wish to dance to a more heavenly tune and have my heart beat to a more eternal rhythm. I wish to be a hero of the spirit rather than a villain of the ego.

This book is written in the belief that the true heroes around us—and within us—are already there, just waiting to be recognized. I believe that the everyday unsung acts that mark the fabric of a dignified human life are what make a hero. And I would urge us all to open our eyes to this kind of heroism, and to let it inspire us to its heights—not just because it is more accessible than the history-making brand of heroism, but because it is far greater. And in the process of living heroically, struggling and defeating the prison of our ego and the incarceration of our selfish agenda, we may—finally—find authenticity and a real sense of self.

4

THE RISE OF THE BIBLICAL HERO

> Even in the darkest of times, we have the right to expect some illumination, and that such illumination may come less from theories and concepts than from the uncertain, flickering, and often weak light that some men and women, in their lives and work, will kindle under almost all circumstances and shed over the time-span that was given them on earth.
>
> —Hannah Arendt

On September 11, 2001, as everyone knows, New York's two tallest buildings were felled by a terrorist attack. When the dust cleared, a new world was visible, and towering over it were again two giant pillars: the figures of New York's policemen and firemen. Sometimes the greatest light emerges from the deepest darkness. Carrying his dusty and soiled fire coat, dragging his weary bones back to the scene of the disaster, wiping the sweat from his blackened brow beneath his battered fire helmet, this new brand of real-life hero dominated the New York skyline.

Prior to September 11, America was a society that focused its attention almost entirely on the famous and rich. We devoured the gossip columns for each morsel of news about Nicole Kidman's latest beau, and we stared, fixated, at HBO for the latest installment in the Carrie Bradshaw soap opera. We worshiped the movie star, adulated the rock star, and lionized the millionaire. These were our all-American heroes. They had initiative, they were entrepreneurial, they vanquished the competition. We closed our eyes and imagined ourselves as them. Awed by their cliffside houses and their glittering, star-studded parties, we looked at our own everyday spouses and felt the shame of ordinariness. We wished for a life more like the ones we were watching on *Entertainment Tonight.* It did not matter how many divorces the average Hollywood movie star had been through, how many illegal drugs he might have abused, or how many abandoned children he'd sired. We followed an ever-changing cast of heroes in and out of rehab, in and out of custody battles, in and out of bed.

But that day in September all this changed. Amid the rubble and the smoke emerged a new breed of hero, celebrated not for his mimicry in front of a movie camera, or her shapeliness in a bikini, or his ability to throw a ball through a hoop. As we stared with sadness, shock, and anger at the devastation caused by the brute terrorists, we began to admire a group of men and women near the bottom of the earning ladder but at the pinnacle of the heroic summit. Our collective consciousness became focused on those who helped others: the firefighter, wracked with grief but firm with resolve; the doctors, nurses, and paramedics who came from all over the city to stand outside St. Vincent's Hospital, waiting to help the wounded who never came.

In the midst of all this true heroism, the deeds of movie stars and athletes seemed so, well, unimportant. Who really cared if someone stepped out in a Versace dress, or if someone's batting average had improved over the last week? Those were negligible accomplishments compared to the heroism of those who were walking through the valley of the shadow of death so that they might bring a soul or two back to the land of the living. Miraculously, in the weeks following the World Trade Center disaster, the gossip columnists cut their columns—aware that the nation was at last transfixed by those who were actually doing something worthwhile.

Most amazingly of all, these new heroes were nameless. They strived not for recognition but for service. In so doing, they bypassed all five characteristics of the classical hero. Contrast the traditional, classical, insecurity-based definition of the hero in the previous chapter with this different definition of heroism. The firemen's strength was of the spirit rather than physical, although they labored mightily and at great risk to themselves. They raised up rather than subdued their fellow man. They received no adulation from the masses, as most remained unknown by name. They received no financial or romantic rewards for their pains. Unlike the cowardly terrorists who perpetrated the act, they were promised no women in heaven, or virgins in paradise, for their pains.

On the contrary, it was the fiendish terrorists who fit the bill of the classical heroes. It was they who used cunning and brute strength to destroy the lives of their fellow man in return for a promise of seventy heavenly virgins apiece for their troubles. Likewise, their memories are immortalized among their fanatical compatriots.

It's no surprise that the heroes of 9/11 didn't fit the classical definition. Plug figures like Martin Luther King Jr. or Gandhi into the definition of the classical hero at the beginning of the last chapter, and you'll see how surely they too fail the test. Both Gandhi's and King's strengths lay in their irrepressible strength of spirit, not in any physical or warlike might. Both subscribed to a policy of complete nonviolence, even to the point of refusing to fight back when their own physical safety was jeopardized, so they certainly didn't overpower their fellow man. They sought to uplift all of humanity instead. They were adored by the masses, certainly, but only by the lowest and most disenfranchised citizens of their respective countries. The rewards Martin Luther King received for his efforts on behalf of humanity were a preacher's salary and a bullet in the neck. Choosing influence over power, he never held public office. While the memories of King and Gandhi are certainly immortalized, their motive was never to write their place in history. Whatever fame they achieved was merely a by-product of their devotion to their respective causes. Like Abraham Lincoln or Robert Kennedy—or Moses—

neither of them lived to see true victory in their causes or the triumph of their ideals. Although Gandhi saw India achieve independence before he died, the two months prior to his death were steeped in violence, bloodshed, and anger as a result of partitioning.

Does their apparent lack of success mean that Gandhi and King weren't heroes? Not if we accept the definition of heroism demonstrated in the Bible, where Jacob wrestles with a mysterious, angelic foe. This untested novice in warfare, weak and unarmed, somehow defeats his superior antagonist. But Jacob's supreme moment of heroism doesn't involve subduing the enemy, but rather forgiving him and allowing him to go free. What is he doing? Is he crazy? Allowing his opponent to escape opens Jacob up to the possibility of further attack. Yet, as Rabbi Joseph Soloveitchik notes, faced with the opportunity to destroy his opponent for good, Jacob decides instead to rise up and become a hero. His heroism is manifest in his ability to overcome his animal instincts to vanquish the enemy and to exercise instead his godly capacity for mercy. He retreats in forgiveness rather than advance in triumph. Imagine that!

Or consider the image of Moses, the great lawgiver. A man with no legions, Moses is armed only with the word of God who, moved by faith and fired by the passion of fighting injustice, brings Egypt—the world's greatest empire—to its knees. Moses proves the power of the word to defeat the sword. Moses, who climbs mountains and speaks to God face to face, is described in the Bible in the only phrase relating directly to his person—as the most humble man who walked the earth.

When God saves the Jews from Egypt and brings them to the foot of Sinai to be His chosen people, they build a Golden Calf. God demands their total annihilation, promising to make Moses into the father of a great nation, like Romulus or George Washington. But Moses will have none of it. Desperate for clemency, he offers the ultimate sacrifice—self-destruction, oblivion, and anonymity—to save the Israelite nation. "And now, if you will not forgive their sin, blot me out, I pray you, from the book that you have written" (Exodus 32:32). What Moses means is: "Purge me from the Bible, remove my name from the history books. Let it never be known that I ever walked the earth. Save the people instead." Moses offers to withdraw from the spotlight, to do the right thing because it is right, to serve the interests of humanity at great personal sacrifice, even though the sacrifice will never be recorded and no one will ever know. What a gesture! There is the biblical hero at his best, rising above questions of ego gratification so that others may shine.

In this context, the actions of Elie Wiesel, Martin Luther King Jr., and Mohandas Gandhi have a greater heroic import. Where the classical hero advances to defeat his enemy in battle, the biblical hero retreats from conflict with his fellow man. Whereas the classical hero battles monsters and dragons, the biblical hero battles his own inner demons. Whereas the classical hero seeks to become a god, the biblical hero teaches all men to know the one true God. The Knights of the Round Table are born for adventure, but the biblical knight of faith is born for service. Whereas the classical hero conquers hundreds of women, the biblical hero is true to one great woman. The classical hero is remembered as an immortal, but the biblical hero is remembered for his morals. Whereas the classical hero is wrapped in splendor and garbed in glory, the biblical hero is naked and innocent before God.

What September 11 ushered in was a return to the biblical hero—a man or woman who operates out of spiritual greatness as opposed to personal insecurity. Maybe eventually our kids will take down the posters of Justin Timberlake and replace them with images of Dan Walsh from Fire Company 5, Ladder 4, on Long Island—or with photographs of their dad, who comes home early every night to help them with their math homework. Then, maybe, with an image of true greatness before them, they will stand a fighting chance of becoming great men and women themselves.

5

❦

THE LONG SHORT WAY

Show me a hero and I will write you a tragedy.
—F. Scott Fitzgerald, *Notebooks* (1945)

The pursuit of happiness is listed in the Declaration of Independence as one of our inalienable rights, and Americans really should be happy. Recession or no recession, our country is enjoying an age of unsurpassed prosperity. We have more money than ever before. Colleges produce graduates who can make $100,000 a year right out of school. We have tons of disposable income to spend on our computers, sports cars, Palm Pilots, Prada handbags, and beachfront homes.

And yet, despite all this success, all this accumulation, we aren't happy. We don't feel good about ourselves, so instead of enjoying the fruits of our labors, we indulge in an orgy of self-help books and luxury spas and gurus, until the journey becomes an excuse for never reaching the destination.

Where did it all go so horribly wrong? We have achieved our dreams only to discover that they're indistinguishable from our nightmares. We have few or no sustaining emotional supports. We are deeply alienated from those who are most dear to us. We work ourselves to the bone only to discover that our careers are fundamentally unsatisfying. We see our children idolizing the shallow men and women of the big screen and scarcely appreciating all that we try to do for them. We think back to our childhoods but can barely remember our own parents. We're bullied at school, and when we get older, we're bullied in the office. We make love to our spouses and think about other people. We watch our spouses having affairs with strangers, then moving out and marrying them. We come home to empty apartments and use our televisions for company. How did we work so hard to reap so little? Is this really a life, or are we all ghosts?

I believe that what we are witnessing today is the final tragedy of the classical hero. In our age, he has reached his apogee. America, with its free society, provides the opportunity. Everyone is free to run his own business, live in a big house, and drive a fancy car. We can wear designer clothes. Young men can hunt young women and get as much instant gratification as they want with scarcely a commitment. We have even invented erection pills we can pop to keep the whole process going.

But it has all begun to unravel. The destroyer of the great dream is insatiability. The land of opportunity makes the pursuit of material prosperity easy—anyone can become "a somebody." But whatever ingredients we put into the mix, the taste is still bad. How can you be a somebody when you always feel like a nobody? How can you feel like you've arrived when you're always looking over your shoulder to see who's catching up and ahead to see who's gone farther?

Look at celebrities. They're the greatest suckers out there. Having your own *E! True Hollywood Story* doesn't mean that the public loves the real you. Those ticket-holders don't actually know you. They don't recognize your unique light. They love your celebrity persona. They love what you do, right until you stop doing it or someone else comes along who does it better. Then you're stranded high and dry, no longer surrounded by those who adored you. Feeling good about yourself because you're a celebrity is like feeling good about yourself because someone married you for your money. There's nothing real about it.

Classical heroism is a losing proposition. Rather than master insecurity, the classical hero is left insecure and unhappy from indulging insecurity's every whim. This is why the vast majority of superstars are reclusive. They begin life trying to get noticed, then live out their days behind sunglasses and concrete walls to ensure that they are not. They start their professional lives wanting to draw people's attention to their talent, but in doing so they grant those people the ability to determine their worth. If millions of people buy their albums or watch their movies, they're important. If the public doesn't bite, they become nothing. After a while, these celebrities wake up and realize that they've made themselves prisoners of the public, and they begin to detest their jailers. And this sense of contempt for the public only increases when they discover just how fickle and disloyal the public can be.

I read once that Donald Trump, one of the richest Americans, gives an inflated estimate of his net worth to *Forbes* magazine every year. He gives them a number, and they go through his holdings themselves, and invariably the number they come up with is some fraction of the one he supplied. It's still an enormous number, but it's not the one he gives them. Every time I think of that, I begin to pity him. This man is not just in the big leagues, but in the really big leagues—and he's endangering his dignity to impress anonymous *Forbes* readers like me? It's a travesty. But can we honestly say that we're different?

Self-esteem is a term we hear a lot, but in truth there's very little that you can do without it. In the Book of Numbers, there's a story about losing your freedom to low self-esteem. Moses sent twelve spies into the Promised Land to see if it truly was flowing with milk and honey. Was it as rich and beautiful as they had heard? The spies returned a short time later. Ten of them were filled with doom and gloom—the land was indeed beautiful, but there were giants there who would prevent them from ever occupying the land themselves. They said, "We were in our own sight as grasshoppers, and so we must have appeared to them." Despite the testimony of Caleb and Joshua, two spies who were sure that the giants could be overcome, the Israelite people withdrew and wandered forty more years. They lost the thing they wanted most because they were nothing more than bugs in their own eyes—how could they expect to conquer anything?

Classical heroism always erodes our self-esteem, because the classical hero's achievements are built on quicksand. He has money, cars, women, houses, but because there's no rock to stand on, all the success he accrues just gets sucked into the bog. When his looks go, or his pitching arm, he has no real relationships or true self-esteem to fall back on, and then he falls apart. Classical heroism can't sustain us because it's not real.

Young athletes are often advised to stay with their education and finish college so that they will have something to fall back on when their athletic career has run its course. The classical hero is like the athlete who has ignored this advice. He puts all his eggs in one basket, surrounding himself with fans and worshipers and allowing them to determine his value. When the people who say you're something turn their backs, it makes you feel like you're nothing. How many times have we seen this? The has-been child star turned junkie? The dot-com entrepreneur who had it all and spent it? The aging actress who mutilates herself through repeated plastic surgery?

These actions are the death throes of the classical hero. No wonder these "heroes" eventually strike out against those around them. When you threaten their success, it's their very life you're threatening. There's nothing else. There's no substance behind the life-size wax model. They don't have the tools to transform their lives.

There's a story told by the rabbis about a traveler who came to a crossroads and asked a small child sitting there which way led to Jerusalem. The boy pointed one way and said, "That's the long short way. The other way is the short long way." The traveler, of course, took the short long way. That road led immediately to the walls of the city, but there was no gate there and no way in. The walls were impenetrable, and he wasted valuable time trying to dig his way in, to no avail. Defeated and dirty, he came back to the crossroads and took the other path instead. It was slightly more circuitous—you might say scenic—but it led him right to the city's gates and inside.

Classical heroism is the short long way. It may promise immediate glory, but a flame-out almost always follows. The classical hero self-destructs: he's destined to be shot down in a blaze of glory. Julius Caesar is the quintessential example. He created the calendar that we use to this very day, and the structure of the empire that he created lasted four hundred years. He defeated the Gauls, was revered by the masses, was declared a god, accrued enormous wealth, dated Cleopatra—the whole classical package. But the structure of his life was an inverted pyramid based on competition, and when the people dedicated themselves to beating him at his own game, they toppled him easily.

When you live by the sword, you die by the sword. Pursued by his own inner demons, haunted by his feelings of helplessness, unable to escape his insecurities, in agony over his feeling of anonymity, the classical hero finds that his triumph is necessarily brief and fleeting. His success isn't the kind that leads to greatness. It has no longevity. And I believe this is why we're in such desperate straits right now.

We *are* in desperate straits, by the way. Like Tony Soprano, the classical hero is spending all his spare time on the psychiatrist's couch. Yes, these people have conquered, but they have no inner peace. We don't live in an age when the average citizen has to work in the mills or the mines and struggle to feed his family on a starvation wage. No, today the average depressed person is someone who has everything he could hope for. The most successful people in the world, the ones living in the largest mansions in the Hollywood Hills, have personal lives that are in shambles. More people take antidepressants today than ever before—25 percent of this country is being treated for clinical depression. The National Association of School Nurses estimates that three million children take Ritalin— our kids have to be drugged in order to be up to the job of childhood!

Americans are less likely to marry, and more likely to get a divorce, than ever before. Sixty-seven percent of all American marriages since 1990 have ended in divorce, according to Dr. David Buss of the University of Texas at Austin. I counsel young people about relationships and am appalled to realize that young women and men believe that falling in love and building a family with another person is an impossible fantasy, the stuff of fairy tales, instead of a reasonable expectation. Our children are strangers to us, and the average age of the first use of recreational drugs is getting lower and lower every year.

When we refer to the United States as the greatest nation on earth, we justly praise its financial prosperity, democratic principles, and freedom. Its emotional health is another matter. The material prosperity of America has not translated into emotional prosperity, and vast riches are no guarantee of stability. Our collusion in the disintegration of our collective emotional health is the only thing I can see that could cause this country's destruction. If we're not happy here, in this Garden of Eden called America, then where *will* we be happy? If we're not happy now, in an era of the greatest political freedom, then when *will* we be happy? Why is there so much unhappiness amid all this abundance and prosperity? Why is it that success cannot bring happiness?

The answer is simple: when we have no real meaning in our lives, we have no intrinsic happiness. The only way we can achieve a fleeting glimpse of happiness or relaxation is to escape our own lives. We live in an age of escapism. The biggest, most successful industry in the world today is the entertainment industry, because it gives people a chance to lose themselves in something else. Sheer financial success is not enough, because it does little to address our inner dissatisfaction. And when life becomes meaningless, we seek shallow and cheap alternatives to meaning.

If we are the successes we think we are, and if our lives are fulfilling the way we intended them to be, then why do we spend most of our leisure time escaping from them? Why do studies show that friends left together at a dinner table will commonly turn the conversation to movies within the first seven minutes?

What is happening today is the collective downfall of the classical hero. We can no longer deny that the heroism we've chosen isn't working. There is something gnawing away at our center that creates this vast void where our souls should be. The way of the classical hero can make us successful, but it cannot make us happy. If we make a deal with darkness, we're going to live in darkness. Our model of greatness, the classical hero, runs fundamentally counter to our nature, and to what we really want to be. We're at war with ourselves. We choose to live lives motivated by fear instead of strength. We won't get better until our inner and outer desires are integrated and working in harmony.

Look at the greatest classical heroes of the ages. Isn't it clear that those men chose their success over life? And where did it get them? They were powerful, yes. But they were also paranoid. They had great riches, yes, but in most cases without love. They lived their lives in prison. Whose life would you voluntarily choose to live? Caesar, dead in the prime of his life at the hand of a trusted friend? Napoleon, who died alone and in exile on a rock in the middle of nowhere? Hitler, whose very name, sixty years after his death, is worse than the worst curse word you could summon? Richard Nixon, whose brilliant foreign policy successes were all undermined by his enemies lists and his excessive paranoia?

In the end, goodness always triumphs. It triumphs because it's real, because it's true, because it's authentic, because it feels good and right. But the secret of success is to combine goodness with maturity—the ability to delay gratification and search for more sublime rewards. The biblical hero ends up with the true victory. The ancient rabbis of the Talmud said, "Who is wise? One who always sees the consequences of his actions." The biblical hero takes the long, but ultimately, shorter way.

6

⁂

DIGNITY:
THE SECRET LIGHT
OF THE HERO

Dignity consists not in possessing honors, but in the consciousness that we deserve them.

—Aristotle

What's the fundamental difference between the classical and the biblical hero? What is it about the path of the biblical hero that can make us happy—and why will classical heroism always make us miserable?

The one attribute that every biblical hero shares is a deep consciousness of his or her higher, godly nature. This is their dignity. We speak of humans having been created in the image of God, and dignity is the very light that God casts on us. Dignity is the thing that separates us from the animals. Animals don't have self-consciousness. They take no pride in their achievements. They don't create. They don't have complex emotions. They cannot feel embarrassment. Human beings can, and this is what makes us special.

When you are truly in touch with your own dignity, you understand that you don't have to *do* anything to be worthy of love. You are born worthy, possessed of infinite value. Your unique gift is evidence aplenty that you are unique and worthy of affection. You don't have to get into Harvard, sell a million units, or become homecoming queen. In fact, you *can't* make God love you more. You can even lead a more righteous life, and that will not cause you to draw closer to God than you already are. It is the fact that we are created in God's image that makes us unique. To be sure, God wants what's best for us, and achievement feeds our soul's need to be productive and creative. But success will never make us more valuable in God's eyes, just as ignoring God will never diminish His affection for us either.

This, then, is the secret of the biblical hero and the key to our liberation as individuals. The biblical hero is free to give his life to something higher, because he doesn't have to use it to convince himself and everyone else that he's worth something. He believes that he was made in God's image and has value as a result. When you are distinguished only by earning or by doing and your sense of self-worth is determined by an ever-growing mound of possessions, then you live by one great law: *don't stop doing*. As the psychologist Warren Farrel has written, we become human *doings* rather than human *beings*. We are all desperately treading water, afraid that we'll sink and drown if we stop. Our dignity is our natural buoyancy—the knowledge that we'll be fine if we stop thrashing around and let ourselves just *be*. Dignity is the recognition of our God-given ability just to float.

For many of us, the cloak of dignity lies buried at the bottom of our mental and emotional closets. We never think, "How can I acquire more dignity?" even though on a subliminal level this question is our biggest motivation in life. We think, "How can I earn more money?" or, "How can I get that big promotion?" or, "How can I win the upcoming election?" or, "How can I get Jessica to marry me?" In fact, the desire to enhance our dignity lies behind each of those questions. The underlying motivation behind all human actions is the question, "How can I be special?"

But you can't acquire more dignity. You can become more aware of it, and you can certainly compromise it, but you can't accrue more, and you can't lose it permanently. It's like intelligence. You can certainly exercise your intelligence by training your mind and gaining more knowledge, but you don't actually get smarter. So the spoils of classical heroism—the beach house, the corporate takeover, the Armani suit, the engagement ring—won't make you happy because they do nothing to enhance your dignity.

In America, where many in society make the mistake of basing things on externals, we have the unfortunate habit of confusing dignity with status. The two are not the same. A janitor may have dignity but no status, while a successful entrepreneur may have status without dignity. Anytime your dignity is dependent on something outside of yourself, you're in trouble. The celebrity culture is pathological precisely because it robs people of their dignity by reducing them to a number. The classical hero lives by the numbers: his time at the finish line, the number of promotional dollars behind his latest project, the Nasdaq, the Nielsen ratings, the commission check. His dignity, his intrinsic value, can be put on a scale and quantified. Even if the status quotient ranks high, however, the determination process is intrinsically demeaning.

In my lectures I often pose this question to the audience: "Who here thinks they're just plain ordinary? Which one of you thinks that there is nothing about you that distinguishes you, that your being could easily be swallowed up by the other six billion people on this planet? Who here thinks that they are nothing more than average, that there is nothing about them that would make them irreplaceable?"

I have asked this question to halls of thousands of people around the world, and no one has ever raised his or her hand in agreement. Chances are, most of the people in those rooms *are* ordinary. Most of them aren't going to find a cure for cancer, or win the Nobel Peace Prize, or accept the Oscar for best actor. And yet all of these people believe that they are special, different from every other person sitting in that hall or inhabiting Planet Earth. And they're right.

The most deep-seated of all human needs is the need to be special and to have our uniqueness corroborated. We long for something that will rescue us from the throes of anonymity. We hover over an abyss of sameness, feeling undistinguished and ordinary and by turns motivated and paralyzed by Hegel's thymotic urge—the will to be recognized. If we didn't feel we were special and unique, we would have no reason to get out of bed in the morning. And yet so often we forget that we need to be recognized, not by the masses, but by the people in our lives who really matter—and by ourselves.

All of us have a special gift that we can give to the world that no one else has. That is what it means to be created in the image of God. God is the one and only—there is nothing else like Him. He is irreplaceable, just as we feel instinctively each of us are. Humans are like a garden. Everything that grows out into the world, whether a flower or a vegetable, adds something different—a smell, a color, a texture, nutrition—and together the elements are beautiful. But each is unique, rooted in its own soil, traditions, and history.

When we recognize our unique gift, we get back in touch with our dignity. When we have an understanding of the unique, one-of-a-kind contribution we're making to the garden, we gain perspective on our own worth. We don't have to become something, because we weren't born a nothing. What a liberating concept!

Imagine how much good we could do if we weren't always out there trying to prove our own worth to ourselves and others! If, on our dates, we didn't try so hard—to impress him, to make her laugh, to say the right thing, to talk her into bed—we might actually have the chance to fall in love. Just as "life is what happens to you while you're making other plans," love is what happens when you stop evaluating the person you're dating and quit trying to impress them. If, in our workplaces, we stopped competing with the cubicle next to us and started focusing on the best way to use our own skills and talents and gifts, we might actually create something we're proud of.

When we're in touch with our real gifts, the internal light that all of us are born with, we can get off the treadmill once and for all. When we recognize that inner light, we don't need the light bounced off our diamonds and shiny new cars and penthouses.

Sometimes our gifts don't appear to be gifts at all, and they may be more hindrance than help in certain situations. Winston Churchill was incredibly stubborn, for instance, and for most of his life this trait made him unpopular with many of his colleagues. But it also enabled him to stand strong against Hitler, even when the whole world was capitulating. The same trait that had driven everybody crazy was the gift that allowed him to say, "I'm here and I'm not moving. We'll fight them on the beaches." History has made it clear that his ability to hold fast was a true gift.

Lyndon Johnson was raised in tremendous poverty, which led to his phenomenal insecurity, and in turn to some very terrible behavior. But his roots in poverty and unique life experience gave him tremendous empathy, and his anger about his early years fueled the imagination and stamina he needed, against fierce opposition, to enact sweeping civil rights laws. Ultimately, it led to his vision of a Great Society.

From major figures to everyday people like us, it's often the case that we discover our unique gifts through just these kinds of trials. I was scarred by my parents' divorce as a child, but I like to think that my early life experience of a fractured family has contributed to my passion for and devotion to true love, relationships, and marriages— my own and those of others.

Unfortunately, when we're out of touch with our unique gifts, we often seek external confirmation of our value. Instead of helping, our quest for those externals puts us in situations where we compromise our dignity instead of enhancing it. Sadly, most human beings become aware of their own majesty and grandeur only when it is taken away from them. Having dignity is like having a heart: you become aware of it only when it begins to malfunction. Its absence establishes its existence.

And yet the Western world today seems bent on robbing people of their dignity. I believe that this crime is being committed so subtly and insidiously that most of us fail to even recognize that it is happening. We applaud and honor people on the other side of the world, like Nelson Mandela, who will fight to the death to restore dignity to their people. Why aren't we more vigilant about it at home? Most of us don't understand that our own culture is fleecing us of our basic humanity and replacing it with something tackier and cheaper.

When Bill Clinton answered the question, "Boxers or briefs?" he diminished the dignity of the office of the presidency and replaced it with a flashier, tackier, and cheaper imitation—celebrity. Instead of listening to his inner light and staying true to himself, Clinton allowed his insecurities to drive him to answer the question. Do you think he'd have answered that question if it had been asked at a press conference outside the G8 Summit? Do you think he'd have answered it if he'd been flanked by Jacques Chirac, Jean Chrétien, and Tony Blair? In different circumstances, he would have known that the question was below his dignity, but he was so insecure about himself and so eager to please, to be popular, to show the MTV crowd that he was hip, that he compromised himself.

I don't seek to pass judgment on our former president. Indeed, I have been guilty of the same thing. When I wrote *Kosher Sex,* I was invited on to many shows that I should have rejected. I loved doing Roseanne Barr's talk show and became a regular guest, but one time I found myself seated in front of a group of scantily clad dancers as I discussed my book. It was no place for a rabbi, but I was more concerned with promoting the book than with my own dignity. Then there was the photographer from the *Times* of London who asked me to sit (fully clad, I hasten to add) in a bed in our home to take a picture to promote the book. He placed a glass of champagne in my hand. I raised it into the air, but my dignity fell to the floor. There was nothing inherently controversial about the photo. But it looked and felt wrong, and I went stupidly along. My own insecurity got the better of me. I was so busy hoping that the attention of the national media would lend me dignity through popularity that I never allowed myself to realize that I was sacrificing my inner dignity.

If I had recognized that I wasn't worthless to begin with, then I would have been able to concentrate on my message instead of stooping to any measures to get the press to notice me.

God gave us a safety mechanism to protect our dignity. Just as a smoke detector sounds when there is a fire smoldering in the house, our shame detector goes off whenever our dignity is melting away. It should be noted that losing our dignity is not the same thing as humiliation. Humiliation has to do with our status in other people's eyes and occurs when someone embarrasses us rather than when we shame ourselves. Other people can humiliate us, but only we can shame ourselves, because shame has to do with compromising our own dignity. Being humiliated by someone doesn't necessarily mean that we've been shamed. Only we can do that to ourselves by betraying our values and ethics or by behaving in an inappropriate or compromising manner. We know when we're doing this, and we must start listening to that alarm.

The essence of being a celebrity is being noticed for the sake of being noticed. Celebrity is not about being a better person or finding ways to help other people. Celebrities often do no more than prostitute themselves so that people will know who they are. Celebrity is so exalted that people have started doing anything to get attention. We confuse celebrity with dignity, to the point that when a producer says to a group of women, "Who's willing to fight to marry a man you've known less than an hour just because he has a few bucks? Who wants to be exposed on national television as a money-grubbing gold-digger?" he has to work hard to winnow the contestants down to a mere hundred.

Unfortunately, celebrity replaces people's inner light with an outer spotlight. People start chasing the spotlight, hoping that it will give them meaning, and they end up snuffing out the light of their soul, their dignity, the godly spark that separates them from the animals. We are not the first generation of individuals who have wished to be famous, but we are the first generation who are prepared to lose our dignity in the quest for celebrity.

The classical hero has always been an unrealistic, insecurity-based model, but there is one significant difference between the classical hero of the ancient world and the classical hero of our own day. The classical hero in the ancient world did whatever he did—conquering worlds, taking prisoners, marrying the most beautiful woman—in his search for dignity and glory. His ultimate quest was for dignity, and his other achievements were by-products. Even recently, celebrity was garnered for doing something: for undertaking a great feat, like Charles Lindbergh's solo flight, or for conveying a message, like John Lennon's "Give Peace a Chance."

Now, it seems, people are famous for what they wear and who

they sleep with. We lionize all these celebrities, but we're not recognizing them for their real gifts either. Tom Cruise may be a good and interesting person, but that's not why his box-office receipts are so impressive. He's rewarded for his straight white teeth, biceps, sex appeal, and ability to pretend to be something he's not. Why is that such an accomplishment? In my book, the man who works hard to raise healthy children and to make his wife feel desirable has made a unique and worthwhile contribution to the world—one at least as important and deserving of recognition as Tom Cruise's.

It seems as though our cult of celebrity does exactly the opposite of enhancing dignity. In fact, we will sacrifice our dignity entirely for a chance to be on television. On a TV talk show, a young woman, at age sixteen, admitted to having already slept with thirty men. She said, "I'm pregnant, and the father can be any one of eleven men." Clearly there was a connection between her behavior and her desire to talk about it on national TV. She slept with the men in question because it made her feel loved, at least for a little while. And she told her story to the camera because that also made her feel loved. Celebrity made her feel important—until the cameras were turned off and she found that she actually had to live with the consequences of her actions.

We compromise our dignity because we don't see the significance in our own lives. We can't see our own heroism because we're using the wrong definition. Until that definition changes, our dignity is forever in jeopardy. That dignity has been banished from our society is a terrible thing, because it is an absolute human essential. Like a bottle of milk that will begin to sour if it is not placed in a refrigerated environment, or a baby who will catch a cold if he's not wrapped in a warm blanket, the human soul becomes ill when it's not wrapped in the protective covering of dignity.

When we take the time to reacquaint ourselves with our inner dignity, on the other hand, everything changes. We start seeing things differently, because our dignity affords us a higher consciousness. The more we come in touch with our own godly nature, and the more deeply we experience our own spirituality, the more sensitive we become to the divinity that surrounds us throughout creation. Simply stated, practicing goodness by conferring dignity upon others trains us to see everything around us as special. Once we give up seeing only how the world can benefit us, once we look at how the world can inspire us, a whole new landscape presents itself, lifting the heart and firing the emotions.

A number of reactions are possible when you see an impressive natural phenomenon, like a mountain. You can say, "It's so big! I'm going to climb it. I'm not going to feel small—I'll dominate it to prove my superiority to myself and whoever's watching." Or you can say, "This is beautiful. I'm going to take a picture of it, or build a ski resort on it. I'm going to get something from it, whether it's joy or money—I'm going to make it work for me." And then there's a third response: you can say, "This is incredible. How majestic! I thank God that this exists and that I'm lucky enough to be here."

When you're in touch with your own dignity, you're not driven by inadequacy and insecurity. Your own dignity enables you to see the dignity in everything around you. Wonder is what rescues you from a superficial horizontal perspective and enables you to have a deeper vertical view. The experience of awe, reverence, and wonder for everything that surrounds us is the natural posture of the biblical hero. Far from wanting to dominate people and the world around him, the biblical hero wishes to nurture people and the world because they are a part of him, as he is a part of them.

7

❧

NICE GUYS FINISH LAST

Goodness is the only investment that never fails.
                    —Henry David Thoreau, *Walden* (1854)

Ask any woman to choose between the following two guys. The first is good-looking, immensely giving, always eager to please, ready to assist at the drop of a hat. He has a good job as an English teacher at a local high school and really cares that his students understand why you shouldn't end a sentence with a preposition. He wears comfortable shoes, drives a 1989 Honda Civic to visit his mother, and lives in a modest apartment.

The second guy is an ego-driven Wall Street bruiser. He works at a Top Six firm and rarely gets home before 2:00 A.M. When he isn't working, he's attending power lunches and cocktail parties, and he is known as a "modelizer" because he won't look at a woman who isn't tall, blond, and starving. He drinks a lot and has no problem doing a line of cocaine to keep the party going. He wears expensive suits, drives a fancy sports car, pops off to Cancun for weekends, and chooses his friends according to their earning power and social position. He has no time for anyone who can't advance his career.

Sadly, an awful lot of women won't even look at the teacher. And it's not just in New York or Los Angeles that this is true.

The greatest impediment to our successful pursuit of biblical heroism is our deep-seated belief that nice guys finish last. We have been conditioned to believe that goodness will stand in the way of our success—that if we do the right thing we will get stepped on, taken advantage of, and end up at the back of the line. We believe that goodness will make us weak. What is the payoff for being good in a world that will only punish us for it? Why bother taking the time to teach children if she's just going to go for the broker? Where is the payoff in this kind of heroism? What's in it for us?

As I write these lines, a whole slew of corporate scandals has broken out in America. From the Enron disaster to the Tyco disgrace to the Worldcom meltdown, American corporate executives are being accused of thievery. The collapses we're witnessing are the natural outcome of moral decay, of the desire to succeed at all costs, of the relegation of goodness to the backwaters of ambition. People today would much rather be successful than good. They don't want to be evil, mind you, and they rationalize their behavior as something that "everybody does." But they have lost their ambition to be moral lights—people that other people look up to.

Why do we associate goodness with failure? Where did this pervasive idea come from? Let's take a look at the high priest of this philosophy. Considered by many to be the most influential political theorist of the past millennium, Niccolò Machiavelli wrote *The Prince* in the fifteenth century in an effort to curry favor with the ruling Medici family. He failed at this goal, but his model for political and material success continues to inspire the darker angels of our natures today.

Machiavelli encouraged those who wish to be leaders to eschew goodness, to focus on winning at all costs. It doesn't matter if you cheat, lie, manipulate, or kill to achieve success. Ruthlessness is key. "All armed prophets have been victorious, all unarmed prophets have been destroyed," he argued. "A Prince wishing to keep his state is very often forced to do evil," he observed. "He who becomes master of a city accustomed to freedom and does not destroy it, may expect to be destroyed by it," he warned. Machiavelli's very name has become synonymous with treachery. And yet *The Prince*, while condemned by people like Bertrand Russell as "a handbook for gangsters," continues to serve as a model for men and women who want to assume power.

Machiavelli never told anyone not to be good, but he posited what he considered to be an unbreachable wall, separating morality and ethics from success and power. You want to be a saint? Go ahead. Just don't complain when you have to live on crusts of bread and wear a hair shirt, because that's all you're going to be able to afford, buddy. Great leaders can't afford to be good, Machiavelli argued, because their achievement is predicated on taking the necessary steps to secure success. They have to be prepared to claw, steal, and cheat their way to the top.

Can we really say that this isn't true? Classical heroes may not be good friends or husbands, but they have certainly left an impressive legacy. Pope Julian II, more warrior than priest, was one of the most corrupt pontiffs in the history of the Catholic Church. But amid all his ruthlessness and bloodshed, he commissioned the St. Peter's Basilica in Rome and hired Michelangelo to paint the Sistine Chapel. If he had been a pacifist pope, would we have even a straw hut to show for it? Robert Moses had unprecedented power over development projects in New York City. The ugly public housing projects he sponsored essentially warehoused New York's lower classes, and now boast some of the highest violence rates per capita in the world. His Cross-Bronx Expressway made a grotesque slash through vibrant neighborhoods, isolating people from services and their neighbors, and that crippled borough is still fighting its way back.

But Robert Moses got things done, sparing no measure to build the roads that helped New York continue to lead the world in commerce. It's interesting to note that no truly major public work has successfully been completed in New York since, the systems that were put in place to prevent another Robert Moses have made sure of that. There has also been no one with the larger-than-life personality, drive, and ruthlessness necessary to get large-scale projects done.

In Machiavelli's world, a person had to choose between worldly success and morality, piety, and ethics. For this reason, those who chose to be truly righteous were rarely powerful. Religious Jews were famous as the world's victims, not as champions. Machiavelli's book taught one how to become a Caesar or a Napoleon; religion taught one how to earn the privilege of being eaten by a lion.

Life, said Machiavelli, is a choice, and it is a choice that cannot be circumvented or ignored. You have to choose between goodness and prosperity, selflessness and wealth, power and penury, love and fear. Goodness and success are contradictory, incompatible, and inversely proportional. In Machiavelli's world, the biblical hero dies under the galloping hooves of Genghis Khan's Mongol hordes, or while helping schoolchildren in Robert Moses' burned-out South Bronx.

Yet, however much we seek to deny it, we still believe that there is truth in the Machiavellian way. No matter how bitterly we criticize mean-spirited political campaigning, politicians whose campaign style is based on character assassination almost always get the better of their opponents. Just ask Michael Dukakis and Bill Bradley how far you get abstaining from smear campaigns.

If you want to climb the corporate ladder, then forget all this nonsense about goodness, right? The boss isn't going to promote the guys who walk old ladies across the street, but those who crush the competition. You're not going to get ahead by respecting your coworkers, but by spreading malicious gossip about them so that they founder under a cloud of grave suspicion. The great robber barons of the nineteenth century—Andrew Carnegie, Cornelius Vanderbilt, Henry Ford—all amassed large fortunes by swallowing up their competitors and creating monopolies. They busted unions, and their workers labored in appalling conditions in the mines and on railroads. In the process these men made millions and millions of dollars, built hundred-room mansions, and achieved elite status in American society. Today we have billionaire Bill Gates, who was accused of using Microsoft's monopoly to gain ascendancy over Netscape, Sun, and Novell. Jack Welch's slash-and-burn, greed-is-good management style is a subject of emulation. Many businessmen continue to destroy other people's livelihoods in order to advance their own position.

We have become a generation of men and women prepared to do almost anything to get ahead. If that means spending long nights at the office and neglecting a spouse and children, so be it. Our stock portfolios are worth more than our marriages, our careers are worth more than our children, and anyone who tells us otherwise can just drive away in his rust-bucket jalopy to the nearest homeless shelter.

To those who still wish to be altruistic and believe that goodness can lead to material and professional success, Machiavelli would say that there is certainly nothing intrinsic about ethics and morals that hinder success—the moral approach can work, however, only in a world where everyone is moral. In a world where so many are prepared to compromise their morality and trample one another in an effort to get ahead, you'd better watch your back. The good guy who is committed to ethical behavior has now got one hand tied behind his back and is at a distinct disadvantage.

Many of us have the same feeling: goodness can work only if everybody's practicing it. Virtually all women agree that it is unethical, not to mention downright stupid, to sleep with a guy on the first or second date. They all agree that it's better to wait for emotional intimacy to develop, or at the very least for the man to pursue them more. But they also reject the advice to wait. One woman told me: "Waiting for sex works only in a dating environment where there aren't other women who are prepared to sleep with the guy. But if you're trying to maintain your dignity and play hard to get, be a prize that he wants to earn, while Lucy down at the office will jump into the sack with him after one dinner, can you realistically expect to compete? Either all women agree not to give sex to a man until he's proven himself a gentleman, or all women jump into bed. It has to work as a sisterhood."

It doesn't take a genius to see that at some level the arguments against goodness are correct. Goodness is a constant struggle. It is hard. It involves sacrifice. And it may interfere with our success. After all, many of history's most powerful leaders followed the Machiavellian model. Is there really any glory in having your subjects rise up and rebel against you because you refused to rule them with an iron hand? Is there magnificence in being chicken fodder for every invading army? It's good to be loved, but it's far, far better to be feared. Isn't it?

Many of the classical heroes we've discussed lived truly Machiavellian lives. Napoleon waged never-ending battles against any and everyone; his life was a real-life model of Machiavelli's maxim that there is no time for peace. Stalin's citizens feared him more than they feared death: he created a state where little children would denounce their parents to the authorities for anticommunism. Hitler also blitzkrieged his way to a mighty empire, until the blue rivers of magnificent, cultured Europe ran red with blood. These men learned their lessons well at Machiavelli's knee.

These ruthless dictators, men who built their empires by maligning, incarcerating, and/or murdering their enemies, wore their successes proudly. Their power was absolute, and though their reigns did not last forever, when they were in power they were formidable. They were princes: goodness was never part of the equation. Happy, no. But successful, by their own rights? Yes.

Even in our own country (and I hesitate to mention an American president on the same page as these other madmen, so forgive the comparison), Machiavelli has succeeded in the highest office of the land. President Richard Nixon had in him much that could be admired. Sadly he showed little faith in the democratic process, preferring to subvert it to ensure his power and his place in history. He was truly Machiavellian in his paranoia about his enemies and in his way of dealing with them. He sent robbers to steal psychiatric records. He ordered the IRS to audit opponents. He arrested student leaders and placed them under obtrusive and uncomfortable surveillance, and worse.

We all want a piece of success, and we crave the "winning attitude" that we think will help us get there. Even though (or perhaps because) it runs directly counter to our instincts, we wish that we were tougher, harder, less easily pushed around. We're embarrassed by our own sensitivity and sentimentality. We like to imagine ourselves squinting through smoke and blood, not getting teary over a Kodak commercial. Even though we know that we really should despise these Machiavellian heroes and consider them unworthy of our attention and our time, we are still fascinated with them. We are more likely to pick up a book of true Mafia stories than the story of a righteous priest who had a couple of bucks and gave it all to the poor. Do you think it's an accident that there are only about two biographies of Mother Teresa on the market, compared with five hundred of Hitler? We believe that goodness not only leads to vulnerability and failure but is also downright boring. Women don't date nice guys—they want a bad boy with tattoos and piercings and a leather-jacket attitude. Women want James Dean and Kurt Cobain, not Clark Kent. They want the man in Armani who speeds past red lights in his Ferrari.

I'm sure we all have personal stories of times when the choice to do something good has ultimately harmed us. We can all relate stories of being hurt or taken advantage of when we've opened our heart. Do we not regularly feel abused by having extended ourselves for others, only to discover that they instantly forgot the favor, or worse, took advantage of us at our most vulnerable moments? Do we not believe that "no good deed goes unpunished," and that we'll inevitably be dismissed out of hand by the big boys for being too weak or sentimental?

Like many of you reading this, trying to be good has interfered with success in my own life. I do wrestle with goodness, and sometimes, when I'm making moral and ethical calculations, other people just zoom by. For instance, dedicating yourself to goodness means that you can't take revenge. I have often been maligned by people, both privately and publicly, who could say whatever they wanted because they were not bound by any kind of morality. I could easily have undermined the credibility of their opposition to me by exposing them for what they were, but as a rabbi committed to godly ethics, I could not do that.

What Machiavelli achieved, even if he didn't set out to, was to relegate goodness to the basement of ambitions. We genuinely believe there is a dichotomy between those who are good and those who are great. So asking people to be good doesn't really seem fair these days. Not only is there no clear reward for being good, there isn't even really any attraction. It's not sexy or compelling. Goodness is hard. It involves sacrifice. It may compromise our success. With these arguments against it, why should we even bother? What is the point of trying to be good in a cruel world that punishes rather than rewards it?

It's a question that has yet to be answered. Most of the time we have to fall back on religious answers, which hinge on promises like the rewards of the afterlife. But there seems to be only one response grounded in the here and now, and it's one I personally find very compelling: the desire to be good sits at the core of human nature. To ignore it is to live in contradiction to our deepest nature and is a surefire guarantee that we will face inner turmoil and unhappiness. Yes, Hitler and Stalin had incredible power. But do we think of them as happy? Does it seem to anyone that men like these ever achieve even a small measure of bliss? *What we're doing right now isn't working.* The way we live, the things we prioritize, aren't good for our world or good for our children, and they're not making us happy.

8

⤫

WHAT DO YOU
REALLY (REALLY) WANT?

A man without ambition is dead. A man with ambition but no
love is dead. A man with ambition and love for his blessings here
on earth is ever so alive. Having been alive, it won't be so hard in
the end to lie down and rest.

—Pearl Bailey

In *The Sixth Sense,* Bruce Willis plays a child psychologist who seeks to
counsel a boy who has the gift of seeing dead people who have remained
behind because they have not come to terms with their death. I am convinced that the enormous popularity of this movie has to do with the
fact that the audience identified with its central theme. We're dead, and
we don't even know it. We are ghosts of what humans are meant to be.
The mold of the classical hero has blunted our hearts, stifled our souls,
and caused our integrity to atrophy. We are all so desperate to get ahead
and beat our colleagues to the finish line that we spend our lives running
and running. We're not heading toward any particular destination, but
away from ourselves and the feeling that somehow we're not worthy. In
the end, all we're doing is burning ourselves out.

What would happen if we stopped? If we took a breather and
asked ourselves what we really want to be? What would give us a
sense of belonging and preserve us from always having to feel out of

place? What would make us happier about ourselves so that we don't have to get back on the treadmill to stay two paces ahead of the feeling that we're worthless?

It isn't hard to see why Machiavelli was as successful as he was, and why *The Prince* continues to be used as a primer for success. The life of a classical hero, even if it does not lead to inner contentment, still seems like a pretty impressive way to spend your days on this earth. We love the aura of power, the radiance that success brings, and the comforts that money buys.

Unfortunately, what everyone discovers eventually is that there is scant reward in the life of the classical hero. Like Machiavelli, I don't believe that there is something inherent in success that precludes goodness. Unlike him, I believe in a world where both are possible. More than that, I believe that they are both necessary. Money, power, speedboats, and trophy wives—these things are not enough for us. Indeed, unaccompanied by depth and virtue they corrupt the soul. Success that's gained by devious methods, or at the expense of human relationships, denies an essential part of us, and it will never be intrinsically satisfying.

This is the poison pill hidden in *The Prince*. The rewards that Machiavelli promised for ruthlessness are fleeting. The classical hero isn't built to last—he's destined to flame out and crash. If Machiavelli was so right about classical heroism, then why is every successful country moving toward democracy? Where are all the great monarchs? The undefeated despots? When the United States was engaged in the cold war with the former Soviet Union, the Soviets thought we were completely nuts. A free press? Protests? How could our government possibly survive if we allowed journalists to openly criticize policy? Students even! How could we expect loyalty if we tolerated open dissent in the ranks?

History has chosen the victor in that particular quarrel. Openness and tolerance—qualities of biblical heroism—carried the day. The preeminence of the United States is hardly the only example. History is filled with successful "biblical" struggles. As Bishop Desmond Tutu has said, "Ultimately goodness, laughter, peace, compassion, gentleness, forgiveness, and reconciliation will have the last word and prevail over their ghastly counterparts. The victory over apartheid is proof positive of this truth."

John F. Kennedy is remembered now not for his ruthlessness in pursuing power, but for the biblical attributes he demonstrated once he got it. He's remembered fondly for his devotion to his young wife and family, not for the hookers and blond bombshells he was seeing on the side. He's remembered for his speeches about reconciliation, inspiration, and peace, and for *Profiles in Courage*, a book about biblical heroism. We remember those aspects of his personality because we recognize those facets of his character as the truly heroic ones.

Machiavelli missed the point. He called himself the ultimate realist, but he was totally unrealistic about people's real desires. All Machiavelli did was to condemn power-grubbers to dark lives of misery. When you use strong-arm tactics to attain power, you know it's only a matter of time before someone else uses the same strategy against you. You can't trust anyone. Like Stalin, you have to begin murdering your own officer corps to make sure that nobody betrays you. Like Saddam Hussein, you kill your best friends, your sons-in-law, never trusting a soul, not even family.

As I write this, one of publishing's big success stories is *The Nanny Diaries*, a book whose humor masks an underlying tragedy. Its pages are peopled with a whole host of classical heroes—the big swinging dicks of Wall Street. Their world, filled with swanky Park Avenue apartments, houses in the Hamptons, and hordes of servants, is horrifying in its dysfunction. The head of the family has cheated on his first wife and married his mistress, and now he's cheating on her. She's always alone and knows something's going on, so she uses her shame and humiliation to fuel her sadistic treatment of their staff. The kid is farmed out to the help, even when they're on vacation. Nobody has any time for him at all. There's no way anyone could read this book and envy these people. They're miserable! They're crazy and unhappy, and they're thoughtlessly spreading their illness to the next generation.

Today's corporate titans and Wall Street's "Masters of the Universe" have followed Machiavelli's dictums to the letter. I know many of them personally. They have ignored friendships and relationships to spend more time at the office. They have ruthlessly crushed the competition and fired employees who had ceased to be productive without a second thought, and they have great material rewards to show for it. And yet they are in real distress. The only people they confide in are their shrinks. Their wives are lonely, their children hurting, their parents neglected.

They come to people like me and complain that they've lost the ability to fall in love. They have no real relationships: they feel disconnected from a healthy, balanced life. They've lost the ability to be authentic. Their wall-to-wall carpeting and country club lifestyles have not brought them—or bought them—any degree of happiness.

Power doesn't make us happy. We go after it hoping it will make us feel satisfied, respected, and loved, but instead it isolates us. It's like a man who attempts to satisfy his craving for intimacy with casual sex. He'll never be satisfied; he'll merely become a womanizer, and soon it'll be impossible for him to have an intimate relationship at all. By chasing the wrong thing, he's cheated himself out of the thing he most wants. Classical heroism is a dead end; it distracts us from discovering and pursuing our deepest desires.

After a football game, any good coach will sit down with his players and review the high and low points of the game. Why can't they do it during the game? Because it's impossible to review the lessons of a game—its successes and failures—until the game is over. The same is true of life. Sometimes we find it impossible to know exactly what it is that we want from life until the game is nearly over. It is an oft-repeated cliché that no one on his deathbed wishes he'd spent more time at the office. Why should we wait until we're dying to figure this out?

Wherever you are in the game of life, take a moment to look ahead to the endgame. We are all mortal, and one day each of us will be eulogized before our friends and community by a member of the clergy or a relative. Try this exercise: take a deep breath and—either on paper or in your head—draft your own eulogy. How is it that you want to be remembered? And how does that correspond to the life you're living now?

Will your eulogy read something like this? "He was a dedicated man who got up at the crack of dawn to sell Japanese futures. His dedication was such that he rarely even ate lunch, and even after work his beeper constantly told him of the goings-on in markets across the world. He loved his parents, but had little time to visit them, although he did manage to find the time to attend his grandmother's funeral. He spent at least thirty minutes every day on the StairMaster before he went to sleep, and he never, ever missed a New York Yankees game."

Or will it read like this? "She did everything she could to make partner at a high-priced corporate law firm and made sure to choose only the kind of friends who could help her advance her burgeoning career. She loved children but had no time to bear one until her late thirties, at which point she had a little girl, whom she gave to nannies to raise. She lived in a beautiful Manhattan apartment with a terrace and private elevator, and she had hidden quadraphonic stereo surround-sound speakers in every room of the house. She was always decked out in Escada or Donna Karan and visited her elderly parents twice a year."

You can laugh at these extreme examples, but I'm probably not that far off the mark.

Wouldn't we rather be remembered as decent and loving people? "He had a law practice of medium size and was scrupulously honest in dealing with all his clients. No matter what the financial hardship, his family's Friday evening Sabbath meal was always brimming with guests. He worked hard to grant his family a decent standard of living, yet he always did homework with his children at night. He never passed a beggar on the street without giving a few dollars from his pocket, and he scrupulously tithed his income to the needy. He only ever had kind words to say about anyone, and he tried never to judge people, even when their worst side was on display. He forgave slights, rarely bore grudges, and was always the first to apologize. He respected the confidences of his friends. And he made his wife feel like a queen."

Aren't these the kinds of things for which we wish to be remembered? And doesn't that prove that this is what we most want for ourselves? When we reach the end of our lives, we want our achievements to be remembered as the lasting kind, the kind that speak to the quality of a man's soul, not his possessions. What we most want is to be good. And this is why we're so unhappy. We're not living in accordance with our deepest nature. It's like being hungry. You can't be happy when your stomach is grumbling, because your need at that moment is to eat. Our need at every moment is to be liberated from the suffocating incarceration of the ego. We need to do good in order to be happy in order to cater to our most deep-seated nature. Otherwise, we're at war with ourselves.

An older friend approached me a few years ago and asked me to try to broker a meeting with his children. This man was sixty-two years old at the time, and he hadn't spoken to his daughter in more than twenty years. I asked him what the history of the relationship was and why he wanted to be in touch with her now. This is what he said:

"Our relationship probably started falling apart years ago, before my daughter was even old enough to realize what was happening. I have always been a workaholic, driven to make my business as successful as possible because I wanted to make enough money to provide for my family in a manner that was decent. Of course, decent can mean different things to different people—but suffice it to say, the standard in my house included a full-time housekeeper and three vacations a year. We sent our children to private schools and exclusive camps and gave them every toy that they ever dreamed of.

"I spent eighteen hours a day at the office to ensure that we could sustain this lifestyle, so I was never there for my children. At first, when they were younger, I told myself it didn't matter because they were too little to notice me anyway. I figured that when they were old enough to notice, I would start coming home for dinner more regularly. But as my children grew, my business became more demanding. I justified my absence by saying that the kids were in school, and when they came home all they wanted to do was watch television and do their homework, so my presence didn't really make a difference. And besides, I had to be earning the money to pay for all those things that they wanted to buy.

"In the meantime, my relationship with my wife was deteriorating and I started having affairs. She eventually divorced me, and I left the house and started traveling overseas a lot. I missed all of my children's high school graduations.

"My kids grew older and more troubled, and (separately) they started going to therapy, where they learned that the cause of their unhappiness was my inability to commit to the family. My daughter confronted me with this ugly fact, I denied it, and she vowed never to speak to me again until I apologized. I have always been too proud to apologize. My son gradually became a bum. I think he's still trying to be an actor, while blowing whatever's left of his trust fund, but his lethargy prevents him from actually picking up the phone and calling me, and my stubborn pride has stopped me from calling him.

"I realize now that I have already lived the majority of my life, and I don't know what I have done with it. I look at all the money I've earned, and my house, with its high ceilings and wonderful furnishings, and it's nice—but it can't ease the pain of regret that haunts me all the time. I want to get to know my family a little better. I want to meet the man my daughter married. I want to find out who my children are and what they are up to now. I feel that this is more important to my life than anything I have done in the past, more important than any wealth I have accumulated, any companies that I have bought or sold. But it seems that the people I want most in my life want me least in theirs."

This man did eventually manage to get together with his children. One day he called his daughter out of the blue and apologized. To be sure, she said all the predictable things: "*Now* you're calling? Where were you when I was growing up? You're a stranger. I don't know you. Don't come into my life just to disrupt it. I learned to live without you long ago." She hung up on him a few times, but he persevered and ultimately broke through the barrier of his children's hostility.

It was interesting to me that he decided to show heroic courage only toward the end of his life. It took him sixty-odd years to realize that he'd been working toward the wrong thing. It took him a lifetime to realize that he'd thrown away the thing he most wanted. And his children responded with their own unique brand of heroism, marshaling the strength and conviction to battle their sense of abandonment and anger to salvage the relationship. Though the initial meeting was awkward and strained, they gradually grew to accept one another.

I have heard variations on this story over and over in my years of counseling. I have also noticed that when people reach a certain age, they become more inclined to engage in spiritually based activities, such as going to synagogue or church. When I worked as a rabbi in London, I found that many of the people who attended my weekly classes were retired. I asked a couple of them whether they were coming because they simply had nothing better to do with their time, or whether they had always been interested in learning Torah. They told me that as young men they had had little time for spiritual matters—they were too busy making sure that their mortgages were paid and their children were doing well in school. Only as they got older did they yearn to know more about life and to find the meaning in the mundane, and so they turned to spirituality.

I will never forget one young man whom I met during this time. He was a lawyer who had discovered a way to save corporations enormous amounts on their taxes, and this discovery (and the wealth it brought him) catapulted him to the heights of London society. He had a beautiful home, married a model—the whole classical shebang. He was in a position, financially and politically, to do good things for the Jewish community, but what he dearly wanted was to become a member of Parliament. Anti-Semitism is alive and well in some circles at that level of British society, and he felt that directly aligning himself with Jewish causes would hurt his chances, so he distanced himself from the Jewish community.

Then it all fell apart for him. Through various mistakes and twists of fate, he lost his job and his fortune, and with it his family and the people he'd thought were his friends. He spiraled into a terrible depression—and that depression was what eventually brought him back to Judaism. When everything he had evaporated, he realized that he needed something solid in his life, something that had real meaning, as opposed to all the stuff he'd surrounded himself with before. He became observant and began attending synagogue, and he found tremendous comfort and a real community there. Eventually he began giving lectures to Jewish students, telling them to learn from his example not to turn their backs on their tradition, not to wait until they'd lost everything to discover their spirituality.

For many people, religion is about knowing where they will go after their death. For others, it is about discovering the hidden mysteries of the universe. For still others, it is about perpetuating a glorious tradition. I believe that all of these purposes are only marginal to religion. The real goal of religion is to teach you and guide you early in life about those things you will only learn later—to help people identify at twenty what life might not teach them until they're seventy or eighty.

In my opinion, religion has no great or profound truths that you cannot discover yourself. Life is the greatest teacher. If you live in this world long enough, you will have ample opportunity to learn that crime doesn't pay, that gossiping doesn't win you friends, and that the important things in life are your family, friends, and God. You will discover that it really feels good to be charitable, and that your kids should come before your business interests. If you live for eighty years, you will discover that your greatest blessings are not your career or your car, but your loved ones, your eyesight, and your health. And you will want to thank someone for all those things, just as Judaism bids us to do every morning.

Given that we can learn all of these things from life itself, then why do we need religion at all? Because religion can help us identify our deepest desires and needs—*before it's too late.* It can teach us the great truths of life in our teens and twenties, so we can live our lives, not squander them. As a rabbi, I see too many people who are living lives of regret. They wish they'd participated more actively and joyfully in the lives of their children. They wish they had known that a life devoted exclusively to materialism is a life of slavery and incarceration. Religion is designed to help us circumvent a life of regret. It teaches us to master life and to be fully human. It's like a sensitive microphone that allows us to hear our own inner desires through all the static and noise of everyday life.

In the Bible, God sends the prophet Elijah to King Ahab to tell him that God will punish him unless he stops worshiping idols. When he arrives, Elijah discovers that Ahab has killed all the prophets, and he runs away to the wilderness, saying to God, "I don't want to live anymore. All the people have become corrupt, and I'm the only prophet left. I ask you to take my soul." God tells him, "Go to the wilderness, and I'll answer you." Then comes a huge storm, with terrible thunder, and Elijah waits for God to speak to him from the storm, but to no avail. Then comes a massive inferno, and Elijah expects to hear something, but again, there's nothing. Then there's an earthquake—and still nothing. And then, after all the madness has died down, Elijah hears God speaking to him, in a still, small voice.

We have to listen for the still, small voice of our own souls—the part of us that communicates our authentic desires. Too often we allow this voice to get drowned out by the din of our everyday lives. But to ensure that at sixty or seventy we end up exactly where we wanted to be all along, it becomes vital to identify our internal will rather than just our external will. In each of us there are two desires. What we want—and in the words of the Spice Girls, what we really, *really* want.

Our inner desires are often obscured by our outer, less serious, and more ephemeral desires. Bill Clinton convinced himself that what he wanted was sex with a young White House intern named Monica Lewinsky. His poor judgment resulted in more than ten sexual encounters in the single most powerful office on the face of the earth. Risking personal exposure and national disgrace, he could hardly deny that, at some level, the forbidden dangers of this liaison had a powerful allure for him.

But after numerous investigations, a congressional impeachment, and the sting of millions of jokes told worldwide, ask President Clinton if those ten sexual encounters were what he really, *really* wanted. Was it all worth it? If he could have heard his still, small voice, would he have done it? If he could go back, would he do it again? Wasn't it his true desire to be a great president and loving husband, a man destined to hold an honorable position in history? Didn't he really want to have as high an approval rating with his wife and his daughter as he had with the rest of the country?

What about you? Do you really think that whatever fantasy you're chasing is going to lead to an authentic life? Is it going to give you joy and make you happy? Or are your achievements and accomplishments simply going to lead to greater insecurity, greater workaholism, evermore drastic efforts to anesthetize yourself against the pain of an inauthentic, meaningless life? Don't you really, really want to be a hero instead?

9

❧

THE PUBLIC AND
THE PRIVATE ADAM

If your success is not on your own terms, if it looks good to the
world but does not feel good in your heart, it is not success at all.

—Anna Quindlen

What will it take for us to be successful, and to take pleasure in
those successes? The Bible tells us that the noble struggle in life is
not for success, but for goodness. The biblical hero struggles to do
the right thing because it is right, not because of what it will bring
him. But does that necessarily mean that we must fail in our worldly
pursuits?

At some level, success is almost beside the point. God doesn't
say, "Do the right thing, and make sure it's received well." He says,
"Do the right thing." My friend Dennis Prager told me once why he
doesn't worry about the number of stations that pick up his radio
show. His job, he says, is to get the word out. If he gets the word out
to one person, then he's done his job. It's all about God. It's not
about him.

Our question is: Can the biblical hero also succeed, by the
world's traditional definition of success? If she plays by the rules,
dominates over the lesser angels of her nature, refuses to gossip, is

honest in business, gives generously to charity, and puts her family first, can she still make a significant impact on the outside world? Can she attain fame and fortune even if these are not her principal objectives?

I believe the answer to this question is a resounding yes. In fact, the synthesis we seek, the confluence of goodness and success, can be found everywhere in the Bible. It's important to remember that the biblical heroes were success stories in the physical world as well as in the spiritual. These weren't shlebby losers. The patriarchs were fabulously wealthy, and the matriarchs were beautiful women. And the heroes of the Bible went on to become the most influential people of all time. Who has more influence today: Caesar or Jesus? Abraham or Augustus? Isaac or Icarus? Jacob or Juvenal? Moses or Marc Antony? Who is more famous? Who is studied more? And if they were alive today, who would be more respected? Genghis Khan or Gregory the Great? Richard the Lionheart or Rebecca, mother of Israel?

Nobody wants to wear a sheet and live in a peasant village when it's much easier to see the rewards of a successful classical hero's career—the McMansion, the sexy girlfriend, the cars and money. It might even seem slightly within reach. But nobody's asking you to trade in your worldly possessions for sackcloth. Obviously, attaining a measure of majesty and dignity in life doesn't mean you have to trade in all your worldly possessions for poverty and deep thoughts. True success doesn't exclusively involve worldly achievement. Nor does it mean just being a good person and a fantastic parent. Rather, it involves a careful balance of both.

As Rabbi Joseph Soloveitchik points out, the need to distinguish oneself outside the home and live a life of professional excellence is expressly mandated by the Bible. Rabbi Soloveitchik referred to it as the need to develop the "majestic" side of our personality. We all want to feel that we've made an impact. There's nothing inherently good about going hungry. If you're sent to represent your company at a meeting and you show up wearing a stained shirt with a frayed collar, you reflect badly on your company. We are God's representatives on earth, and we need to comport ourselves accordingly. God doesn't want you to live a life of poverty and self-denial. How can you have dignity if you can't feed and clothe and shelter your children properly?

I find an answer to this in an unexpected corner: the very opening of the Bible, with its storied account of the birth of man. Though the Book of Genesis is one of the Bible's most celebrated and familiar passages, one aspect of its text that may have escaped many readers' notice is that it offers two different versions of the creation of Adam. Through subtle but telling variations in their language, these two versions reflect the two different visions of the role of man in the universe.

In the first chapter of Genesis we encounter the first of these two Adams—the one I think of as the Public Adam. This Adam is described as having been created in the image of God; he receives a mandate from the Creator to "fill the earth, subdue it, and have dominion over it."

In the second chapter of Genesis, however, Adam is reintroduced in quite different terms. This Adam, we learn, is created from the dust of the earth. And rather than achieve dominion over the earth, he is instructed to "cultivate the Garden of Eden and to nurture it." This is the Private Adam.

The history of man, in my view, is the story of the struggle of these two Adams.

The Public Adam sees his humanity realized in conquering the world, in the scientific harnessing of nature to man's service, in military victory and pushing back the frontiers of space. These creative and technological pursuits lend dignity to man and symbolize humankind's uniqueness in the cosmos. An animal's existence does not possess the same dignity, for an animal is helpless. Only humans are blessed with dignity. The Public Adam works to improve his position in relation to the environment by mastering it.

The Private Adam, on the other hand, sees his distinctiveness expressed through sharing and relationships, not domination and conquest. Unlike the Public Adam, the Private Adam is created solitary; vulnerable and alone, he feels the weight of insignificance pressing against him. Instead of conquering and acquiring, he turns to his soulmate Eve, with whom he builds a covenantal relationship.

This relationship, and his cultivation of it, is what makes him feel unconditionally special.

Surely we can recognize these warring impulses in ourselves. And we can also see how these opposing impulses might contribute to our pursuit of both classical and biblical heroism. But the challenge is not to choose between the Public and the Private Adam as a model for our own behavior; neither is the "right" choice. Rather, what's required is a careful synthesis of the two.

Yes, we need to seek heroism through our achievements. We must build, create, succeed in the outside world—but we also need to find heroism by nurturing our most intimate relationships and the inherent dignity that those relationships afford us. Our cultural preoccupation with the spoils of classical heroism has forced our focus out of balance. We don't believe that we're heroes until we hear the cheers of the crowds. But the Private Adam knows something the Public Adam overlooks. It doesn't take fifty thousand people cheering at you in a sports arena to make you feel special. Indeed, the knowledge that they will cheer when you win but forget you when you lose can exacerbate your feeling of worthlessness. The Private Adam knows that it takes only the love of one woman to make a man feel special, as long as that one woman believes he is the most special person on earth. The Bible describes Eve as having been created from the Private Adam's rib. How fitting that the Private Adam, after experiencing unbearable solitude, contributes part of his own being to the formation of his soulmate.

The Public Adam, on the other hand, knows the considerable value of building beautiful buildings, making great art, and discovering vaccines that can save children's lives. These are also manifestations of goodness, and they are essential—a biblical hero's take on classical heroism, if you will. Perfection is attained when the two Adams harmonize as one, when we are able to find the careful balance between being good accountants and good fathers, good managers and good mothers.

I believe that we are so unhappy today because instead of harmony we have conflict and inner tension. The Public Adam has turned into a recognition-hungry monster, and he has almost completely vanquished the Private Adam in all of us. Because our Private Adams are suppressed, we allow our public side to run amok. People desire money and celebrity today above all else. Instead of using our public side to create good working environments for our staffs, to divert a percentage of profits to charity, to create good public works, we're chasing celebrity, money, press—the booty of classical heroism.

With every passing generation the victory of the Public Adam becomes more and more complete, and the model of the classical hero prevails. If as a student you're taught that getting straight A^+s is more important than what happens when the whole family sits down to dinner together, then you'll likely grow up with the desire to distinguish yourself in the public arena—even if it means compromising stable relationships. If your mother never comes to your swim meets because she's too busy being a star at work, you're going to treat your children the same way. And your children will grow up even more insecure than you are.

The desire of men today to distinguish themselves primarily outside, rather than inside, the home explains a curious phenomenon that has long perplexed me. How is it that the world at large, the macrocosm, is evolving into a better place, while the world of man, the microcosm, is devolving—becoming worse and worse? There is a much greater distribution of resources in the world than there used to be. Wealthy countries are taking more responsibility for poorer ones. Disease is being pushed back on all fronts, and war is receding, with international bodies jumping in to settle disputes almost as soon as conflict erupts. But our private lives are falling apart on all sides. Husbands and wives are falling out of love at an alarming rate, depression is higher than ever before, and our kids shoot one another at schools.

Could it be that we're spending more time on the world's problems than the ones that await us at home? The doctors who are curing disease want to win a Nobel Prize, so they burn long hours at the lab. Great for us, but lousy for their kids. The diplomats shuttle between Protestants and Catholics in Northern Ireland and Arabs and Jews in the Middle East, but they're not shuttling their kids between school and football practice. And can the reason for this be that the public sphere provides recognition, but the private sphere does not? Could that be the reason that we're investing ourselves in public works at the expense of private failures? Is a man given the Presidential Medal of Freedom when he does homework with his kids, or when he negotiates a truce between warring parties in Northern Ireland?

Why must we envision these accomplishments as mutually exclusive? It is in our power to do otherwise—to bring these opposing sides of our personalities back into balance and harmony. The Public Adam is the honorable side of classical heroism, and we must recognize that his achievements are valuable and important. But we must also bring the Private Adam out from the dark dungeon in which he is currently incarcerated and reinvest him with his lost status as a hero. We must recalibrate these two sides of our personalities so that they share even weight. Society can once again show phenomenal respect for men who work hard, nine-hour days to make the world a better place through industry—and then leave, no matter what, to go home to their kids. We can stop lavishing such disproportionate financial rewards on investment bankers whose jobs demand that they never see their families and instead lavish greater rewards on professional men who simply want to work hard without being obsessed by the acquisition of wealth.

This synthesis of the Public and the Private Adams is the answer to the question we posed at the beginning of this chapter: Is it possible to be successful *and* good? Of course it is. It's not only possible, it's essential: we can never be truly successful, by any meaningful definition, as long as our Public and Private Adams are in conflict. As we will see in the next chapter, we cannot ever truly be successful unless we are also good.

10

⌘

AMBITION: HEROISM

If one advances confidently in the direction of his dreams, and endeavors to live the life which he has imagined, he will meet with a success unexpected in common hours.

—Henry David Thoreau, *Walden* (1854)

M y friend Mike owns an electronics business that employs three hundred people. His innovative business plan? He believes that his workers are actually people, and he works to honor their humanity.

At your very first interview with his company, you're told: "Your job as a parent is more important than your job here." And Mike keeps his promise. Nobody is asked to work late. Family photographs are encouraged in the office, and Mike knows every child by name. The company has formal policies that support families as well. Each employee gets a certain number of hours per year to be spent in support of his or her children. This can be spent going to children's school concerts or Little League games or spending time at home with a sick child. The employees don't need to provide proof that they are taking this time off to spend with their kids. It's not a voucher program: all you have to do to get the time off is to make the request in advance.

The children of employees are invited to an annual Halloween party at the company. Everyone eats candy and parades around the building showing off their scary costumes. A small thing, right? But behind the sugar high there's an important principle. Mike wants his employees to feel like their families are a part of their career and important to the business. He also wants the kids to feel good knowing that their moms and dads work at a fun place.

Mike knows that he's doing this not for his employees, but for their children. "Everybody has these moments of clarity in their life. I suddenly saw that I had the ability to have impact on the lives of hundreds of children based on a company policy. I have children of my own, and I make every effort to attend all their events, the school plays and the birthday parties and the sports events. It didn't seem right that I should have an opportunity to do that because I was the boss of the company, and therefore had more leeway about the hours that I did not have to be in the office. I don't think that having the ability to be a good parent should have to be a perk. I don't know why I reached the conclusion that this was what I wanted to do, but I definitely thought that this was one way that I could have an impact."

Mike's company also strongly supports employees who become involved in community activities. "We have people who do Meals on Wheels, and we don't count the hours spent there as time off. Somehow they always figure out how to catch up on their work, and so even if they are leaving during business hours, we look the other way because we know how vital it is that they are able to do things that help build the community. People who have good jobs and stable families have an obligation to make an imprint on the community, and as a business owner, I want to support that any way I can."

Even though success isn't what motivated these policies, Mike feels that these policies have brought his company immeasurable benefits. It turns out that there's more than enough room for both work and family; you don't need to strangle the Private Adam in order to create a space for the Public Adam to flourish. Mike's employee retention levels are very high, not because they have the highest salaries in the industry, but because the company's philosophy makes them want to stay. He gives them the freedom to develop their families, and they give him the freedom to pursue his business, knowing that they'll be working hard and supporting him all the way. And they're all investing in the best (401)k of all—the next generation. Mike knows that his program is having an outstanding impact. "If you can infiltrate one person's thinking at a time, then you can change the world."

Success may not be a motivating factor behind this kind of goodness, but it's certainly a happy side effect. Contrary to Machiavelli's belief, businesses don't suffer when they take an ethical outlook and treat their workers with dignity. A Watson Wyatt Worldwide survey showed that employees who feel that their companies conduct business with honesty and integrity show markedly higher levels of commitment—68 percent—than those who rate their companies low on these values (12 percent).

Companies that are known for their philanthropy and fair working environments, like Ben and Jerry's or the Timberland shoe company, do better with the public as well. The Watson Wyatt Worldwide survey effectively demonstrated this relationship by noting that companies whose employees rated them high on the honesty and integrity scale had a total return to shareholders of 101 percent averaged over three years. Companies rated low on the honesty and integrity scale averaged only 69 percent. A report published in 1999 by Cone/Roper described a five-year survey of Americans designed to determine how strongly they identify with companies that integrate social issues into their business strategies. According to the report, 83 percent of consumers say they have a more positive image of a company that supports a cause they care about. Further, if price and quality are equal, they are likely to switch to a brand or retailer associated with a good cause.

Goodness can be done in today's business world without a loss of success. While our Public Adam searches for distinctiveness in a life of professional excellence, our Private Adam must carefully balance this by seeking distinction through sharing and creating enduring relationships. Of course the biblical hero can achieve success. In fact, he *should* achieve it. But first, we need to stop defining the successful man as the one who has a billion dollars in the bank and three ex-wives. At most, this man is only half a success. The man who has domestic tranquillity and modest financial success is a complete success, because he has brought that all-important balance into his life.

Ethics only leads to failure if we take a short-term view. Maybe goodness does make you dependent on others. That's a bad thing, however, only if you're working with a flawed definition of strength. Is dependency so bad if it means that you come home every night to a loving spouse and a solid relationship with your children? If your employees are loyal because you have a reputation for fairness and loyalty to them? The biblical hero doesn't feel shame in admitting that he's dependent on other people. He's proud of those relationships, because he knows that they're the only ones that matter.

We may never free ourselves completely of our insecurities, but we can control the kind of ambition they encourage us to pursue. Eleanor Roosevelt spent her entire life feeling self-conscious about the way she looked, but instead of letting her insecurities chase her into a cycle of desperate acquisition and disappointment, she was able to transcend them by relentlessly crusading for the rights and dignity of the disenfranchised. In spite of her crippling shyness, she translated her fear into freedom by pursuing a life of service. She became one of the most powerful, influential, and beloved women in the world—*because* of her goodness, not in spite of it.

Princess Diana tried to ameliorate the suffering of hundreds of thousands of people worldwide, despite her own troubled personal history. When she publicly hugged a child with AIDS, she taught the whole world to love those suffering from that terrible disease. She walked across ground riddled with land mines to show the world the dangers that ordinary people face on an everyday basis. This was a person plagued by eating disorders and depression so severe that she had made attempts on her own life, and yet she never allowed her pain to block out the suffering of others. Instead, she extended her royalty to others. She sought value and found self-worth through alleviating the pain of friends and strangers alike, and she became a heroine.

It's only self-doubt that tells us that we can't get ahead without engaging in competition and ruthlessness. The difference between the classical and biblical concepts of success isn't about accumulation: you can have a biblical hero and a classical hero living right next door to each other, sending their children to the same schools, wearing the same clothes, and driving the same cars. The difference is in how you achieve your success, and what you do with it once you have it. There's nothing wrong with achieving a level of material success in this world. But the classical hero uses his success to feel godlike, to supplant God. The biblical hero offers his successes up to something greater than himself.

I would encourage you not to bury your ambition, but instead, to direct it toward greatness. When the British left India in 1947, Mahatma Gandhi proved that goodness is a force to be reckoned with that can be used to change society. Martin Luther King Jr. wasn't a conqueror—he wanted to change the way people think, and he acted through nonviolence. Equality, a distant dream for so many blacks in the American South, became a reality for millions of African Americans as the direct result of his life. Goodness and dignity can be more powerful and long-lasting than hatred and violence. When our goals are great, then goodness is the only way to achieve them.

The ideals of biblical heroism aren't difficult to apply to the real world, but we have to be conscious of our actions. Moreover, we need to reward goodness when we see it—for instance, in ethical politicians or responsible businessmen. One of the most sobering dot-com stories I know concerns an online travel agent who made a point of donating a portion of his profits to charity. Despite the findings of that Cone/Roper poll, his company went under because people stayed away—travelers wanted a cheaper ticket more than they wanted to do something good for others. What a tragedy.

What we're learning now is that goodness is not simply a private affair. The real heroes of this world, as we are starting to realize, and the people who can make changes, are those who seek to integrate their inner desires with their outer ambitions. The biblical hero is again beginning to dominate the world stage. Great men and women are leaving their mark on a world that is witnessing, as a result, the spread of liberal democracy, a global war against terrorism, and a global war against poverty, and those who are spearheading this movement are achieving wealth and fame in the process. They are changing the world through influence rather than power. In the classical book of heroism, it was James Earl Ray who had the power. Holding a high-powered rifle, he could enact the ultimate form of political censorship by assassinating Martin Luther King Jr. But there are voices that can never be silenced, and the biblical hero will prevail.

Goodness doesn't mean the end of ambition. Goodness is not the opposite of success, as Machiavelli wanted us to believe. To the contrary: we *have* to strive for goodness, for that is the only way we can be truly successful.

11

❦

THE URGE TOWARD GOODNESS

Goodness does not consist in greatness, but greatness in goodness.
—Athenaeus

The question remains: Are people inherently good or inherently bad?

On the one hand, we see people behave in the most extremely mean-spirited manner. On the other hand, those same people can suddenly show tremendous compassion. Before September 11, New Yorkers would just as soon swear at you as look at you. In the days that followed the tragedy, there was such an outpouring of generosity and love that the blood banks had to turn thousands of people away.

So what's the truth? I contend that there's a third possibility. People are neither good nor bad. Born innocent, our actions dictate whether we are angels or scoundrels. But every human being is born with the *desire* to be good, the desire to reconnect to our godly source through saintly action. That's why people feel so horrible about themselves when they do something mean (that is, until they have completely desensitized their conscience). When we act badly, we feel innately that we're sinning against our own nature. Being a person who behaves badly is not who we want to be. What we really, really want is to be good.

Every person has a soul that burns like a candle. And just as a candle flame inclines toward a larger flame when they are put in close proximity, our soul bends inward toward the heavens, drawing us toward something better. The instinct to holiness is innate to us all. It's the reason that sex between two loving people is infinitely better than cheap sex with a prostitute. It's the reason that a man and woman who give their kids a lot of quality and quantity time feel really good about themselves, and it's the reason that we get a bounce in our step whenever we help someone in need. Being good is authentic to us. When we're good, we're catering to our most deep-seated desires.

Furthermore, I believe that the connection we make with our authentic nature when we're good is the first step toward true heroism. When we chase classical heroism, we're actually being chased by our own weaknesses and insecurities. We're the prey, not the predator. This chase for the spoils of classical heroism—the promotion, the paycheck, the symbols of success—distracts us from our true goals.

We're like onions. On the outside we have the coarse layer, easily removed. This layer attracts the dirt and the dust—it is most susceptible to its environment. Similarly, we are attracted to what is around us—whatever it may look like. We may coat ourselves in dirt to the extent that it becomes part of our outer layers. However, our many outer layers protect an inner core that is white and extends upward along the length of the onion. Our soul is pure inside, and at our very core is a godly spark that animates and enlivens us. This part of our soul yearns to return to its source. We cannot deny this part of ourselves; it is intrinsic and it is essential.

We all want to be seen as good people. Otherwise, why would people go to such great lengths to defend and protect their good names? The Talmud says that of all the crowns available to mortal men, the crown of a good name is the most precious of all. The shame of scandal is worse than the pain of failure. Why? Because we want to be thought of as good.

The politician John McCain was accused (though completely exonerated in the end) of being one of the Keating Five, a group of senators who used their position to give favors to a savings and loan magnate. McCain later said that although he was a prisoner of war for five years in the Hanoi Hilton, where he suffered torture and the most inhumane deprivations, that pain was nothing compared to the accusation that he was a dishonest man.

Similarly, the legendary Israeli war hero Avigdor Kahalani was accused of passing state secrets to an Israeli newspaper editor when he was Israel's minister for police. Kahalani is one of only five men to receive Israel's highest military honor, appropriately named "The Hero of Israel." In the 1973 Yom Kippur War, his small tank brigade helped turn back more than two thousand Syrian tanks, saving the north of Israel, and his own tank singlehandedly wiped out ninety of the Syrian tanks. Although he was later cleared of the charges against him, he told me that the year he spent with the cloud of suspicion hanging over him was the worst year of his life. Even the pain of losing his brother in battle and the horrific injuries that he himself sustained (his tank was blown up, resulting in first-degree burns to 80 percent of his body) never came close to the pain of being thought of as a dishonest politician. There's a similar story about Thomas Jefferson, who was accused of being a coward during the Revolution. He later said that he never recovered from the accusation.

If these men aren't examples of our deep desire to transcend classical heroism and become biblical heroes, I don't know what is. These men had accrued the highest honors, the glory, the military parades and decorations from heads of state. McCain is a senator and one of the most respected men in American politics; Kalahani is revered by military commanders around the world; Jefferson was president, one of the Founding Fathers. Yet all of these men's achievements paled before the most important thing of all: the preservation of their good name.

At the beginning of his book *How to Win Friends and Influence People*, Dale Carnegie says that the best way to flatter people, even better than praising their intelligence or their accomplishments, is to tell them you think they're good. We all want to be thought of as good people. This applies not only to the most virtuous but also to the most sinister people in society. Take an extreme form of evil, like the Nazis, as a case in point.

I had always wanted to visit Auschwitz. I wanted to be in the place where millions of my people perished simply because they were Jews. Arriving at the death camp in 1998, I was violently shaken by the sight of thousands of shoes, bearing witness to the thousands of victims who would not return to reclaim them. In another room thousands of innocent victims suddenly acquired names, and a holocaust of six million suddenly became a personal tragedy of individual victims. Here were the remaining pieces of luggage, the suitcases and bags, bearing the name of each person who had arrived in Auschwitz. Eighty percent of them were dead within two hours of arriving at the camp.

Where did all these people go? The answer, of course, was to the crematoria. With my guide in tow, I went from Auschwitz I to Auschwitz III, known as Birkenau, to see the infamous machines of death. And here was the most surprising thing of all: nothing remained of Crematoria I and II other than blown-up rubble. Of Crematoria III, IV, and V, nothing remained at all. The Germans, on Hitler's personal orders, had destroyed the death machinery of Auschwitz in an effort to bury the crime. At Belzec, eight hundred thousand Jews were incarcerated and murdered, but there is no evidence of it today. The camp was completely dismantled by the Nazis, who planted trees over it and converted it back to forest. Even today it retains its haunting silence, its horrible secrets buried deep beneath its majestic veneer. The Nazis had literally covered up their fiendish crime.

Why did they do this? Likewise, why was there not even a single written document directly linking Hitler with the order to exterminate European Jewry? I asked myself a simple question: If the Nazis truly hated the Jews, weren't they proud of their hatred? Didn't they advertise it to the entire world with their repulsive Nuremberg Laws and public pogroms like Kristallnacht? Why not make the crematoria and death camps into national shrines advertising the ultimate triumph of the Aryan over the Semitic race? Rather than destroy the concentration camps, why not make them into triumphant museums? I had always assumed that the Nazis reveled in their evil—that they were as proud of their murders as mothers are of their children. Even in their moment of defeat, I could not see why they had wanted to destroy the evidence of their destructive power before the world could witness it.

You see, even the Nazis, the greatest beasts of all time, wanted to cover up their crimes—even the *Nazis* were concerned about their reputation! Murderers always provide rationalizations for their crimes. The Timothy McVeighs and Unabombers write manifestos explaining their actions to the world, hoping that they will ultimately be understood to have been acting in the interests of justice. They don't want people to think that they have acted cruelly without reason.

We want to be known as good people. But I believe that we also want to *be* good.

If we look at the lives of some of the most well-known criminals, we see that even they struggled to be good in some way. Jesse James, the famous outlaw of the Wild West, was a Robin Hood figure, someone who was always ready to help out some poor cowpoke who was down on his luck. John Dillinger and his gang, who robbed banks during the Depression, would empty a bank of its money, but while they were there, they would also steal and destroy records of mortgages that people were finding so difficult to pay. They saw their crimes as a service to society.

The infamous Jewish gangster Meyer Lansky once boasted proudly that "everyone who came into my casino knew that if he lost his money it wouldn't be because he was cheated." One of Al Capone's biographers writes: "Although he preyed on other people's weaknesses for a living, his reputation and standing in the community mattered deeply to him. The deeper he went into racketeering and all its associated sins, the more he idealized his family, as though they, in their innocence, were living proof that he was not the monster that the newspapers later insisted he was." Capone was a devoted father who doted on his son, and he saw himself as a source of pride to the Italian immigrant community, a generous benefactor and an important fixer who helped people. He provided employment to thousands of poor Italian immigrants through his bootlegging operations. He gave a considerable amount of money to charity, and in 1930 he even opened up a soup kitchen that served three free meals a day. "Public service is my motto," he once told a reporter. Decades later, New York gangster John Gotti followed in Capone's footsteps, becoming beloved in his community for his generosity.

If we want to be cynical about it, we can argue that these criminals benefited from the public support and good PR these actions brought them. But I would also argue that these criminals toyed with being good because they liked the way it made them feel. They too struggled with the balance between their Private and Public Adams. Their ruthlessness brought them no peace, no matter how much money they made robbing banks, or how many illegal saloons were pumping dollars into shoeboxes for them. They craved the simple pleasure that being good brought them. So they gave a lot of money to charity, and they helped a lot of people. Sure, they also tommy-gunned people to death, but that didn't give them pride. They didn't take pride from being heroes in the classical sense; even they wished they could be heroes in the biblical tradition. Business was simply business, but goodness was a source of satisfaction.

This is the most joyful aspect of the argument for biblical heroism. Being good makes us happy. It's that simple, and it's this that Machiavelli didn't understand. His theories run counter to our deepest ambition for ourselves—they're toxic. We can't absorb his philosophy without making ourselves sick.

My own story is the best example of this that I know. I have been fortunate to have achieved modest success in some aspects of my career, and I expected happiness to follow that success. But it didn't, which caused no end of wonder. Why wasn't writing a popular book enough to satisfy me? Why did appearing on television shows leave me with such a fleeting feeling of achievement? So I adopted a new strategy. I talked myself into thinking that happiness is a foreign god, not worthy of pursuit. What is happiness, anyway, other than a feeling of inner contentment? And isn't contentment merely the hallmark of mediocrity? When you are content, you no longer aspire to anything more. If you're not itching on the inside, you have no compulsion to act on the outside. Isn't inner peace just a prison designed to preclude the opportunity for further achievement?

As I have matured, I have regained my will to be happy. And I feel that I have discovered one of life's greatest secrets: that you *have to be good* in order to be happy. When I spend an evening playing with my children, I go to sleep a contented man. This is true even if my work responsibilities have piled up. Before the Bible and my Judaism reshaped my dreams, I wanted to be the guy who is recognized by strangers when he walks into a restaurant. Now I know that the real hero is he who is greeted by his children when he walks through the door at night, because he comes home at a decent hour to play ball with them in the yard rather than staying out late and trying to win over the rest of the world. I now understand that so many of the people I looked up to as heroes were really weak and ordinary men whose lives were impelled by a desperate need for attention in an attempt to comfort their lacerated egos.

Happiness is predicated on inner and outer harmony. Since our innermost desire is to be good, we can't be fulfilled unless our outermost actions reflect that desire. We need to achieve synthesis between those two desires. Goodness, as we shall see, is not just a moral imperative, but a psychological necessity as well. It's what we really want.

12

IN PRAISE OF THE STRUGGLE

When the freedom they wished for most was freedom from responsibility, then Athens ceased to be free and was never free again.

—Edith Hamilton, *The Greek Way* (1950)

If I'm correct, then the secret to a fulfilling life, and the first step toward true heroism, is to master the art of goodness. If the will to goodness is the quintessence of human nature, then a question naturally follows: Why aren't we better people? What's getting in the way of our innermost desire being manifest in our outermost actions? If the desire to be good is so innate, why do so many of us fail at it? Answering this question is crucial to our happiness because, as I have said repeatedly, wars bring no happiness. When you are experiencing inner conflict—feeling disappointed about the way your life is turning out, with your outermost actions grating against your innermost desires—you have no hope of achieving contentment or happiness.

The first and foremost reason we fail at being good is that it's hard. Being a really good person is a struggle for many of us. It is for me anyway. Unlike many of the people who surround me, it has never come naturally to me. I am not the type of person who naturally thinks of getting up and washing the dishes when I finish eating. I have to remind myself and push myself to do so. Nor was I, in the past, the kind of person who naturally gave rich and poor the same amount of time and attention. For many years, when I ran the L'Chaim Society in the United Kingdom, I was the sole fundraiser for three large student centers. I had to find our operating budget every single month. And that conditioned me, like every fundraiser, to spend much of my time courting wealthy individuals who might take an interest in our organization, to the exclusion of worthier people I might have helped.

My wife, Debbie, has no such problems. I married someone whose capacity to give is infinitely greater than my own. And with her it comes naturally. Through all the controversy that my book *Kosher Sex* generated—not everyone thought it appropriate for a rabbi to pen a book by that title—Debbie stood by me like a rock. She gave superhuman support without which I could not have continued, and all she asked for in return was my undivided affection. Yet because she is such a good person, I find myself having to defend her all the time. I make sure that nobody takes advantage of her, because she finds it very difficult to say no to all who ask of her.

When I am with Debbie, I wonder to myself, how can she be so good? And why am I not naturally like that? I have tried to live a good life, to be true to my religious convictions and available to all those who are in need. But it has often been an uphill trek. I have dedicated my life to counseling others and making their paths easier, but it used to be important to me that people know about those efforts. Only in the past few years have I made great progress in doing good deeds and purposely keeping them silent.

Ironically, I have never resisted the rituals of the Jewish faith. To be sure, eating kosher food in all places, even when I'm traveling in Singapore, is no easy practice. I've gone hungry much of the time and have had to learn to survive on tuna fish and lettuce. Likewise, remembering to pray and don my tefillin every morning, even when I awaken to a hundred urgent responsibilities, can be immensely trying. But I've learned to do it. It has become a part of my day, and the experience of dedicating time each day to something other than myself and my own suffocating agenda can be very liberating indeed.

Goodness, however, is different,. No matter how many times

you do the right thing, the next time will still be a struggle. Every interaction and situation in the course of a day requires that you make choices about your behavior, and it is tremendously difficult to choose to do the right thing every time. You'll somehow manage to rein in your temper today, only to discover tomorrow that the beast within is just as potent as the day before. Giving ten dollars to a homeless person on the street feels really good. You have struggled against yourself and triumphed over your selfish inner nature! But goodness doesn't get much easier. It will be as hard tomorrow to give up that ten dollars as it was today. There's no end to the transformation. We are constantly in the process of "becoming good." Our survival instinct, which isn't our core nature (we know this because people will give up their lives for a cause), somehow always seems to get in the way and makes us feel that our interests ought to come first.

It's a struggle, but there is glory in that battle against ourselves. The ancient rabbis said, "In the place where a man who has changed for the better stands, the completely righteous are not allowed to stand." The struggling everyman, the person for whom goodness does not come naturally and who wrestles daily with his selfish inclination, holds a place of honor much higher than that of the most venerated canonized saint. The rabbis were quite serious when they wrote this; they recognized the strength in the struggle.

The classical hero is known for making it look easy. He easily surmounts the moral challenges he faces and is never in doubt as to his purpose. In the movie *Gladiator,* Russell Crowe's character wipes out all the other warriors with barely a struggle. His triumph comes easily to him. That's because the classical hero is always portrayed as superhuman, a man who makes most others seem pitiful in comparison.

In contrast, the biblical hero has no desire to be anything more than human. He finds greatness in maximizing his humanity, rather than transcending it. If someone were to offer him some elixir—a heroic Viagra that would make it all easy—he would turn it down because he revels in the struggle, knowing there's nothing greater than the fight to be a good man. He seeks his own triumph rather than someone else's assistance. As the ancient rabbis asked, "Who is a hero?" Someone who conquers the world? No, they said. "It is someone who conquers himself."

In comparison, the classical hero is a washout. He may struggle against adversaries, but he never struggles with himself. Since we continue to worship people who are always good, always above the moral fray—what I like to call the Mother Teresa variety of hero—we do not feel ourselves capable of true heroism. We struggle on the inside, so we think we're unworthy.

We're mistaken. It's not our innate goodness that makes us heroes, it's our willingness to do battle against ourselves every day. Look at it this way. If you make $100 million a year, giving a thousand to charity is a good thing to do, but it's not heroism. If you make $17,000 a year, giving that same thousand dollars is suddenly heroism. To give that kind of charity, you have overcome phenomenal internal resistance. Biblical heroism, true heroism, requires that you struggle against your baser nature.

Look at all the celebrity idols we worship in Hollywood, all of our modern classical heroes. How many can you find who can be said to have really struggled against themselves and triumphed? Britney Spears recently opened a large charitable foundation to help the needy. Yet she made the money she uses to help the needy by exploiting American teenage girls, encouraging them to dress and flaunt their bodies like she does. Where is the heroism there? Does her meteoric rise speak to her innate talent, or are she and her handlers just manipulating vulnerable girls and lecherous men? Whatever she gives away will represent a small fraction of her overall net worth. This is not to minimize the goodness of setting up a charity—that is surely a good thing to do. But it is not heroism, because it requires no struggle.

Celebrities have conquered the world, but they haven't come close to conquering themselves. I want to see a movie starring Private Adam. I want to see a major Hollywood celebrity married for fifty years. I want to see a leading man who isn't a ladies' man. I want to see a guy who, impressive as he is at getting millions of people to see his movies, is equally impressive at overlooking the massive adulation given to him by fawning and willing women. If a man like that doesn't exist, can any of them be called heroes?

A woman once came to see me, terribly distraught. She had been out at a party with her husband, and she noticed him eyeballing the other women at the affair. She wanted to know if she could still trust her husband. I told her, "If he wrestles with his nature to be faithful and monogamous, then not only can you trust him, but you should be honored to be married to him. He loves you so much that he fights himself to be completely devoted to you. But if he just excuses his being distracted as typical male behavior and makes no concerted effort to change, then you are married to a weak man who may cause you considerable pain in life."

When a man is attracted to women other than his wife, and she to strangers as well, yet they both choose to come home happily to each other, they both win a daily contest. Their affection for each other is reaffirmed daily. If they choose each other under the wedding canopy and then never need to reaffirm their choice, they will become irrelevant to each other and the relationship will lack passion. In a relationship, the highest compliment a man can give to a woman is to tell her that he wrestles with his nature daily to be a better man—to be focused, caring, dedicated, and faithful. This tells her that she is worth fighting for. The highest compliment is to be chosen anew every day.

The same thing is true about our relationship with God. The Zohar, Judaism's foremost mystical text, says that God does not wish for people to be righteous, but rather to constantly subdue evil. In other words, struggle is superior to righteousness. God wants to be relevant in people's lives. What relevance does God have in the life of the completely righteous, the total saint? The battle is won; the conquest is finished. God may now be carefully laid by the wayside, since His hegemony is assured in the life of the righteous. There is no inclination toward anything else. The righteous never have to fight for him. With no inclination toward evil, they are not choosing God so much as following their own natural instinct for goodness. They don't have to battle their nature to be good, so how precious can goodness be to them?

It's the money donated when we really can't afford it, the phone call taken from a friend in need when we're already late, and the compliment given when we're tired and irritable that make us heroes. We really triumph over ourselves when we choose to do good, and we need to understand that this struggle against ourselves to be good is what life is all about. The struggle affirms our humanity and highlights our values.

We have to be inspired to goodness. Goodness cannot be imposed from above either, because that is not true goodness. This is a mistake made by many world religions. Goodness needs to be nurtured from within. We are not robots or automatons, programmed by God to do whatever He commands. For that, God has angels. The struggle for goodness shows Him that we are desperately trying to be in touch with our deepest nature.

The difference between three biblical heroes demonstrates how much glory there is to be found in the struggle. There are three patriarchs of the Jewish people. Of the three, Jacob is the most significant. The Jewish people are not known as the children of Abraham or Isaac, but as the children of Israel, the name the angel gives Jacob after he defeats it in battle.

Jacob's not a shoo-in, however, for the most significant biblical hero. At first glance, Abraham seems to be the greatest of the three. After all, it was Abraham who first discovered God in the starlit heavens of Mesopotamia, and it was Abraham who disseminated that knowledge and began winning converts. It was Abraham who unhesitatingly prepared to offer up his son on God's holy altar as a sacrifice. Isaac also represents an extremely righteous ideal, for he was prepared to give up his life as a sacrifice to God. At a glance, Jacob seems to be the least worthy of the patriarchs. He is the one who first tricks his brother into selling him his birthright in exchange for a bowl of soup. He then later fools his father into believing that he is his brother, Esau, in order to receive the first-born blessing. And although this connivance is done at the behest of his mother, he still goes along with the trick. Later he favors one wife, Rachel, over the other, Leah, as well as one child, Joseph, over his other twelve children. This is a hero?

But the greatness of Jacob, which by far transcends that of Abraham and Isaac, derives from being the first hero in the Bible forced to struggle with his ideals in the practical world. Abraham and Isaac are brilliant idealists. They have faith in God and they love God, but they are not part of the larger world. Abraham is depicted as a loner who separates himself from the corrupt vices of his neighbors. He will pray for Sodom and Gomorrah, but he will not live with them because he believes his values are superior to theirs. That's how he earns the name Abraham the Hebrew, which means "he who is separate." He represents the kernel of an idea, the seed of faith, which needs isolation to grow and develop because strong winds could topple the sapling.

This life of isolation is continued through Abraham's son Isaac, whom the ancient rabbis referred to as a "holy sacrifice." Since Isaac was brought up on God's altar, he cannot mix with unscrupulous elements. He is the cherished son of Abraham's old age, the ideal prince. He has the perfect parents, is fortunate to marry a wonderful woman, and is wealthy to boot. A righteous man, he has nothing in common with the wicked. Indeed, Abraham and Isaac are both portrayed by the Bible as men of great wealth, which meant that they were entirely independent of their neighbors. They live separate from the rest of the world and stand firmly on the side of righteousness. And while they are good men, their contribution to the world is mostly personal.

Jacob is the first man who is challenged with the task of translating an ideal into something real, a philosophical thought into a practical mode of living. He is the first man who has to find the balance in his life between pie-in-the-sky fantasy and reality. Perched between heaven and earth, his will be a life of struggle: between the nefarious forces of the world, on the one hand, and the godly tradition he is charged to uphold on the other. He begins life wanting to be just like his forebears. The Bible calls him "a wholesome man who likes to sit in tents." He too wants to be an enlightened man of learning, inhabiting the world of theory, leaving the corrupt world to its own devices.

But he is not as lucky as his father and grandfather. He is born with a violent and conniving brother, Esau, who plans to run off with the family silver. His mother, Rebecca, sees the wicked character of her elder son and wants to ensure that Jacob will inherit his father's spiritual legacy instead. She fears the dire consequences when Esau—the hunter-gatherer, the classical hero—receives his father's blessing and inherits the earth, vanquishing Jacob, the biblical hero, the philosopher-king. So she comes to Jacob and says to him, in essence, "Get out of your tent. You will not be like your father. You will be forced to fight for your ideals. Your life will be the life of struggle. Your integrity will be tested on a daily basis. Your ideals will be given practical challenges. For you, there is no other way." So Jacob dons the goatskins that will fool his blind father and lead him to believe that Jacob is Esau. For the rest of his life he will walk a razor-thin line between morality and necessity. He would rather study, but he must fight. He cannot permit the thugs and tyrants of the world to dominate.

Those who believe that the classical heroes are the really good guys have traditionally been very critical of Jacob. They portray him as an unscrupulous schemer and conniver who fooled his father and robbed Esau of the mantle of firstborn. This position has most recently been taken by my friend and colleague Rabbi Harold Kushner in *Living a Life That Matters*. Kushner sees Jacob as a man prepared "to get what he wanted by whatever means it took." He sees Jacob as a man "at war with himself. Part of him takes pride in his ability to use his cleverness to fool people and get what he wants. But another part of him is uncomfortable with all that cleverness and the realization that people resent and mistrust him for it." At the end of the book Kushner writes: "The young Jacob believed that, in order to make his mark on the world, he had to take advantage of people—his blind father, his hungry and unsophisticated brother. He thought that if he could find the other person's weakness and exploit it he would win and his rival would lose."

I believe that this characterization is far from the truth. It ignores Jacob's Herculean struggles to do the right thing amid extremely trying circumstances. What would Rabbi Kushner have Jacob do? Cede the world to Esau because he wants to remain above the fray? That would be moral cowardice and false piety. Heroism is not where you save your skin and let everyone else perish. It reminds me of all those people who say that the Jewish people are compromising their morality in the conflict in the Middle East. To be sure,

Jews around the world mourn the loss of innocent civilians who are sometimes harmed in Israel's attempt to elliminate murderous Palestinian terrorists. But what would they rather the Jews who live in Israel do? Should they pack up and say, "Living in this neighborhood is too risky to our morality?" Should they move to the moon? Righteous men or women do not shirk their responsibilities to protect life and uphold justice. They struggle to do the right thing, even when doing so causes them to straddle a very fine moral line.

When we look at how Jacob behaves, we see a man who desperately tries not to stain his morality. The ancient rabbis point out that Jacob is super-careful with his language when he is pretending to be his brother, trying to use the least possible trickery to get the job done. He goes as far as he has to, but never any further. Jacob is not happy with what he has to do, but the world is inhabited by forces of good and evil and it's not enough to simply bask in the light. A hero has to defeat the darkness—a job that neither Abraham nor Isaac engaged in with any significant immersion.

Throughout his life Jacob will be forced to wrestle. He will fight the angel that tries to kill him, and he will even be given a new name, "Yisrael," which translates as "he who wrestles with God." His is not an easy life. He is himself tricked by his father-in-law out of seven years of work. He lives in fear of his brother, Esau, exterminating him and all his family. His daughter is raped, and his sons respond violently. His ten eldest sons harbor immense jealousy for their younger brother, Joseph, and kidnap him. Joseph disappears for the next twenty-two years, and Jacob believes that his favorite son is dead.

Jacob does not have the opportunity to enjoy the tranquillity of his forebears, so his is a higher heroism. His faith is tested and stands fast. Abraham and Isaac were more of the heavens than the earth, more angels than men. They move away from the earth on the ladder in Jacob's dream, untouched by it. Jacob is a homegrown, earthly hero. Although he has to struggle mightily his whole life, he and his children are entrusted with establishing the Jewish nation as a lasting entity and going concern, bringing God into the real world of commerce, politics, and everyday life.

Those of us who have inherited the struggle of Jacob are born to complain. We wish life were an endless string of vacations and parties, complete with a money tree growing in our backyard. But there's only one problem with that vision. It would be a leisurely life of mediocrity. If we're never challenged, how can we know the thrill of victory? The husband and wife who've given up the struggle and divorced may not argue any more, but they're also alone. The trust-fund baby has it easy, but he'll never know the pleasure of an honest day's hard work.

Abraham Lincoln was a biblical hero like Jacob. For four long years in the White House, he wrestled with the angel. He was subjected to vitriolic attack, not just from the South but from the North as well. He was despised by nearly every significant political faction in the Union. It's extremely difficult to stick to your moral guns when everyone is against you. Other presidents presided over periods of great prosperity and coasted to reelection. But none of them had the immense satisfaction of seeing men and women emancipated from slavery as a direct result of their efforts.

The willingness to engage in the struggle on an ongoing basis is what makes a hero. Goodness is a constant aspiration rather than a goal to be reached. There is no culmination: since we are constantly becoming good, we are constantly engaged in the struggle. In her writings during her campaign for democracy and human rights in Burma, Aung San Suu Kyi, whose husband, Michael Aris, was an acquaintance of mine at Oxford, observed that "the quintessential revolution is that of the spirit. It is not enough merely to call for freedom, democracy, and human rights. There has to be a united determination to persevere in the struggle, to make sacrifices in the name of enduring truths, to resist the corrupting influences of desire, ill will, ignorance, and fear." Similarly, Thomas Jefferson said that the tree of liberty must be constantly nourished by the blood of patriots. The biblical hero is one who has embraced that struggle.

13

❧

THE IMPERFECT HERO CAN
CHANGE THE WORLD

Better a diamond with a flaw, than a pebble without.

—Confucius, *Analects*

It's important to note that we may not always be successful in our struggle. Our generation is guilty of believing that imperfect people cannot help perfect the world. We basically believe that the imperfect man should first clean himself up before he dares to try to help those around him.

The biblical hero is not immune to the lure of the classical. During John McCain's five years in a Vietnamese prisoner-of-war camp, he was offered early release; his father was the Supreme Commander of American Forces in the Pacific, and the gesture was a cynical public relations move by his captors. But McCain chose, despite his horrendous injuries, to stay in the rathole instead of jumping the line to go free because of his connections. Still, when he was finally released to a hero's welcome, he admits that it went to his head. He went over to the classical side, divorcing his wife, marrying an heiress, and going into politics. But then his true colors started coming out again. He started campaigning for real reforms. He and his wife adopted a little girl from Cambodia and refused to make it an issue during the campaign. I believe that he is one of our most valuable and honest politicians today, and a real example of a classical hero successfully converted to biblical heroism.

Obviously, we're all capable of being both kinds of hero, and we choose every day which kind we will be. Being a bona-fide biblical hero doesn't prevent us from becoming a classical one. But neither does a slip negate the good we have already done, and it doesn't preclude us from getting back on track.

The world defines a hypocrite as someone who doesn't practice what he preaches. A man is considered a charlatan if he advocates one thing in public yet does the opposite in private. By this logic, however, a man who finds it difficult to give to charity has no right to encourage others to give, nor even any right to celebrate philanthropy since he doesn't practice it himself. The absurdity of this conclusion is self-evident. It suggests that those who lie cannot extol the virtues of truth, and those who are materialistic cannot promote the redeeming qualities of spirituality. A world guided by such principles would be one where someone who once made an anti-Semitic comment would not be allowed to condemn the Nazis. In short, this kind of moralistic stand is hopelessly extreme and prevents real progress in the world.

Lyndon Johnson was a racist by the accepted definition of the term. He used the word "nigger" to describe blacks on countless occasions. His maiden speech to the Senate as a freshman senator from Texas in 1949 was a passionate defense of racial segregation. His closest ally in the Senate was the legendary Richard Russell, the architect of the South's perennial legal defense strategies against the cessation of segregation. Yet amid all of this, Johnson, both as Senate majority leader and president of the United States, ended up pushing through the broadest and most comprehensive civil rights legislation of all time.

There is a great difference between hypocrisy and inconsistency. A hypocrite is not merely someone who has been known to fall short of his beliefs, but also someone who doesn't even believe what he preaches, regardless of how fervently he claims otherwise. A hypocrite takes stands for public consumption that he would scorn privately if he thought he'd never be caught out. You're not a hypocrite if you condemn anger but then sometimes lose control. That just makes you human. A hypocrite is someone who condemns anger but secretly believes that screaming at people is the only way to get anything done. A hypocrite is someone who extols the virtues of forgiveness but considers those who overlook slights to be weaklings and pushovers. A hypocrite is someone who advocates the equality of mankind but looks with contempt on the underprivileged.

By these lights, even a person who has publicly made flagrant mistakes in his behavior, like Bill Clinton, has every right to advocate a principle like family values so long as he is sincere in his convictions. We lose something immeasurable when we discount such people simply because they have not been perfect in their own lives. What we should be seeking from our public leaders is all that we expect from ourselves—not perfection but sincerity, not flawlessness but struggle. Men and women are not perfect. Human fallibility is a valid excuse for not always doing right; what is inexcusable is saying things that you don't believe just because it's going to get you ahead.

Of course, what we most want to do and what we actually do aren't always the same thing. But we can't use the excuse of the struggle as an excuse not to perform good deeds. A husband comes home every night, too exhausted and demoralized from his job to be affectionate to his wife. His fatigue is understandable, and thus his excuse is valid, but he still has to find a way to make it work. His wife can be infinitely understanding, but the marriage will not survive if all he has to offer her are excuses for his lack of affection. Judaism puts a great deal of emphasis on action, on the completion of a deed. It is important that we are ambitious and successful in our struggle as well.

The heroes of the Bible are clearly tortured in many cases by the decisions they must make, but their heroism lies in their ability to come through on the side of goodness. When God commands Abraham to sacrifice his son, Isaac, surely Abraham is engulfed by mental and emotional torment, yet we know nothing of his inner conflict. For Abraham that conflict is important—for us, not so much. What matters is that he successfully carries out the will of God even though it directly contradicts his own self-interest. The same is true of Joseph and his inner fight to forgive his brothers for their attempt to murder him. We hear very little of his struggle. The important thing is that Joseph is able to overcome his hostility and heroically reaches out to his brothers when he could have chosen instead to do them serious harm.

None (or at least very few) of us are going to become Mother Teresa overnight. The majority of us can't immediately summon the moral fortitude that such monumental sacrifice requires. But neither do we have to. That's not our destiny. We still have before us the noble challenge of practicing kindness and goodness, of working to love our fellow man as we would ourselves. We don't have to live on the streets of Calcutta to make a difference by helping a homeless person who asks us for money on the street. If we can't find a cure for AIDS, we still have an obligation to visit our friends in the hospital. Likewise, even if we never become Don Juan in our marriages, we should try to never miss the opportunity to compliment our spouses and we can strive to never take them for granted.

With every moral battle we fight and win, we come closer and closer to the ideal of biblical heroism. Every time we refrain from gossip to avoid hurting a friend, we are victorious. Every time we give to charity instead of using that money for a trip, we reach the heights of heroism. Every time a woman away from home chooses a late-night phone call to her husband over the flattering flirtations available to her in the hotel bar, she will have the joy and honor of knowing she has grown as a human being.

The best of us comes out when we are engaged in the battle. We should revel in our struggle to be good, rather than feel constantly guilty about it. Most of us think the fact that we need to struggle to do the right thing is proof of how distant we are from goodness. The opposite is true. The fact that we choose to fight shows how deeply we care about bettering ourselves as human beings. Our fallibility just makes our choice to be good all the more inspiring. Although there is no heroism without goodness, goodness in itself isn't heroism. It is the struggle to *choose* the good, in a world of infinite possibility, that makes a hero.

14

❦

ACHIEVING SERENITY

The struggle to reach the top is itself enough to fulfill the heart of man. One must believe that Sisyphus is happy.
—Albert Camus, *Le Mythe de Sisyphe* (1942)

So will being good make us happy?

In a lot of ways, that's the wrong question. Happiness should be not the goal, but the outcome of life's struggle. Happiness isn't something we can effectively aspire to so much as something that naturally evolves from an authentic life in which our deepest desires are met. In other words, happiness is the natural outgrowth of inner harmony and peace, the total integration of the self.

The biblical hero possesses not only dignity but vision. When you choose heroism over cowardice, goodness over selfishness, and love of humanity over love of personal gain, it changes the way you see the world. Have you ever wondered why the true biblical heroes of our time seem so calm? How is it that people like Martin Luther King Jr., Gandhi, Mother Teresa, the Lubavitcher Rebbe, and the Dalai Lama are able to achieve such genuine grace, even under great physical and emotional strain? The reason is that theses heroes— those rare people who have thoroughly absorbed the tenets of biblical heroism—have achieved complete serenity. Their insides match their outsides. A glass that has been broken will always bear the scar of the break, but you cannot find a seam between the inside and the outside of the biblical hero.

People often questioned whether Martin Luther King Jr.'s unflappable serenity was genuine; at times it was hard to believe that he could be as patient and as good as he seemed to be. Then, one day, while he was speaking, a man rushed up to the podium and hit King in the face with a closed fist, so hard that he fell to the floor. People were astounded, but all the more so when they saw what happened next: Martin Luther King picked himself up and kept speaking. He also demanded that the man not be harmed. He never lost his serenity. When you have peace at your center, it cannot be shaken out of you.

On the night before he was assassinated, Martin Luther King said he wasn't afraid to die, and I believe him. For all the self-involved among us, death is the worst thing that can happen: it means the literal end of you. But if what moves you is not your own self-interest but your cause, then the only true impact of your death is the impact it makes on that cause. The classical hero is torn between his inner light and his selfish quest for money, power, and all the accoutrements. Martin Luther King was so fully dedicated to his cause that despite his tumultuous life and violent death, he enjoyed an untouchable sense of inner peace.

The same is true of the Holocaust survivor Victor Frankl. In his international best-seller, *Man's Search for Meaning*, Frankl writes that even amid the horrors of the Nazi death camps he was able to maintain his dignity by maintaining choice. The Nazis could strip him of his happiness by murdering his family. They could strip him of his home by incarcerating him like an animal in hell. They could strip him of his name by placing a number on his arm. But there was one thing they could never take from him, which he retained throughout the horrors of his time in the death camps: how he chose to respond to each new indignity. While they could take away his bread, they could not take away his determination to share whatever crumbs he had with his fellow inmates. While they could take away his future, they could not take away his capacity to give hope to his fellow prisoners.

By maintaining his hold on his own reactions—and thus his dignity—in this way, Frankl prevented the Nazis from turning him into an animal. He could feel degraded, as they clearly intended, or he could retain the option of seeing himself as a man, despite everything that was happening around him. The second option was obviously more difficult, but it was the one that Frankl chose. When you have your dignity inside, it cannot be taken away by anything happening to you on the outside. The Nazis could determine where Frankl was, but they could not determine *who* he was. That was a choice that only he could make.

Reading Frankl's Holocaust testimony is very different from reading many of the other haunting memoirs of Holocaust survivors. Some other survivors, like Bruno Bettelheim and Primo Levi, distinguished as they were in their illustrious professional careers, never recovered from their experiences and took their own lives many years after their liberation. But Frankl, amazingly, maintained his path. A great serenity, a deeply embedded calm, pervades his prose. I am convinced that the sanity Frankl retained, and the healthy mindset that characterized him in the half-century he survived after the Holocaust, was due to the choices he was able to make even in the cauldron of Auschwitz. This is heroism's highest point: the ability to remain your own master even when all the forces of the world are arrayed against you.

Finally, lest there be any misunderstanding, I would point out that, for all his serenity, Frankl did not accept his fate. In fact, he never stopped struggling internally against what was being done to him. I believe this is the secret to the serenity we see in many of the biblical heroes we've discussed, including Martin Luther King Jr. A biblical hero isn't serene because he refrains from the struggle—he's serene because he recognizes the struggle as part of life.

15

❦

HOW CAN WE KNOW WE'RE
DOING THE RIGHT THING?

I think of a hero as someone who understands the degree of
responsibility that comes with his freedom.

—Bob Dylan, from an interview, 1985

Even if we're committed to the struggle for goodness, it's sometimes hard to know the right thing to do in any given situation. One
of the problems with goodness is that the terms in which it's defined
have tended to be influenced by the place and time in which it's
being practiced. So how can we know what is the right thing, the
heroic thing, to do? Various philosophical systems, each with its
strengths and weaknesses, have tackled this particular question
through the ages. What follows is a brief survey of some of those
benefits and pitfalls.

The Rewards Are in the Afterlife

It's hard to talk about goodness without doing so in the context of
Christianity. Christians believe in a very personal, primarily introspec-
tive, idea of goodness. It's a transcendent philosophy: through piety
and prayer, the soul will eventually leave the earth for the heavens.

Consider this quote from St. Augustine: "In this all true believers daily make progress, seeking to acquire not an earthly kingdom, but the kingdom of heaven; not a temporal, but an eternal inheritance; not gold and silver, but the incorruptible riches of the angels; not the good things of this life, which are enjoyed with trembling, and which no one can take with him when he dies, but the vision of God, whose grace and power of imparting felicity transcend all beauty of form in bodies." It's clear that, for the Christian, the game of life is being played so that we can collect our rewards in heaven.

Of course, there is much to be praised in the Christian emphasis on charity and good works. And yet what's interesting to me is how completely opposite this one aspect of Christianity is from its counterpart in Judaism. A belief system like Christianity, which puts souls over bodies, the internal before the external, carries an inherent risk: by valuing motivation over action, it can be used to excuse immoral action if it is precipitated by moral intention (as happened, for instance, during the Inquisition, when heretics were burned at the stake because it was believed that saving their souls from eternal damnation was preferable to saving their bodies from earthly flames). The ends, put simply, were used to justify the means.

Moreover, the Christian notion of original sin and the fall of humanity suggests that goodness cannot ultimately triumph in our world. Christian theology sees ours as a fallen world, where the evil prosper and the good suffer. The soul, crafted from a spark of God's holy throne, is viewed as superior to the body, born as it is of carnal sin. Suffering brings redemption, the rewards of which will be manifest in the next world. Christianity, Islam, and other religions hold that there is no certain reward for goodness in our world, only in the hereafter. We must be good in this world in order to receive the world to come. The believer must do his or her best to withstand the predilection to evil that runs rampant in our world.

Anyone who actually values this world and all the good it has to offer might understandably wonder about this part of the theory. What good is goodness if it can only be appreciated in the world to come? If we say that goodness can have no place in our world, aren't we saying that goodness is irrelevant here in our world? And if goodness is irrelevant, then what responsibilities do we have? If goodness is beside the point, we might as well start reading *The Prince* and planning our paths to power.

Other major world religions raise similar questions. Buddhism and Hinduism both focus on the transcendence of the spiritual over the physical, the belief that goodness is an ethereal, celestial quality. This life, this world, is nothing but a portal of entry into the world to come. It's hard not to consider, when confronted with the teeming hovels of Calcutta or the Sudan, whether the world's dominant religions have contributed to this denigration of human dignity by downplaying the importance of our lives in this world. Overlook your suffering here, they promise, lead a meritorious life, and gain entry into the afterlife. Yet why must our bodies always suffer? Isn't this world itself worth the effort? Is it not better to hold that goodness needs to be earthy and strong, and that it should concern itself with the everyday, not just the starry heavens?

Following the Ten Commandments

For many of us, the Ten Commandments are the most profound and comprehensive code of goodness ever presented, comprising the sublime secrets of decent human living. Who is a good person? Someone who doesn't lie, cheat, steal, murder, fornicate, commit adultery, lust after another man's wife, envy another man's possessions, or use God's name in vain (though not, of course, in that order).

Needless to say, the world would be a better place if more people followed the wisdom of these laws. The problem is that most of us have a very superficial understanding of the Ten Commandments, and simply following them to the letter can distract attention from many of the subtleties of the laws they contain.

For example, if we understand the sixth commandment, "Do not kill," as simply meaning never to kill anyone, we might miss an important distinction: the word used in the Ten Commandments is "Tirzach," which literally means murder. Murdering someone is not the same as killing someone. Murdering someone requires premeditation and planning; killing in self-defense, on the other hand, cannot be understood as sinful. There are even cases where a premeditated murder might be considered righteous. If Colonel Claus von Stauffenberg had succeeded in killing Hitler in the summer of 1944, for instance, would his action truly have been a sin? Similarly, if we are scrupulously careful never to steal or to lie, we might balk at those moments when stealing and lying constitute moral acts. It would be a mitzvah—a good deed—to steal ammunition from a Nazi death squad, for instance, or to give a lynch mob false information about the whereabouts of an intended victim.

Another, perhaps greater, problem with a simplistic understanding of the Ten Commandments as a code of goodness is that it results in a morality defined entirely by negatives. Not hurting others and not violating the basic tenets of morality may be necessary steps in avoiding immorality. But are these acts sufficient to leading a good, moral life? As Dennis Prager points out, not acting immorally makes you only a neutral person at best. You aren't bad, because you don't hurt people; but you aren't truly good, for you haven't helped anyone either. We hear people making this mistake all the time. They say, "Yeah, I'm a good person. I don't cheat on my wife, I don't rob my customers." But that doesn't make you good. Where is the selfless gesture, the act that benefits others at your own expense?

The Ten Commandments were designed to be prohibitive. They are rules for living in a civilized society and avoiding sin. But simply following their path cannot make us good. Notice that the Ten Commandments prohibit stealing someone else's articles but do not command giving to charity. Neither do they command that we come to the aid of someone whose life is in danger. And is refraining from committing adultery the secret of a good marriage? Of course not. If you never cheat but you never show love either, you'll probably end up divorced. There are very few positive commandments listed among the Ten. There is a commandment to believe in God, to honor your parents, and to honor the Sabbath. While the commandments that are included are of vital importance, surely they alone do not constitute a complete code of morality and goodness.

We might say, then, that the Ten Commandments were designed not so much to inspire heroism as to save us from cowardice and prevent mediocrity and immorality. Their purpose is to prevent society from descending into anarchy more than to inspire altruism. The man who steals may be a coward, but the man who refrains is not necessarily a hero. Being good, as King David says in Psalms, involves not only "turning away from evil" but also "doing good."

The Ten Commandments were meant to function as collective laws addressed to the community rather than the individuals within it. They are prescriptions for a just society rather than for a righteous individual behavior. That's why the famous golden rule of the Bible, the positive commandment "Love your neighbor as yourself," is found in the Book of Leviticus, which is in a later section of the Bible that discusses "sacrifices." The Ten Commandments are found in Exodus, where the Bible discusses civil law.

A society cannot mandate or legislate that each individual should give to charity, clothe the naked, shelter the homeless, and act with constant kindness. It can legislate that every individual has a responsibility not to murder, not to steal, and not to violate other people's marriages or destroy families. And it can mete out punishments for those who violate these cardinal rules. But such legislation will never be enough to inspire the ordinary person to stop craving Machiavellian success, nor will it provide him with any impetus to allow his good conscience to get the better of the little voice inside him that encourages him to abstain from doing good.

Utilitarianism

Jeremy Bentham was a political and legal theorist in the eighteenth century, and one of the founders of utilitarianism, a prominent theory of goodness. Utilitarians define goodness as the maximization of happiness (the absence of pain and the presence of pleasure) for the largest number of people. In other words, the virtue of an action can be determined by what will cause the greatest amount of happiness for the greatest number of people. It is the ethicist's version of democracy, allowing the majority to make the decisions for the minority.

The problem with utilitarianism is that it has no inherent moral framework. It is based on the idea that morality is not absolute but relative, anchored in the changing whims and caprice of public opinion. It is goodness based on happiness: anything that makes the majority of people happy will, by default, be good. It is not hard to find examples that glaringly refute the logic of utilitarianism. If the majority of the public believes that happiness comes from practicing cannibalism, then cannibals they will be! Or perhaps the majority enjoy ingesting Ecstasy tablets, which cause memory loss, and sometimes death, but do a good job of inducing temporary feelings of happiness.

I'm not confident that the majority of people can be trusted when it comes to determining morality. The pull to be part of a crowd, to be a member of something, can be much stronger than the desire to make sure that you're doing the right thing. Of course, we have seen the devastating results of utilitarianism in our lifetimes. In Nazi Germany, many people—the majority, in fact—were "happy" that Jews were being gassed and persecuted. In Palestinian society today, many dance in the streets when they hear news of more innocent Israeli civilians being murdered, just as they danced before the eyes of the world when they learned of the events of the morning of September 11. In a society where morality can swing like a pendulum, it would take very little to make evil the dominant mindset.

Another major problem with utilitarianism is that it assumes that the minority who do not find happiness in what makes the majority happy will disregard their feelings of dissatisfaction. I feel pretty sure that a utilitarian society would be a terrible place to live if I disagreed with the majority-chosen happiness. With no recourse for dissent, those unhappy with the imposed happiness would be bound to be dissatisfied with it. Consequently, it's hard to imagine the minority feeling any compelling reason to follow the dictates of the majority—for after all, it hold no rewards for them. And if these people couldn't see that doing something would make them happy, then they wouldn't be compelled to be good either.

Utilitarianism is inherently flawed, then, because it puts the cart before the horse.

Natural Selection

Another more scientific school of thought divorces the concepts of good and evil from their moral connotations. Professor Bentley Glass has determined a series of so-called objective guidelines that define good as that which is good for the development of the species. What is not good for the species is, by definition, evil. Glass does not make clear in every case what he means by "good for the development of the species," nor does he provide criteria that determine what should be excluded as simply neutral. So those of us with less precise minds might feel free to argue, for example, that to permit people with limited intellects or physical challenges or disease to produce children is bad for the species. The rights of the individual get lost when the species is the focus, and these seemingly harmless theories can have devastating consequences.

Adolf Hitler remains the most widely studied, and perhaps the most puzzling, man of the twentieth century, because deep down, like these scientists, he haunts us with his logic. Why should we not kill the mentally handicapped? Is there a rational reason for allowing men and women who will always be a burden to the state and their families to continue to live? If they will never surpass the intellectual maturity of a five-year-old, why should they be kept alive? If we have to make difficult choices between who gets treatment and care, isn't it right that we decide against those who cannot, or no longer, contribute to society? Fidel Castro incarcerated people infected with HIV. Isn't there a part of us that wonders if he's right? Why should the rights of one be allowed to jeopardize the lives of many?

The hero within us knows that we cannot allow our individual rights to get lost in the struggle for goodness. What these scientists fail to understand is that there is a difference between us and a pack of animals, who will leave the weak and the young and the sick behind, and that difference is our dignity, the recognition that each of us carries a piece of the divine. Surely we can do better than this as a definition of goodness.

Secular Humanism

There is another approach to goodness that many people have promoted. Secular humanism is predicated entirely on the idea of empathy. We extrapolate beyond our own pain and imagine the pain of another. If you don't like being stolen from, then don't steal from others.

Furthermore, the argument goes, if you steal from someone else, what's to stop that person from turning the tables and stealing from you? By pursuing this illegal course of action, you render the effective workings of civilization impossible. We understand that if we create a world where people can freely steal from one another, the world will be insufferable, and life unlivable.

At its best, humanism can inspire a man to assist his fellow man in need or refrain from causing pain to him, but this is true only so long as such actions don't involve personal sacrifice. If I harm society, then as a member of society I am in essence harming myself. Since my sense of self motivates my good deeds, it is a contradiction to harm society to the denial or detriment of myself.

So where does altruism fit into this picture? Altruism takes spirituality and a divine imperative as its motivation. It can demand that man make a personal sacrifice on behalf of his fellow man. It can even demand that he lay down his life for his fellow man, since, in the final analysis, it is God who gave us life, and He has the right to specify the ends to which it should be put, even if that means sacrificing it entirely. Secular humanism can create a negative morality that prevents people from harming one another, but it cannot inspire altruism. And because its basis is human experience, created as it is by and on behalf of human beings, secular humanism can be modified in accordance with human whim.

Another thought: if we keep stealing from one another, society will devolve. But what if I steal from you and nobody finds out?

There is a need to appeal to something higher in human beings, a moral conscience, that works whether or not we're being watched.

Personal Moralities

In a secular age, when religion has lost much of its moral authority, the option of establishing our own individual moralities has become increasingly popular. In other words, we create our own criteria for goodness and try to live lives of decency and respect. We do the right thing based on our own understanding of what that means. And yet it's abundantly clear that one person's virtue is another's vice—which makes it completely impossible to create a viable society based on this system. More important, a system of personal moralities makes authentic human relationships and interactions unworkable. Relationships are based on the idea that humans have something deep and transcendent in common—namely, their shared humanity. If we can't even agree on how that humanity is expressed, then how can we all get along?

This is the most common refrain that I hear in marital squabbles. What one spouse considers sound, another considers sinful. They can't agree on who's right, so they argue into the wee hours. A friend of mine in England worked hard to provide his wife and four children with the good life. As a businessman with a small music publishing company, he went to all the music trade conventions in search of partnerships and more business, and he started taking his young secretary with him. The first time he didn't even tell his wife. She found out, and she was livid. They fought. He promised that the next time he would get her permission. So the next time he called her to tell her he was bringing the assistant to an important convention in Nashville, as he was incapable of tracking all the people he met and ensuring the follow-up by himself.

His wife objected. "She's not going. I don't want to hear about it again, and I don't even care if you don't go. But she's definitely not going with you." He blew up. "I work hard to give you a good life, and I never complain. I've never given you a second's worry over my fidelity, and this is how you reward me for it? You know I'm not attracted to my secretary. You know how much I love you. I'm taking her for the sake of the family. There's no one else who can do her job, no one else who knows the business. You're interfering with my ability to support this family." But his wife wouldn't budge; worse, she was furious at his obliviousness. She felt that her objection was so evidently legitimate and justified that it should have gone without saying.

Who's right and who's wrong? Both invoke the needs of the family to bolster their position in this argument. If their positions are based on their personal moralities, these two will never reach a consensus. They called me for my opinion, but as I told them, my "opinion" is irrelevant to their marriage. I said to them, "In Jewish law, the wife has a right to determine how close a husband gets to another woman, even for professional purposes. And your wife is clearly uncomfortable. However unreasonable you think she's being, you're not the final arbiter of right and wrong."

Even the very best men, the greatest biblical heroes of them all, have demonstrated that they are in need of an external code. Even Martin Luther King Jr., whom I consider the most accomplished American of the twentieth century, had some personal shortcomings. Thomas Jefferson, who behaved heroically in instances both personal and political, owned slaves and may have had sexual relationships with some of them, resulting in children whom he refused to claim. As a result, it's tremendously difficult for many African Americans to recognize him as a hero.

Imperfect heroes can change the world, but not all of their behavior should be emulated. Even these men, who surely had strong and innate tendencies toward heroism, needed something greater than themselves to tell them how to behave. Even a hero needs a code by which to live. I totally reject the notion that people don't need an overriding moral code—absolute measures of good and evil rather than shifting estimates of right and wrong. As a rabbi, I am often asked by nonreligious Jews why religion is important. "I'm not interested in keeping all those esoteric laws that you talk about so much," they say. "I don't care about keeping the Sabbath, and I have no great desire to eat only kosher food. Why should I have to? I'm a good person. Are you better than me just because you don't eat pork?"

These people are right. I'm almost certainly not better than them. But I don't believe we can rely on our own personal morality barometers for guidance on how to behave, because they are subjective and arbitrary. I believe that, at any given moment, it can become almost impossible for us to know what is good. The human mind is infinitely capable of rationalizing the bad things we do. Do you think for one moment that Hitler thought he was a bad person? In his mind, he was saving Germany. Stalin killed twenty million people, starved them to death—in order to collectivize Russian agriculture. In his mind, he was saving them from starvation by industrializing a primitive country. Pol Pot, who murdered a million Cambodians—one-quarter of the population—in the killing fields in the early 1970s thought he was reeducating a backward people for their own ultimate good.

The Talmud even says that the first time you do something bad, you acknowledge it as bad. The second time, it becomes neutral, and the third time you talk yourself into believing that it's a good thing. That's why we need a higher code to tell us the way to behave.

Moreover, there is no guarantee that those who are passionate about their own rules of morality will in the end adhere to them. The rules we make and enforce ourselves are often broken with impunity and little sense of risk or consequence. We negotiate with ourselves all the time—"If I have this ice cream, I'll do an extra twenty sit-ups tomorrow"—and it's easy to play fast and loose with the lines we draw. "This company is so huge and so rich, and I work so hard and make so much money for them with so little compensation. I deserve that overtime, even if I wasn't actually working over the weekend." Laws of good and bad are replaced by your likes and dislikes, depending on personal whim and practices.

So what is the answer to this thorny question? How can we know how to be good?

Religion is certainly no guarantee against atrocities. Indeed, it is demonstrably responsible for many. There's a lot of religion out there without much God in it. In a lot of cases, religion has become about something else: power, or money, or politics, or control. Man becomes the center, not God.

That said, I do believe that a blueprint for goodness can be found in the stories that make up the Bible. Remember that the Ten Commandments are delivered by God in the form of two separate tablets. The first one deals with laws concerning the belief in, and absolute respect for, God, and the second with morality and prescriptions against indecent behavior. The two tablets are meant to be equally indispensable: without God, there can be no goodness, and without goodness, belief in God becomes a farce. It is for this reason that a definition of goodness must embrace God and find the divinity in all of humanity.

The Bible teaches us goodness through stories of heroes who struggled against their own baser nature to be good. I believe that even today the key to a wholesome life—and a life of biblical heroism—is to struggle to maintain and honor our own dignity and to do everything within our power to confer dignity upon others.

The definition of goodness is indeed the ability to confer dignity upon as many people, and as many things, as we can in our lifetime. Making people feel important, clothing the naked, feeding the hungry, honoring God's earth, never causing cruelty to animals, are all essentials of being good.

II

❧

THE PATH
TO BIBLICAL
HEROISM

16

✦

A THOUSAND HEROES

I'm not an American hero. I'm a person that loves children.
—Clara Hale, as quoted in *I Dream a World,* by Brian Lanker, 1989

Once, I was on my good friend Joey Reynolds's radio show in New York. With me as a guest was the author of a book about finding your calling in life. When Joey asked him why he wrote his book, he said that he felt America had lost its purpose. "The last bold American achievement," he said, "was back in 1969, when we put a man on the moon. Now here we are, more than thirty years later, and we have yet to put a man on Mars. We don't dream anymore. We don't aspire to heroic action."

He was getting my juices going, and I jumped in. "What was noble about landing on the moon?" I asked. "Of course it was inspiring, and it advanced the cause of science. But after all, we discontinued the moon landings because we no longer saw the point. What is it that would really be motivating us to land a man on Mars? The technical advances it represents, or the ego boost? There are everyday acts of heroism on the part of *ordinary* Americans that are the equal of the great moon landings."

Here's another way of posing the same question. Certainly every astronaut is courageous. But is theirs the only kind of heroism we can honor?

We don't need to look to the heavens for bold gestures. Martin Luther King Jr. changed the world by restoring the abused dignity of his people through the power of the spoken word alone. That's heroism. The unarmed students who stood in front of tanks in Tiananmen Square in Beijing to demand that their voices be heard in one of the most oppressive regimes in the world were heroes.

Okay, so Dr. King is a slam dunk. But there are millions of equally noble, everyday, unrecorded heroic acts that have taken place since 1969. Pessimists like the author I met that night find it easy to diminish personal, private heroism, making our own everyday struggles to feed our families and love our children seem insignificant. Yet those are the real acts of heroism from which the fabric of society is woven. These are the real heroes: the doctors and nurses who give tirelessly of themselves to save the lives of their patients; the policemen who walk dangerous streets in order to keep their communities safe; the scientists and laboratory technicians who stay up late at night in search of cures for disease; the everyday businessmen who offer quality service to their customers at an affordable price.

For me, this is the most beautiful part of biblical heroism. You don't have to sell forty million records, or jet across the world, to know that your life has meaning. The heroism of the Private Adam is an accessible heroism, one we all can achieve. Yes, the biblical hero is the fireman who lives in a blue-collar neighborhood in Long Island but unthinkingly risks his own life to save an investment banker who makes more in a year than he will make in a decade. The biblical hero is also the teenager who makes a special effort to walk his grandmother home every time she has dinner with his family, even when he has homework to do and friends to instant-message. So is the woman who goes to buy a sandwich for the hungry, homeless woman at the corner.

Unfortunately, our culture trains us to overlook this kind of heroism. Note the *Merriam-Webster's* definition of a hero:

1a: a mythological or legendary figure often of divine descent endowed with great strength or ability; b: an illustrious warrior; c: a man admired for his achievements and noble qualities; d: one that shows great courage.

2a: the principal male character in a literary or dramatic work; b: the central figure in an event, period, or movement; 3: an object of extreme admiration and devotion; an idol.

Notice what stands out in this definition. The hero is a god, a great warrior, or a venerated idol. If, perchance, the hero dares to be human, then at the very least he is the *principal character* in this context. The literary hero is the protagonist of his story; the historical hero is a famous personality who defined his era. Not coincidentally, in *Webster*'s definition, heroes are all male.

Do you see why it's so difficult to envision yourself as a hero? How could any man living a normal life live up to such a definition? (And never mind any woman.)

To be sure, there have been individuals who believed from their earliest years that they were destined for greatness. According to legend, in his late twenties Julius Caesar lamented the fact that Alexander the Great had conquered the world by his midtwenties, and wondered when his turn to prove himself in a similar arena would finally come. But any average twenty-something today harboring such dreams from the confines of a desk job would be dismissed as delusional at best.

The "great man" definition of heroism has led the vast majority of us to underestimate the importance of our own lives. It has given all of us a deflated sense of our own potential. Unable to envision ourselves as central to any important historical drama, we have no compunction about burning four hours a day of our lives passively plunked in front of the television set. The thinking goes, "If I can't be a Napoleon, or a Dan Rather, or a Matt Damon, why even get off the couch?"

As the example of Julius Caesar suggests, heroes of all kinds need role models. It's become commonplace today to lament the loss of the great heroes, the great leaders. We all complain that we have no one to look up to. My students at Oxford used to ask me, "Where have all the heroes gone?" I say the same thing to you that I said to them. Look around you. They are everywhere.

Beliefnet, a spiritual website I've written for, had a contest inviting people to nominate the most inspiring figure of 2001. To be sure, all the big names were there: George W. Bush, Pope John Paul II, the Dalai Lama, the passengers who brought down Flight 93 in Pennsylvania, and Rudy Giuliani.

But amid these expected names came postings that were more surprising:

I would love to nominate my mother, Minnie L. Mathews. She has been a constant inspiration not just to me but to her grandchildren as well. She has helped me and others all her life . . . even raising her younger brothers and sisters. Her charity work at church, constant giving, and advice have helped me become a better Christian today.

And another one:

The most inspiring person in my life, and this year especially, was my mother. Always one to put others first, Mom's courage in her battle with pancreatic cancer really helped me cope with caring for her and accepting the fact that she would soon be gone. The extraordinary part of this story is that Mother was not bitter and rarely complained of her illness. She worried about my dad, her three daughters, her grandchildren, and several friends who were ill also. She even sent flowers to my sister-in-law who was having back trouble!! And all the while she was dying.

The author on Joey's show was wrong. He was looking for classical heroism. You don't have to walk on the moon to feel tall, and you don't have to land on Mars to feel like you're out of this world. Only people who are bored with the everyday, who find no magic in pushing a child on a swing or in comforting a mourner at his home, need the entertainment of moon rocks. And that's a great shame. That is not to say that we should cease building the international space station or quit exploring the solar system. It is to say that these should not be the only endeavors in which we take pride.

The person who admires the biblical hero doesn't need to live vicariously through him or her. We're inspired by such figures in our lives, not intimidated. Their greatness lies in part in their very accessibility. They are available as models whose example can change our lives, not put us to shame.

We need to realize that the rush of pride that comes from grand heroic gestures—finishing first in a marathon, saving a puppy from a burning building—isn't the only sign of a heroic act. We need to start seeing the magic in the everyday. No marriage, for example, succeeds solely on the basis of its anniversary celebrations. A marriage is constructed of little daily gestures that conspire to make something infinitely bigger and grander. Daily compliments, to show appreciation rather than taking things for granted. Good-bye kisses in the morning and comforting conversation in the evening. A cup of tea fetched in response to a cough. Flowers brought home for no reason. Sudden passionate sex on a regular old Wednesday evening. When a marriage is devoid of the small moments, or when the small moments start to feel inferior to the big moments, it has lost its inner spirit.

The same is true of the world we inhabit. The social programs of the United States to educate every child and to offer food stamps to poor families are infinitely more heroic than even the noble gift of landing a man on the moon. If we could end hunger on earth, we would be the greatest heroes of all time. If we could put an end to racism, we would truly be men and women of distinction. If we could banish loneliness by giving more love into the world, we would be immortalized forever.

Ellen is a friend of mine. She is the single mother of four children, one of whom has a very serious form of cancer. A former model, she now works two jobs to keep her kids fed and housed and pay her daughter's medical bills. I can say, without qualification, that this woman is a hero. The position she holds is as important as the highest office in the nation. She is as courageous as any four-star general, and as resolute as the most powerful CEO in the country. But she doesn't know it. When she comes home at the end of a long day, she turns on *E!* or reads *People* to catch up with her own heroes, Julia Roberts and Meg Ryan. She wishes that the face that looks back at her from the mirror had fewer bags under the eyes and lines around the mouth, like theirs, which benefit from the staffs of trained professionals working around the clock on preservation efforts. When she visits our home, she talks to me about her career with the sadness and weariness of someone who feels that she has missed out on life, that somehow the gravy train has passed her right by.

And yet, compared to her, those movie stars are ridiculous—flimsy, plastic imitations of the real thing. They have not struggled to juggle two jobs to clothe their children. They haven't had to turn down dates because they couldn't afford a baby-sitter. Julia Roberts should be reading stories about *Ellen* in the newspapers; perhaps it would help put her own accomplishments in perspective. Julia and Meg are entertainers; Ellen is the real deal. I have a soft spot for people like Ellen. My own mother raised five children by herself by working two jobs. There is no movie about her sacrifice, and President Bush hasn't called yet to award her a Congressional Medal of Freedom, but she is a hero, nonetheless, and I remember the sacrifices she made.

Soldiers have hard lives, but they get medals pinned to their chests that tell them—and everyone around them—that they're heroes. Their accomplishments are applauded. Athletes push themselves through an astonishing amount of pain to do what they do, but they are celebrated—and paid well—for their trouble. People like Ellen don't feel heroic because flashbulbs don't go off and they don't get millions of dollars every time they parade down the red carpet to read *Goodnight Moon* for the two-hundred-and-ninth time.

One goal of this book is to get people like Ellen to realize that they're already heroes, much more so than the people they lionize. My friend needs to be able to look at her tired face in the mirror and tell herself: "I take pride in what I have achieved. I take strength from the fact that I have never given up or let my children down. I envy no one. There is glory in what I do every day." That people like

Ellen have been made to feel they have somehow missed out on life—that the dance floor or the secluded spa is where the real action is—is a travesty and a tragedy, one that desperately needs to be corrected. Ellen needs to tell herself she is a hero, and believe it— because it's true, and because knowing that will give her the inspiration to continue.

One of the most memorable speeches of the last few decades was George Bush Senior's "thousand points of light" speech. True, his pursuit of the ideal may have left something to be desired, but the metaphor is wonderful. It allows for the possibility that mankind is not saved by one great hero, but by the great light produced by a thousand heroes. The metaphor recognizes the small heroic gestures that are normally taken for granted. The brilliant thing about the biblical model of heroism is that it allows all of us to be heroes every day. Classical heroism is about one guy, one savior, one big event. Biblical heroism allows for an endless number of heroes, using their unique gifts, together and separately, to cultivate their gardens and heal the world. The Jewish concept of the messiah is similarly focused around a single individual who will galvanize the contributions of many.

I'd like to call for each of us to recognize a thousand heroes around us. Put aside your belief that there are no models for great leadership anymore and train your eye to recognize the heroes in our midst. The New York transit worker who greets everyone politely as they buy their Metrocards is a hero. So is the college student who works a night job to get an education, the NFL safety who gives up an enormous salary playing pro ball to serve his country in the military, the public school teacher who passes up a private-sector income to keep working in the inner city, the small businessperson who goes to parent-teacher conferences to hear progress reports on his kids, the ordinary wife who balances a demanding job and even more demanding kids with grace and humor. What extraordinary people, and how much they give of themselves so that others may prosper!

When we shift our focus slightly and embrace these small gestures as acts of heroism, it changes everything. We can learn to become heroes ourselves by seeing every small moment in our lives as an opportunity to perform an act of heroism. And we can—we must—reward others for their heroism. The reward doesn't have to be more than a smile, a remembered name, a letter or e-mail of admiration, a compliment, a joke, a thank-you, or a seventy-five-cent cup of unsolicited coffee. We must not ignore heroism when we see it.

Once we begin recognizing people for their contributions rather than their acquisitions, the magnificence of our human lives will come brilliantly into focus. Heroism on a truly great scale is every-where around us if we choose to recognize it, and it is within our reach if we choose to make it our goal. Not many movies will be made about such acts, and few books will be written (except for this one, of course). But if the everyday biblical heroism of the Private Adam is the kind of heroism we aspire to, then all of our endless pining for role models will be over—replaced with a recognition of the heroism in ourselves and the extraordinary people around us.

17

❦

CONFER DIGNITY
UPON OTHERS

One's dignity may be assaulted, vandalized, and cruelly mocked, but cannot be taken away unless it is surrendered.

—Michael J. Fox

In *Ethics of Our Fathers*, the Jewish collection of rabbis' observations on moral behavior, the question is asked, "Who is honored?" The answer given is, "He who honors his peers."

Bestowing dignity upon someone else is the equivalent of giving them life. One of the qualities of life is the ability to have an effect on the environment. A stone is not alive, since its existence is inert and brings about absolutely no changes to its surrounding landscape, but a plant grows, photosynthesizes, and thus changes its environment. When we make people feel that they matter, that their existence is noticed and essential, we lend them dignity and make them feel alive. On the other hand, if a wife looks across the breakfast table and sees that her husband hasn't heard a word she's said, she feels dead inside. If she stays at the office late working on an important project and her boss never once compliments her work, she feels useless. Without dignity, she feels no better than an inanimate object. She exists but she doesn't live.

And since the highest definition of goodness is to preserve and enhance life, it follows that the essence of goodness is to enhance and preserve dignity. Who among us can honestly say that we enhance and preserve the dignity of everyone whose lives we touch over the course of a day?

The highest honor a person can receive is not becoming a king or a president or a rabbi or a scholar or a rock star. These are the people who receive public honor in our society, but the rabbis are careful to note that real honor doesn't live in these externals. If we want true honor, something that will last when we are no longer the toast of the *Vanity Fair* crowd or sitting at the head of the boardroom table, we need to learn to respect others and bestow dignity upon them.

To bestow dignity on others is to recognize a divine spark within them and seek to honor them. It can mean giving a starving man a piece of bread to eat or giving clean clothes to a homeless person, and always in such a way that the other person feels dignified receiving your gift.

Bestowing dignity means educating people, giving them the tools and confidence to make the best choices in their lives. You cannot have dignity if you have no choices. There's no dignity in slavery—no matter how well slaves are treated, they have been robbed of choice and therefore of their dignity. Slaves aren't in control of their destiny—they have no resources, no independence, no autonomy, no ability to act on their own behalf. They're reduced to plant or animal status, limited to instinct.

Giving the disenfranchised the right to vote is giving them dignity, because it enables them to let their voice be heard. Listening when someone talks is bestowing dignity for the same reason. When you listen attentively, you are telling the speaker that his thoughts and feelings and opinions matter. The only way to be good in this world is to make sure you are bestowing dignity on all things around you, from people to the environment.

Born in Eritrea, Nikki Tesfai survived a brutal and abusive marriage at a young age, a terrifying African prison, and a refugee camp. She escaped this early life of terror and incarceration and has now opened two homeless shelters in Los Angeles especially intended for African women and their children (although all are welcome). Her organization provides beds and clothing, designs programs to sensitize the LAPD to the special issues faced by African women in domestic violence situations, and provides access to job training, education, legal aid, and health care to the women who stay in the shelters. Tesfai, who has spent much of her life fighting for her own physical freedom, knows that having a safe place to lay your head is just the first step to survival. She takes care of people's physical needs, but she's also in the business of restoring dignity.

We always have to be careful to preserve dignity, even when we're doing good. The ancient rabbis of the Talmud said that although charity is a virtuous act, it becomes good only when we uphold the recipient's sense of dignity. In other words, a charitable act that leaves the recipient feeling beneath the benefactor is not a good deed. The ancient rabbis listed seven levels of charity, and at the top of the list was the anonymous donor who gives to an anonymous beneficiary. This kind of charity bestows on the recipient the most dignity possible.

Incidentally, fewer than 10 percent of gifts over $1 million are given anonymously in America, according to the Center on Philanthropy. The Public Adam always expects recognition for his good deeds. I am reminded of the story of a heroic man who founded a chain of airport duty-free stores and accumulated a massive amount of wealth. After setting aside only a comparatively modest sum for himself—around $5 million—he gave away the rest, over $600 million. The only string attached to the gifts was that his identity be kept completely secret. He was so anxious to keep the gifts anonymous that he didn't even take the tax deductions he was eligible for. The story was broken, against his will, by a journalist, but the man never did an interview on the subject.

So important is the concept of dignity in Jewish charitable law that in an astonishing legal ruling the Talmud says that if a man who was once so wealthy that he had fifty servants running in front of him becomes impoverished, the Jewish community must restore the fifty servants to him (that is, if they can afford it) until he gets back on his feet. Otherwise, he would suffer a diminishment of dignity, which Jewish law cannot tolerate. In other words, the ancient rabbis valued dignity as even more essential than the staples of life, like food, clothing, and shelter.

Sadly, most people don't see the world this way. They think of charity as a matter of giving only token sums, if that. In London I knew a wealthy man who, through a string of bad investments, had landed on hard times. He lacked the funds to continue to send his three children to the very expensive and exclusive British boarding school where they were students. I and a few others took it upon ourselves to approach some benefactors discreetly to ask for help defraying the tuition cost. I went to the office of a wealthy property executive who was well known for his philanthropy. When I told him what we were collecting for, he said outright that he was unsympathetic. "My own kids don't go to a school that good. Why would I pay for someone else's kids to go there? Ask me for money for an operation for someone in need, Shmuley—then I'll help, you know I will. But you have the nerve to come to me and tell me that some guy wants his kids to go to a fancy-shmancy school—and that I ought to pay for it?"

But this man was missing the point. I was asking not that this man "put" someone else's kids into a fancy school, but that he *assist* in an effort to help three children maintain their dignity by helping them remain at their current school. I tried to explain the degree of shame these children would face if they were forced to leave their school and their friends because their father could no longer afford the tuition, but he would not be persuaded by my argument, and I left his office empty-handed. This well-intentioned man's simple mistake was that he failed to appreciate that dignity is as necessary as food and shelter. If the kids had been starving or naked, he would have helped, but saving them from humiliation was not something he considered essential.

Look at your own life and the way you give to others. Have you ever noticed that when one person gives change to a homeless person on the subway, many people in the car will be roused to follow suit—but if no one gives, the homeless person will often pass through the car without receiving a single dime? It's hard to be the first person to dig into your pockets. It attracts attention, something we're conditioned to avoid. It can be even harder to make eye contact with the person you're giving the change to, to touch their hand as the change passes between you and accept their thanks graciously, allowing even a moment of connection between you. But it is essential to give that money, to start the reaction, and to treat the person with all the dignity and respect they deserve. To behave in a way that preserves the homeless person's dignity also enhances yours.

But conferring dignity isn't just about giving charity the right way. We enhance another person's dignity by making him feel special and worthy. Every time we listen to someone—really listen and take her seriously, as opposed to waiting for her to stop talking so we can pitch in with our two cents' worth—we confer dignity. When we inconvenience ourselves to make someone else's life easier, or show gratitude, or forgive, or fall in love, we confer dignity on the other person.

Too often we succumb to the habit of treating people who are providing a service to us as if they were their jobs. *Newsweek* once asked a number of people what their New Year's resolutions were. It was probably the first time (and maybe the last) that I'll be mentioned in the same article as (the man then known as) Puff Daddy. I said that my resolution was to really listen to cab drivers. It seems like a small thing, but I had noticed that I had a habit of getting into a cab and immediately opening a magazine or getting on my cell phone. When you do that, you're telling the person driving you that they're no better than a mule. I spend a lot of time in cabs, and it's good working time for me, so I'm not prepared to get into an hour-long discussion every time, but I do try to make an effort now to ask one (nontraffic-related) question and to really listen, with all my concentration, to the answer. Listening to people is one of the most important ways in which we can establish authentic relationships, because for that one moment you abandon your own personal agenda and dedicate yourself to being a receptacle for someone else's thoughts, opinions, and problems. (Just a thought: our New Year's resolutions always seem to be about ourselves. This year perhaps you'd consider making some that involve your behavior toward others?)

But is this kind of thing really such a big deal? So we chat with the woman ringing up our groceries—are we really supposed to expect a medal for it? Well, no. The rewards we have in store are different, and far more valuable. When we treat another person with dignity, we recognize his or her deepest essence, and by doing so we corroborate the divine inside ourselves. When we make a cashier feel like more than her job—because we see her as more than her job—we confer dignity. When we make a subordinate feel like a colleague—because we have started to see him as a collaborator instead of as someone whose only role is to serve us—we confer dignity.

A young Brazilian woman who helped my wife with our children lived with us for a period of time. During that period Brazil won an important game in the World Cup. When I heard the news, I thought, "Oh, I should call her to congratulate her on the win!" A call is the kind of casual contact you make all the time with your friends, to tell them that they mean something to you and you were thinking of them. But then I felt silly—I was in Italy at the time on a book tour. Should I make the effort all the way from Europe? But I called and congratulated her on her country's win—and she was pleased that I had thought of her.

One of the students I knew at Oxford became involved with a very worthwhile cause, a halfway house for troubled teens. The organization badly needed funds, and this student asked a wealthy family friend to contribute $25,000 in order to save it. He was wracked with anxiety about his request, ashamed to have to ask, and sure that if he wasn't rejected outright, his relationship with this family would change. What happened was a delightful surprise, both for the student and for me. The billionaire was not only happy to donate the money to such a worthy cause, but he thanked the student profusely for the opportunity. "Not only should you not be embarrassed to ask, but in fact I'm in your debt. Thank you for bringing this worthy cause to my attention, and thank you for having the courage to approach me on its behalf. Wealth can be a burden when you don't have good things to do with it. And you have helped to unburden me."

The man could have turned the student down, or he could have given him the money in a way that exacerbated his embarrassment instead of alleviating it. What he did was to go one step further. The young man left the house not just with a check but with his dignity enhanced.

Again, this is about turning all the moments in our lives—the big and the small—into opportunities to practice heroism. I have found that the concept of conferring dignity upon others provides a terrific framework for many of the "What should I do?" questions I've been asked over the years. Putting our ethical dilemmas to this test has a pretty good success rate: Will your actions rob another person of dignity or bestow it?

A married woman sits waiting for her friend in a bar. An attractive man offers to buy her a drink and starts making conversation. What's the harm? She loves her husband and will happily go home to him. This stranger isn't a real threat. But how would her husband feel if he could be a fly on the wall of that bar?

Maybe your daughter is acting out during a dinner party at your home. Instead of taking her aside and speaking with her in private, you lose your temper and chide her in front of your guests, telling her to shape up or you'll send her to her room like a baby. She'll get over the embarrassment eventually, right? But not with her dignity intact.

We must work hard to confer dignity on others—and by extension, we must fight to preserve others' dignity against any perceptible threat. Refusing to humiliate a friend in public and taking care not to litter in the woods are two gestures with something essential in common: both reveal a fundamental reverence for the matter in question. When you litter, you are saying that you're indifferent to whether the world is contaminated, stained, ruined. The same is true for zinging your friend—you'll get a laugh, but at an extraordinary expense. This is why fidelity is so important. When you take wedding vows, you're telling the world that you'll sacrifice the opportunity to be with anyone else. When you cheat, you're telling your spouse and the world that you're willing to gamble on finding someone who's better-looking, more desirable, better in bed. When you step outside your marriage, you are ripping your spouse's dignity away.

In other words, "What should I not do?" can often be as important a question as "What can I do?" It takes so little to wound someone else's dignity that we have to be ever-vigilant about monitoring our own behavior and the effect it can have on others. Every time we snap at an assistant or visibly display boredom when talking to an elderly neighbor or play for a laugh by making fun of someone's outfit behind their back we are stealing their dignity from them—and thus committing a sin. More than that, we're compromising our own dignity in the process. Take a step back. If you could watch a videotape of yourself behaving in any of these ways, would you be proud or would your face burn with shame?

The preservation of dignity at all costs is a theme that recurs over and over in Jewish law. According to the Talmud, the single greatest sin—worse than killing a person, more nefarious than spilling human blood—is to rob a person's dignity by humiliating him or her in public. The Talmud writes that whoever causes a person's face to turn white in public—causing the blood to rush away from his or her face in embarrassment—loses his allotment in the world to come. Why is it such a grievous sin? What is a little embarrassment compared with the horrors of drawing a gun and shooting someone?

It is bad enough to murder someone, but it is far, far worse to make him wish he were dead, and when we lose our dignity we no longer wish to live. When we are embarrassed in public, we pray that the earth will just open beneath us and swallow us. The most painful moments in life are those that involve a loss of dignity. Every schoolchild knows what it feels like to be humiliated in front of the class. It's the agonizing feeling that haunts you when you do poorly on a college exam and the scores are posted for any passerby to see. It recurs when you are fired from a job, despite your belief that you were providing a valuable service to the company. Or when a lover calls you up to dump you because he's found someone who may be more attractive than you, somehow more deserving of love. When these things happen, the pain and the anguish are so severe because it's our humanity that's being threatened.

It is worse to humiliate someone than to kill him or her because the only thing worse than being someone's murderer is making that person into his or her *own* murderer. When we have lost face or lost dignity, not only is life no longer worth living, but we are not capable of living. To be robbed of dignity is to be robbed of the life force. Tolstoy's great heroine Anna Karenina kills herself, not because she loses Vronsky's love, but because she is a woman scorned. She cannot face the humiliation of rejection. After risking everything for Vronsky, she finds that being cast aside and made to feel superfluous is more than her constitution can handle. Her dignity is destroyed by the rejection, and she is offended and hurt in a way that cannot be healed. She loses her reason to live.

A successful lawyer I knew was once accused of tampering with a witness, and though he tried to defend himself, in the end he was disbarred. He couldn't find other work and sank deeper and deeper into a depression. Then, finally, his wife, a journalist, started having an affair with her editor. Her husband killed himself. He was unable to be productive, and he'd lost his wife to another man. He felt his dignity had been stolen from him, and he couldn't live without it.

We can steal someone's dignity by stealing his or her freedom as well. In many countries, prisons are deliberately designed to rob a person of their dignity. One of the main arguments that southern slave owners made for preserving the institution of slavery was that they were practicing charity. Blacks were an inferior race, they argued, who needed to be taken care of, and every day, in exchange for work, the owners fed and housed an entire population of unfree men, women, and children. "Just compare the life of the blacks in Africa to the South," they hollered. "In Africa they would have starved to death, but here in the American South they have everything they need." Well, everything except freedom. The slave owners refused to recognize that their actions were not granting people dignity but robbing them of it.

Fifty percent of black students at universities may now choose black dorms, but it was the struggle to win that choice that was at the center of the civil rights movement. What Martin Luther King Jr. understood was that the struggle was about more than economic equality, that it was also about dignity, the central human right of all, and one worth dying for. You can't have dignity if you don't have choice.

Robbing another human being of dignity is a sin against yourself, for a denial of one human being's dignity is a denial of all human dignity. What makes you special is not your wit, intelligence, or money, but the divine spark within you. And if that isn't enough to inspire you to confer dignity on all of God's creatures, then you are essentially bereft of dignity as well.

My definition of goodness, therefore, is that any action that promotes human uniqueness is by definition good, and any action that makes people feel subordinate and ordinary is quintessentially bad. Apply this definition to every single situation in your life, every tangled moral conundrum, every tortuous ethical dilemma. Doesn't it always lead you to the right answer? It involves a constant, everyday struggle against our baser instincts to seek out, recognize, and enhance the dignity in someone else. But this, as we shall see, is the fundamental quality of the biblical hero—the way of the Private Adam.

18

✦

HONOR YOUR PARENTS

Children begin by loving their parents; as they grow older they judge them; sometimes they forgive them.
—Oscar Wilde, *The Picture of Dorian Gray* (1891)

How can we learn to embrace the posture of the biblical hero by conferring dignity? I believe that there is much to be learned about everyday heroism from the men and women who raised us.

After all, why wouldn't we learn from the same people who taught us how to tie our shoelaces and to say "thank you" and to look both ways before crossing a street? Those people who got up at night with heavy lids to change our diapers when we were babies, went to work at eight in the morning for forty years to provide for us and send us to college, and continued to love and stand by us even when our spoiled behavior and actions made us unworthy—surely they have something to teach us? If parenting isn't heroism, then the concept simply doesn't exist.

The Bible says, "Honor your father and mother." The Bible could have told us to honor the leaders of our generation—to venerate the great rabbis, priests, and presidents of our times. But instead, it reminds us to honor our parents, to take our lessons from their behavior and look up to them as heroes. There was a time when a young boy's greatest hero was his dad, a young girl's greatest heroine her mom. We heard kids saying all the time, "I want to grow up to be like my dad." But in the generation gap that has developed in the last half-century, what has been broken is the idea of a living tradition of heroism.

My father's family emigrated from Iran to Israel in 1952. Like so many other Israelis, many members of the family became Westerners and no longer completely rested on the Sabbath. They enjoyed their nightlife and sometimes went to the cinema on the Sabbath eve and to the beach on the Sabbath day. My father always remained observant, but in a modern way. But as I grew older, I saw my father becoming more and more observant. He put us into a Jewish day school and raised his family to strictly observe the Sabbath. He started reading the Bible with us every Saturday after synagogue. I asked him what had changed in his life, and he said he was haunted by a vision of his departed father.

You see, every morning his father would rise early, put hundreds of pounds worth of carpet on his shoulders, and go to the marketplace to sell it so that he could feed his thirteen children. When he had made enough money to meet their needs for the day, he would return, spread out a carpet, and read from the Torah. When he reached the passage of the Bible in which Moses is described as the most humble man who walked the earth, he would burst into tears, inconsolable. My father told me that after he had realized his life-long dream of making money and owning a big house, he had re-embraced his father's example. After all those years, my father understood. His own father had become his hero. That old man, poor and weak, had become rich and strong. To be sure, my grandfather had long since passed away. It was not he who had changed. It was my father who had begun to see.

Our parents show the kind of selflessness that is deserving of greatness, and we should do everything we can to emulate them in our dealings with the world. They fed you when you were helpless; now go and feed the hungry stranger. They clothed you when you were cold; now go and dress the naked. They saw your beauty when everyone else saw your ugliness; now go and make all of God's creatures feel special. These unsung acts of heroism should be the ones that inspire us in our lives.

The key to the heroism of the parent, beyond all the little and big things they do for us, is the fact that it is done with no thought of recompense, reward, or recognition. It's pure love, the highest form of heroism, precisely because it's not quid pro quo. They give their children their love as a free gift, with no strings attached.

Many of us in modern times, though, have had less than ideal relationships with our parents. It has become normal today for children to judge their parents, to hold them accountable for whatever deficits of love or attention they feel they've suffered. Instead of honoring our parents, we refuse to allow them to disrupt our lives. We find their opinions irrelevant, and sometimes we tell them so. We calculate the cost-benefit balance of their love and act accordingly. Your father was neglectful during your childhood? No harm, then in giving him only 5 percent of your valuable time. No Easter and Christmas this year—just Thanksgiving.

It is true that many of our parents left something to be desired in the role model department, but this is where I think children owe their parents. Our parents gave us life, after all, whatever their other flaws. Of course bringing a helpless creature into the world involves the responsibility to raise and care for it—a burden most parents assume, even if imperfectly, and even if their children show no gratitude. And if children owe nothing else to their parents in this life, surely they owe them that one fundamental gift: gratitude. Children must show thanks for all their parents have done for them, rather than focusing on what they might have missed or messed up.

To fully realize our own potential as heroes, we all must first be healed of our past, and the only way to do that is to show forgiveness—one of the essential traits of the biblical hero.

The first giant step I took toward healing my own spirit—a spirit nearly crushed by the breakup of my parents' marriage and an insufficient connection with my father—has been through forgiveness. I used to be extremely judgmental of my father. My parents divorced when I was eight years old. At the time we were living in Los Angeles, and my father stayed there while my mother, my four siblings, and I moved to Miami. The transition was hard. The six of us lived in a one-bedroom apartment, and my mother worked long hours to support us. My father and I were separated by thirty-five hundred miles and a lot of emotional baggage. I missed him terribly, and I unfairly blamed him for visiting this unnecessary pain on me. I had a hard time adjusting to school in a new city and felt stigmatized by the divorce. The pain of it stayed with me long into my adult years; it became a defining event of my life.

One of the most beautiful rabbinical teachings proclaims, "Never judge a man until you are in his place." Or, as Atticus Finch put it in *To Kill a Mockingbird,* "You can't really understand a person until you walk around a bit in his shoes." When I grew up, I tried to walk around in my father's shoes. Sometimes I would recall my uncles' memories of him, a ten-year-old boy who left the house in Iran at dawn, staggering under the weight of very heavy carpets and materials, to help his own father support his siblings. They remember a boy who would use his fabric scissors to poke his legs, sometimes even allowing blood to flow, just to stay awake so he could keep on working. I thought of the stories that people who knew my father told me after we moved away. For years, they say, he walked around, lost and distraught, over the loss of his family. They say he was a shell of a man. In my youthful ignorance, I had thought he did not miss us as much as we missed him.

As an adult, and as a parent, I realized that I could not be a whole human being, nor a parent capable of giving fully committed, unconditional love, until I had put to rest the demons of my childhood. As long as I was angry at my father, I could not love to my full capacity. It was as if my heart were a measuring cup—as long as this feeling of bitterness filled half the cup, my love could only fill the other half. I wanted to fill the cup with good. I did not want to waste the valuable space that was being taken up by my past. When I walked in his shoes, I understood that I could never fully appreciate my father's suffering. When I did, it was the first step toward really becoming a son.

It is impossible for us to truly honor our parents as heroes until we can forgive them. This is not an easy lesson to learn. We react passionately to this question of forgiveness. We ask: "How can I forgive those who hurt me when I was defenseless and unable to fight back?" We cry out, "How can I ever absolve someone who has had a profoundly negative effect on my life and my spirit?" We associate forgiving with forgetting. We assume that to forgive is to allow for the wrongdoings of others, and hence to let them continue. We say that we cannot forgive, for to do so would allow the villains to be victorious.

I challenge you to rethink forgiveness. Contemporary scholars of forgiveness remind us that to forgive does not mean to pardon. Nor does it mean to forget. The theologian Marjorie Suchocki asks us to reimagine forgiveness, not within the "forgive and forget" model, which suggests both denial and avoidance, but rather as an "action of will towards the well-being of both yourself and the person who harmed you." She puts forth the revolutionary idea that we can achieve this ability to forgive by choosing an attitude of supreme love toward the human race. Robert Enright, a developmental psychologist at the University of Wisconsin, has actually founded an institute dedicated to the study of forgiveness. Recognizing that the collective holding of anger and resentment in humanity has been malignant to the human spirit, he created this discipline as a response to the "pervasive anger in society at large." Goodness and anger are almost always incompatible. When you're angry, you're judging someone else, and that automatically means that you're alienated from him or her. You're demanding that the other person earn your love and deciding that he or she has come up short. That judgment fundamentally denies the other person dignity. Conferring dignity on someone involves loving that person like a parent loves a child—no matter what.

Enright calls forgiveness the opposite of anger and suggests that we think of forgiveness as "giving up the resentment to which you are entitled, and instead of denying and suppressing the pain inflicted upon you, offering to the persons who hurt you friendlier attitudes to which they are not entitled."

Such a choice does two wonderful and transforming things. We are empowered by making a choice that the forgiven person has not actually earned or required. The choice to forgive releases us from the victim position, which is a tremendous liberation, and automatically restores dignity to us. Second, our choice challenges the forgiven person to live up to the ideal that has been presented to him. It makes for a win-win situation, but it is not easy. Mahatma Gandhi said, "The weak can never forgive. Forgiveness is the attribute of the strong."

How can we do this? We have to approach the matter from three directions. The first is memory. We do not block, deny, or evade the past. When we avoid our memories and feelings, we simply ingest the hurts that have been inflicted upon us and make them a diseased part of ourselves. The question of memory is one that has been dealt with extensively within the Jewish community when confronting the atrocities we have endured throughout history. We ask, how can we forgive the horrors done to us without forgetting them altogether? The answer? We remember. We tell our stories and we pass them along. As one Zen Buddhist teacher advises, "Whatever forgiveness is, it is not putting an end to the matter. It is not marking an episode closed and completed—out of memory, out of mind. Forgiveness does not end bearing witness. If anything, it deepens the process of bearing witness."

It is important that we stay in touch with feelings of anger and neglect as a result of our childhood, if only in order to keep us vigilant about repeating the same mistakes with our own children. But just as it is dangerous to raise a child with blind ignorance, it is dangerous to raise a child with deep-rooted distrust—with a perception of humanity that contradicts the belief that the human being is formed in the image of God. So the second pillar of being able to forgive is empathy—concern for the well-being of both the victim and the violator. This sounds impossible, but it is not. I have read of a man who was advocating against imposing the death penalty on a sixteen-year-old girl who had killed the man's grandmother. For a long time this man held the girl at a distance. He allowed himself to see her only as the terrible Other. His anger manifested itself in a substance abuse problem and a strained relationship with his wife. Then he wrote a letter to the girl in prison. She wrote back, and they eventually exchanged two hundred letters. The girl earned her high school diploma, and the man healed his marriage and quit drinking. When he chose to see this young woman as a human, when he allowed himself to feel empathy for her and to understand that she was herself the victim of unthinkable abuse, he was able to heal himself. Now to be sure, I am not in favor of forgiving cold-blooded murderers who must indeed pay for their crimes. But what the man discovered about *this* murderer was that she was a sixteen-year-old child, a minor, who had transferred her own abuse onto an innocent victim. And that perspective at least allowed him to try and empathize with her. Surely if this man was capable of forgiveness, we can forgive our parents! Like I said, it is not easy. But it is necessary.

The third and final pillar of forgiveness is imagination—envisioning a "well-being not yet achieved," according to Marjorie Suchocki. In other words, forgiveness requires that we see with the vision of the biblical hero, someone who sees the divine in everything. This clarity of vision releases us from the past and enables us to imagine and create a new and better future. It allows us to close the book on our last chapter and turn to a fresh new page, where we can write a new and better story.

When we choose to forgive our parents, then, we are not denying that they wronged us. We are not whitewashing their sins or making saints of sinners. We're not forgetting what happened to us during our childhoods. Our parents will not be better people as a result of our forgiveness. They will not suddenly come forward contrite and start showering their grandchildren with love and affection to make up for that which was denied to us. We cannot undo what was done to us in the past, nor can we forget it. We're not changing anything *but ourselves*—and that's the hardest and most important victory we'll ever achieve.

Many of us will always feel that our childhoods were intrinsically unfair, and that nothing we do can change that. That's true. Many of us have suffered through difficult, lonely, even abusive childhoods. And there's an important distinction to make here: in recommending that we forgive our parents, I'm not saying they *deserve* to be forgiven. Indeed, they may not. But to my way of thinking, that is all the more reason that we must forgive them. In a strange way, if they deserved to be forgiven, they wouldn't really need our forgiveness. It would happen in and of itself. It's precisely because we believe that they don't deserve it that we must find the strength to do it.

The more you make the choice to forgive, the more you get in touch with compassion and realize your own need to be forgiven. Forgiving is essential in a society where survival is based upon interdependent relationships. It's optional only when we think we no longer need one another—a truly fatal assumption.

The theologian John Patton claims that at the core of forgiveness is the discovery that the injured person could commit the same evil as the wrongdoer. In other words, there but for the grace of God go I. We have to forgive our fathers because we too need to be considered as human beings greater than the sum total of our sins. We are something greater than the deeds that we do: we have the light of our dignity and the undiminishing flame of our potential, which cannot be extinguished through an act of carelessness or malice or deception. It is always our trespasses that we ask God to forgive. It is for the deeds we do that he forgives us. When it comes to the kind of people we are, we simply want God to love and accept us.

There's a story about a man on a train. His children are running wild, racing up the aisles and screaming, while he sits staring out the window. At the end of the trip, another passenger approaches him and tells him how appalled he is—by the children's behavior and by his failure to quiet them and show respect for the others on the train. The man apologizes profusely and then says, "We're coming from their mother's funeral. I'm sorry—I'm having a hard time, and I don't have the heart to discipline them today." You can't judge someone by their actions unless you know the context—and you can never truly understand the lifetime of context each person carries each day.

If there's an underlying reason the Bible exhorts us to honor our parents, I believe it's that we can't afford to shrink our parents to the tiny size of any individual deeds. We show someone honor by refusing to judge them. We show someone honor by never degrading them, never shaming them, and never robbing them of their humanity. And the prima facie example of robbing someone of their humanity is to strip them of their human personality and reduce them to nothing but the actions they commit. I want my own children to be forgiving of their childhood, of whatever mistakes I inevitably make. I want them to acknowledge somehow that I did my best, even if my effort fell short. I hope they will see in me the humanity that I am trying to see in my own father. I hope they will not let the burden of their childhood cripple their lives, and I hope they can break free and walk on their own. If I want my children (or anyone else) to see the humanity in me, then I have to at least attempt to see the man in my father and the woman in my mother. I need to see them as more than just their shortcomings. Forgiving them is what gives me the ability to do so.

I'm not advocating that we forgive our parents because we have come to understand where they were coming from. Rather, I want us to forgive them specifically because we don't understand. Doris Lessing has said, "If you understand something, you don't forgive it, you are the thing itself. Forgiveness is for what you *don't* understand." If our parents had a plausible reason for behaving like they did, then what would they need our forgiveness for? We could just excuse them without hesitation. Even if we went over our parents' childhood with a fine-toothed comb, we would probably still never come to understand quite why they behaved the way they did toward their own children. Hindsight has certainly not made the past clearer for me. But maybe it's better that way. Maybe true understanding would preclude forgiveness. Thankfully, we don't need to understand in order to forgive.

But even though we don't understand them or their trials, and although we may believe that our parents may not deserve it, we must freely offer our forgiveness in order to free ourselves of every burden. I can speak for myself in saying that I want the weight of my past lifted from my shoulders: I want to be free to step into the rest of my life unburdened by the precedent of a loving but incomplete childhood lived out in the environment of a broken but loving home. There is an old English proverb that anger is more hurtful than the injury that serves as its cause. When we hold on to wounds and allow them to fester longer than they should, we harbor not only the pain from the original wound but the multiplied injury of the festering resentment. As our minds and hearts relive the hurt we suffered years ago, we nurse the pain like a baby, feeding it, almost reveling in the sore comfort, until it grows to be a despicable adult, running amok and adding to the world's pain.

The Bible is nothing if not realistic. You'll notice that it never commands us to "love" our parents, but to *honor* them. The Bible understands that there are things that our parents do to us, or neglect to do for us, that would make love an unreasonable goal in the short term. But even in those moments we must honor them. We must place their actions in the larger context of the life we possess and the love we've received. It may be a struggle to overcome our anger and bitterness, and it will certainly come up over and over again in our contacts with our parents. But we must struggle against impatience and bad temper with equal persistence. In our ongoing struggle to do good, we must constantly learn to forgive.

I had a disagreement with my father recently. I wanted him to do what I thought was a small gesture, but it did not work out. I was upset with him, but as we got off the phone I swallowed my disappointment, told him I loved him, and respected his decision. He's my father. It's my responsibility to be a good and loving son, no matter what.

It's relevant to note that when we forgive our parents, we get them back as models of real-life heroism. How can we think of our parents as heroes when we reconstitute them in our minds as nothing more than harbingers of pain and conduits of neglect? When in my heart and mind I made peace with my father, I was able to recognize his strength as a boon rather than a deficit, and I was able to use his unshakable strength as an inspiration. Today we are a loving father and son. I confide in him constantly and he gives me valuable guidance about life. I look up to him as a great man and feel proud to be his son.

Forgiving our parents allows us, finally, to grow up. Furthermore, when we forgive them, we are making a statement to the world: my past will no longer determine my future—and my future is wide open with potential and grace. I am able to replace the anger and resentment with love and compassion, and as a result I can feel healthy and new. Indeed, the National Institute of Healthcare Research found that the act of forgiveness is linked to lower depression and anxiety. The need to forgive is our heroic obligation, and the right to rise to heroism is a right we must choose to exercise.

Although I can only speak for myself, I would like to put in a plea. I want children not just to forgive their parents, but to *cease judging them*, to understand that they have no right to judge them. For who are we, the beneficiaries of our parents' kindness, the recipients of the gift of life itself, to ever pass judgment on them?

I once counseled a very successful businessman who had long been estranged from his father. He felt that he bore emotional scars because his father had pushed him to study and prepare for a career, at the expense of giving him a "normal" childhood and all the innocence that those early years should offer. But I often told him, "Your father grew up during the Depression. His father may have shown little affection toward *him*, and raised him and the rest of his family with an iron fist. Has it ever occurred to you that your father pushed you so hard because he didn't want you to have the same life he'd had? He didn't want you to have to work in a factory, beholden to others to earn your daily bread. You've never tried to see it from his perspective. And amid all the pain of your lost childhood, think about everything you've attained as well. Where would you be without him?"

What I wanted him to know was that he simply didn't have the right to judge his father. Now that I am a father myself, I have given a great deal of thought to my own children, and how I want them to think of me when they grow up. To be sure, I would like them to remember how I always wanted to be with them, even when I had to travel for lectures and book tours—which, after all, was how I supported them. But as adults, coping with their own emotional scars, they may still ask, "Why wasn't our father around more, like the other fathers who never had to travel? Why was he locked in his office typing on so many nights, instead of playing with us as we asked?"

I pray that my children will give me the benefit of the doubt, that they will say to themselves, "Our father did the best he could— no, more than that, he did the best anyone could have, based on the challenges and unique circumstances he faced. He may not have been perfect, but he was a warm and decent man who tried to give us all the love in the world." I hope they will always focus on the positive things, the sacrifices I made for them, not on the sacrifices that circumstances may have forced upon them, or the errors I've made (and no doubt will continue to make) in raising them.

My hope that my children will not judge me unfavorably leads me to think of my own father—and I am forced to admit that he always loved me very deeply, although he often had a difficult time showing it. When I remove my own ungodly predilection to judge, I remember countless gestures that show that he did what he could. My father grew up in utter poverty in Iran, a land where Jews were persecuted and oppressed. From a young age he had to leave school to go with his father to the market daily in order to help feed his many siblings. He was a breadwinner before his eleventh birthday. Is it any wonder that he found it difficult to show emotion? Is it any mystery that he hardened his heart and raised his ramparts? He understood that life involved serious responsibilities, whether or not he was old enough to meet them. He would have to lower his shoulder to the plow and discharge those responsibilities. Finding happiness in life or enjoying himself as a teenager were concepts utterly foreign to him. He did what he had to do, and had no time to do things he would have enjoyed. What choice does a man have, when every day is a struggle just to get by?

But rather than focusing on any shortcoming in his parenting, I want to focus on all the positive things he did for me, and on his own personal challenges. I have begun to see that even my father's toughness was a kind of love—an imperfect love, to be sure, but love nonetheless. Until I stop allowing myself to equate who my father *is* with what he did, I cannot hope to successfully impart this critical lesson to my children or to heal myself.

And now, with time, rather than bitterness, I feel blessed. In place of anger, I have found absolution; in place of rancor, reconciliation. And my initial resentment has slowly given way to forgiveness. But I want to take it to the next step. More than forgive my father—for who am I to mete out forgiveness to my father?—I want to stop judging him.

And that's what I'm asking all of us to do. Live up to the fifth of the Ten Commandments. Honor your parents *by not judging them.* They did the best they could, as you and I will with our children. If we never recognize that we have no right to judge them, we will be forever trapped in an unyielding cycle of hurt and resentment.

As I've said, we'll never know our parents' struggles, torments, and frustrated dreams. It's very likely that our parents have suffered just as much as we have. But at some point it becomes incumbent upon all of us to say that the cycle of pain stops here. We cannot continue it by raising an angry generation. We must choose to live in redemption and to reach a rapprochement with our life source. Treat your parents with respect in your every interaction. Don't rush off the phone with them, or snap at their opinions, or use your busy life as a way to avoid spending time with them. Treat them as thoughtfully as you would a friend. Listen to their thoughts and share yourself and your own opinions and interests with them. Lastly, teach your own children, by word and example, to respect their wisdom.

If we do not forgive our parents, we are doomed to crawl through life. But if we can summon the heroism to rise above their imperfect example and show compassion toward them, then we can walk and run like spirited adults. Consider your parents heroes. We must all dream the dream of the hero—that one day parents will wake and discover there is no need to wander in search of treasure, because the greatest treasures of all, their children, are sitting right there in front of them at home.

19

*

FORGIVE FREELY

Forgiveness is the answer to the child's dream of a miracle by which what is broken is made whole again, what is soiled is again made clean.

—Dag Hammarskjöld, *Markings* (1964)

Forgiving our parents can be a crucial first step, allowing us to rise above our childhoods on the path to embrace heroism. And like other behavior patterns we learn within our families, taking this first step can teach us how to forgive those in the world at large as well. Forgiveness is one of the most sublime manifestations of biblical heroism there is.

Why is forgiveness so important? Well, how great is a man if he lacks the capacity to rise above the scarring of the past and turn toward the promise of the future? How free is a woman if she remains forever trapped in the deadly sepulchre of revenge and recrimination? How vital is a man or a woman who has grown old under the weight of wrongs inflicted by others? And how great is a man or a woman who has been shrunk by slights and insults?

The classical hero is celebrated for being the opposite of a forgiver. Nobody dares step up to him. He's a real man, who doesn't overlook slights. Anyone who insults or disrespects him will be hunted down and punished. He'll defend his honor to the point of death if necessary. He challenges people to duels and shoots them down to avenge slights to his honor. How principled! How noble!

How pathetic!

Did it ever strike you that this characteristic of the classical hero reveals him as someone so limited that he can't help but be offended? He is so weak that everything pierces him, everything offends him. He can't overlook anything, can't rise above anything. This guy can't evade a single arrow. He is like a child who sulks when someone tosses an unkind word his way. Neither can he deal with everyday disputes in a mature and responsible way.

In the movie *Schindler's List,* the evil commandant Amon Goeth rises every morning, takes his rifle, and begins shooting indiscriminately at the camp's helpless inmates, killing a few every day. One morning Schindler says to him, "You don't understand. You're the one with the power. To shoot innocent people is not a sign of power. It's a sign of insecurity. To forgive, however, that shows real power."

Modern culture is quietly returning to the model of the classical hero, not only in our interpersonal relationships and in business but also in our relationship with the world around us. Our automatic response is combative, aggressive, judgmental. Wherever we turn today, something is available to offend us, something that offers a challenge: a politician we don't like, a colleague who gets on our nerves, a child who's been disrespectful. We spend our lives writing to the producers of Howard Stern's radio show instead of just turning the radio off. It's as if we have all developed some sophisticated, offense-finding radar calibrated specifically to seek out stimuli that make us unhappy.

We can't seem to rise above such offenses. If someone pushes past us in a subway car, we won't relent until the entire car of commuters is embroiled in our drama. If a television host offends us, rather than doing the most beneficial thing and simply turning off the tube, we write and complain and exert every effort to get the host taken off the air. If our spouse has an annoying habit, rather than politely and diplomatically informing him of how best to change, we harbor an inner resentment and wait for the opportune time to strike back. "I'm not going to lower myself to having to tell him to stop. He should be more considerate. He should know on his own that he shouldn't keep watching television when I'm trying to sleep. This proves he doesn't love me. He's too selfish to love anyone but himself." Rather than immediately making the situation better by stroking his hair gently and asking him lovingly to turn off the TV, instead we plot our revenge. Tomorrow we'll read late into the night, the reading lamp burning brightly over his shoulder.

There's a story about a young student who once came to Rabbi Menachem Mendel Schneersohn of Lubavitch, known as the Tremach Tredeck, complaining that all the other students in the yeshiva were mistreating him. "Wherever I go they step on me," he said. The great sage responded, "Who asked you to spread yourself so thoroughly over the entire yeshiva so that wherever anyone steps they will inevitably be stepping on you?"

Are you holding a grudge against someone or something? Your parents, your spouse, your boss, a neighbor, a whole political party? To let go of these grudges is a form of forgiveness. An inability to forgive traps us in a welter of unhealthy, stagnated emotions. I once counseled a man who had fallen out with his brother ten years before over a bad business deal. It was the eve of Yom Kippur, the holiest day in the Jewish calendar, and a time when it is traditional to ask and to give forgiveness. This man was tortured by his fractured relationship with his brother, and I urged him strongly to call and try to mend the break. He picked up the phone in my office, dialed the number, and hung up. The next time he tried he was able to stay on the line long enough to hear his brother pick up the phone. "Call back," I said. "Speak to him." He said, "I can't. I just can't do it." Not "I won't," or "I'd rather not," you'll notice. He said, "I *can't*." I was struck by his choice of words: this man had lost his freedom and was incarcerated in a prison of his own creation—his inability to forgive.

When we exercise the power of forgiveness, we are completely free. And this heroic choice is always available to us. Over the course of a lifetime we will be betrayed by people, hurt by those we've sought to help, abandoned by those we once loved. We confront this on an everyday basis: a colleague decides to tell us off, a relative comes down on us with harsh criticism, a date we were interested in simply never calls again. We can't control those things. What we can control is how we react to them. Will we be distracted from our heroic path and enslaved by our desire for revenge? Do we want to involve ourselves in an ever-revolving circle of resentment? Will we bear grudges or withhold our love from others in self-protection? Do we really want to give as good as we get?

Or do we want to rise above the disillusionment and the hopelessness and reach out to others, enriching them and ourselves in the process? Wouldn't you rather sidestep the arrow, or even allow it to puncture you, even as you rise above the wound? "I guess there's some truth in what you're saying, and I appreciate your bringing it to my attention. I know you're saying this for my edification. So thank you." Or, "I'm sorry you're so upset. I assure you I intended no malice. Is there something I can do to make you feel better?" There, you said it. The world didn't come to an end. More important, neither did an important relationship you care about preserving. You may not have the opportunity to remedy the situation. That promising first date didn't call to ask for a second? Your best revenge is to keep your heart innocent and trusting and to believe as passionately in true love as you did when you were fourteen years old.

Dignity, as I have said, is fundamentally about freedom. There are different kinds of freedom. There's juridic freedom, when a man is able to liberate himself from physical or political incarceration. And there's typological freedom, when we're freed from our own limitations and scars and insecurities, when we can move past our self-abnegation and low self-esteem and truly experience life. When we're hung up on false pride, wounded by everything, obsessed by judgments, and dedicated to revenge, we imprison ourselves. As Jesse Jackson has said, it's easy to take the man out of prison, but harder to take the prison out of the man.

I experienced the liberation of forgiveness recently during an argument with my sister with whom I am extremely close and whom I love with all my heart. Neither of us was able to apologize until I came to my senses and realized that this stupid fight was denying me a sister! My own self-righteousness was going to bar me from one of the most important relationships in my life. I apologized, and my sense of relief was immediate and explosive. I've made an effort to remember how good it felt to do that so that I can call upon the feeling the next time the stubborn classical hero in my psyche gets in my way.

Of course it's often difficult to follow such a path. But biblical heroism provides us with many real-life examples of people who have risen above trials and tribulations much greater than our own. When I find forgiveness difficult, I think of Nelson Mandela, who sat down with the attorney general who was responsible for his life sentence. His greatness empowered him to forgive even this man, the person responsible for robbing him of so many years of his life. When asked what they spoke about, he joked that they'd told war stories, as old lawyers tend to do. Clearly moved, the attorney general called Mandela a saintly man. This story is an inspiration to me every time I think of it.

Forgiveness can also help us to stick to our plans. As you'll have noticed, the biblical hero has a fundamental dedication to his or her path. I've told the story of the Reverend Martin Luther King Jr. getting punched in the face during a speech. King picked himself up and kept talking—he stayed on course. His path before he was punched was to spread the word to the group he was speaking to, and his attacker punched him in order to knock King off that path. But King was a free man in every sense of the word. His ancestors had been slaves, and he wasn't about to turn the clock back. He wasn't about to imprison himself on the inside with feelings of anger and revenge. He was going to continue on the path he had chosen— of nonviolence, of dignity—rather than become the hostage of someone else's agenda. If King had hit back, or started an altercation, or even changed the content of his speech to acknowledge the incident, then the other man would have won. King was so focused on the message he was delivering that he didn't even seem to feel the blow. It was like a gnat bite to him compared to the importance of the task he had at hand.

Again, this is one of those tremendously powerful stories that we can all use to inspire us to do the right thing. King was a great man, and he was greatly tested. The simple fact that the rest of us face less awe-inspiring challenges, however, doesn't give us an excuse to treat our smaller challenges as anything less than opportunities for heroism. Perhaps a pedestrian example from my own life will illuminate this. Not long ago I was on a book tour, and my publisher had sent the plane tickets for the next leg of my tour to my hotel. They called my assistant to tell her that I should pick the tickets up before leaving for the airport . . . and my assistant forgot to tell me. Since I didn't hear otherwise, I assumed I had an electronic ticket. Only when I got to the airport late that night, expecting to be able to walk right onto the plane, did I discover her mistake—and learn that there were no extra seats available on the plane.

You can understand that my first impulse might have been to express anger. Keeping my travel plans straight is a significant part of my assistant's job, and her carelessness had not only inconvenienced me but jeopardized a public appearance in another city. In short, I was about to lose the respect of a lot of people and incur the anger of my publisher by not turning up in the next city as planned. I could have expressed my outrage by calling my assistant up and giving her a piece of my mind, and part of me wanted to do just that.

But I enjoy working with this person, and she is devoted to me and generally as professional as I could possibly hope—and I want her to know that I appreciate everything she does for me. More than that, I want to be a considerate colleague, the kind of person who can show forgiveness and tolerance, and not just when it's convenient for me. Her error was just that—an error, not an act of malice. Was I going to let her error affect the kind of person I wanted to be? Was I going to let other people's opinion of me disrupt this special relationship? Was I going to rob her of her dignity in an effort to save my own? I gained control of my emotions, called her up, calmly told her that her mistake was no big deal, and waited for the next plane. It might not sound like much, and maybe it isn't, but that night I went to sleep feeling like a hero.

The biblical hero Joseph—"Joseph the Righteous"—faced an inner battle that eclipsed any that ever took place on a battleground.

In some ways Joseph seems cut out to be a classical hero. He is blessed with a title and wealth as the Viceroy of Egypt and given a highly prized woman by the Pharaoh. Ultimately, he finds himself in a situation typical for the classical hero—facing his long-term adversaries in a potential battle for their lives. But the adversaries are his own brothers, who tormented him early in his life and sold him into slavery. The situation is reversed: Joseph has made good in Egypt, and the brothers are desperately searching for food to take back to their own country, which has been struck by famine. They don't recognize Joseph, so he decides to test them. After giving them food and money, he hides a silver cup in Benjamin's pack, then accuses him of stealing it. The brothers band together to defend Benjamin, their youngest brother, and Joseph is so moved by their clear change of heart that he reveals his identity to them and grants them protection and sustenance.

A familial relationship alone wouldn't have stopped a classical hero: it was not unusual for a newly crowned king to destroy his entire family preemptively, to ensure that none of them killed him in an attempt to seize the throne. Even in our time, of course, some of the worst, most bloodthirsty fights happen between relatives. But for Joseph, things aren't so simple. He has had a dream, in which the balance of power has shifted and his brothers are his servants. It would be easy to use the dream as evidence that he's destined to take dominion over his brothers, but Joseph deliberates and withdraws. He denies himself the "satisfaction" of revenge and chooses forgiveness and love instead. He knows that everything is happening in accordance with God's plan for him. "You intended to harm me, but God intended it for good."

We control how we allow external events to affect our plans for ourselves. Joseph decides for himself what kind of hero he is to be. The Talmud states that every dream is open to analysis. Our character is defined not by what we actually dream, but by how we choose to interpret these dreams. Joseph takes his dream as a challenge rather than a decree. And he accepts the challenge as an opportunity to elevate his brothers to his own level of righteousness, rather than sinking to their level. He views his brothers as worthy of elevation because they too are members of the human race. Joseph values their lives as he values his own.

We all have dreams. What defines our lives is how we decide to interpret these dreams. We dream of greatness, but what *kind* of greatness do we pursue? The greatness of the Public Adam, strong and imperious, or the greatness of the Private Adam, humble and fair and, yes, "righteous"? The choice is our own.

The story of Joseph is frequently interpreted as a test of the repentance of Joseph's brothers. Had they changed? Did they regret having sold him? Would they run out on Benjamin to save their own hides? To me, it seems clear that the greater test is of Joseph himself, of his capacity to show empathy, compassion, and forgiveness. Joseph passes the test with flying colors, like the colors of his vibrant coat. He earns his place as the first hero of the Bible whose greatness is determined entirely by his ability to place love and acceptance before bitterness and revenge. He has won the most difficult of all battles, the one with himself.

Is there a battle you're waging with yourself that remains unwon? Is there a grudge against someone or something that you're finding difficult to let go? When we prioritize forgiveness—in our working relationships, our marriages, even our relationships with a forgetful assistant or politically inflammatory talk-show host—we ultimately win that battle with ourselves.

20

⁊

SERVE A HIGHER PURPOSE

Many persons have a wrong idea of what constitutes true happiness. It is not attained through self-gratification but through fidelity to a worthy purpose.

—Helen Keller

There's a story about one of the greatest Jewish sages, Rabbi Yohanan ben Zukai, who began crying on his deathbed. "Why are you crying?" asked his students gathered around him. "I don't know where I'm going," he said. Was this man, the greatest rabbi of his generation, actually worried he wasn't going to make it to paradise? Was he really so foolishly humble? No. He had spent his entire life with a single-minded focus on the goals of his human life. The first moment he took to reflect on his own future came on his deathbed, when he had no more energy to focus on the world and the impact of the uncertainty alarmed him.

Imagine that someone flatters you, or intimidates or shames you into giving money to charity. You do so because of the pressure. So you've done a good thing. No matter what the circumstances, giving money to the needy is a good thing to do. But you haven't been a hero. You've simply surrendered to someone else's plan for you. All you've proven is your ability to be manipulated. The biblical hero's role is to find goodness within himself, within his essential nature and translate it into a program of action in the wider world, rather than allowing another to determine the course of his life.

This is why revenge is one of the most toxic activities there is. Someone wrongs you, and you decide it's payback time. So you put aside all your plans, all your hopes and dreams and activities and relationships, and devote yourself full-time to avenging another's misdeeds. Aren't you actually compounding the wrong that's been done to you by allowing your life to be further derailed? Wouldn't the real revenge be to forgive and move on, keeping your eye on the things that were important to you before you were wronged? Forgiveness allows you to rise above the slight and to continue along on your path.

Think of Alexander Hamilton, the man who was the first U.S. secretary of the Treasury and one of the framers of the Constitution. George Washington considered him the most valuable member of his cabinet and thought he was even more brilliant than Thomas Jefferson. Hamilton allowed himself to be goaded into a battle with former vice president Aaron Burr. Two classical heroes met in a duel, and Hamilton was killed. This man who essentially invented American capitalism is remembered for dying like a dog on a little landing on a river in New Jersey that today you can't even swim in. Not for his fiscal brilliance or his incalculable contributions to our country's history, but for a petty quarrel. It's profoundly depressing that someone so great could have been so easily distracted from his purpose. What's more, Hamilton's son Philip was *also* killed in a duel—defending his father's name. The classical hero never learns. The biblical hero isn't in competition with his fellow man, and certainly not with God, so it's not a problem for him to subsume his own self-interest for the greater good of the cause.

The biblical hero necessarily has a fundamental commitment to the course he has chosen for himself, and it is that commitment that sustains him. There is a remarkable story about Rabbi Elchanan Wasserman, a great Jewish scholar who lived in Vilna in the first half of the century. When the Nazis invaded Vilna and rounded up all the Jews there, Rabbi Wasserman realized he was going to die.

He also realized that his death would be an innocent one, and therefore a martyr's death sanctifying God's name. So when the Nazis came to get him, he said to them, "You have come to do your duty, and I am going to do mine." He dressed in his Sabbath finery, put on his gold watch, and walked erect through the streets of Vilna.

Although the guns were at his back, vicious dogs were barking at him, and Nazis were shouting orders and abuse, he walked tall and proud in the image of God. He knew that even if they took his body, his soul—that godly spark that separates us from animals—was something they could never take. When all the Jews were ordered to stand at attention near the mass grave, he told the commandant to wait. He explained to all the Jews there the laws of dying in God's name, and he calmly, carefully, and gently explained to them the thoughts that should be going through their heads when the bullets started flying. When he finished, he turned to the commandant and said, "I have done my duty, now you can proceed to do yours." They opened fire.

Although the Nazis were doing everything in their power to make Rabbi Wasserman feel inferior, he held tight to that godly spark and showed them that true dignity is internal and those who possess it are worthy to walk down the street with their heads held high. He never wavered from his purpose, even in the face of cruelty and complete injustice. Not even the evil within man could break his attachment to God. Not even cold-blooded, heartless murderers could degrade him in his last moments of life.

The Israeli writer and journalist Yaakov Kulitz tells the story of how, nearly sixty years ago, in a burned-out house in the Warsaw ghetto that was being shelled every moment by the Nazis, a man named Yossele Rakover, in his last moments of life on this earth, pulled out a pen and wrote a letter to God. He had already witnessed the murder of his wife and ten children by bullets and starvation. He held in his hand his very last Molotov cocktail to stave off the Nazis, and he knew that within a few moments he too would be dead. In his letter he expressed his anger at God and his sense of having been abandoned. But rather than be defeated, he ended his letter with defiance. "My God and God of my father, You may insult me, You may strike me, You may take away all that I cherish. But I will always believe in You, I will always love You. . . . You have done everything to make me renounce You . . . but I die exactly as I have lived, an unshakable believer." Like so many millions, he departed with the ancient words of faith on his lips, "Hear, oh Israel, the Lord is our God, the Lord is one." Here was a man so heroic that not even God could get in the way of his devotion to God.

I hope that none of us ever have to marshal these kinds of resources against this kind of evil to stay true to our inner purpose. There are many times in our lives, however, when we find ourselves in environments that are not of our choosing. Too often we allow such situations to affect the way we act. We get caught up in the heat of the moment, abandoning our own beliefs for the current mores. This influence of our environment on our behavior can come in obvious ways. One only has to look at the crowds in Arab countries who cheered when the World Trade Center was attacked, the racism of the Depression-era South, the anti-Semitism of Nazi Germany, or the frantic purges and witch-hunts of Communist Russia to see how easy it is for ordinary and otherwise good people to become caught up in the mood of the time.

The biblical hero draws upon his own inner dignity and moral convictions to stay the course and do the right thing, even in an environment that is unfriendly to his beliefs. The biblical patriarch and hero Jacob lived in his father-in-law's house for more than twenty years. Laban was a notorious cheat and a thief, and he used wily tactics against Jacob many times. Jacob was an extraordinary shepherd; he could easily have used Laban's own laziness against him to skim sheep off the top of the flock for himself. And he just as easily could have joined forces with Laban in a crooked crusade against others. Despite this, Jacob maintained the highest integrity. "These twenty years I have been with you; your ewes and your female goats have not miscarried, and I have not eaten the rams of your flocks. That which was torn by wild beasts I did not bring to you; I bore the loss of it myself; of my hand you required it, whether stolen by day or stolen by night. It was like this with me: by day the heat consumed me, and the cold by night, and my sleep fled from my eyes. These twenty years I have been in your house; I served you fourteen years for your two daughters, and six years for your flock, and you have changed my wages ten times."

Corruption is feared because of what it does to us as human beings. The corrupt individual is not born bad, but rather has the opportunity to be good and chooses instead to thwart morality and conscience by acting fraudulently. It is this kind of corruption that Jacob girded himself against—showing us that biblical heroism can help us move beyond the fray to find goodness.

We don't have to go with the status quo if the status quo is bad. We don't have to take our problems and exacerbate them. I have a friend who took a job as a stockbroker on Wall Street, working in a small firm that he discovered practiced insider trading with some regularity. There were even partners of the firm who sat on boards of companies that they would then recommend to their investors, advising them to buy or sell stock when new developments occurred. These partners also had connections with business journalists that they would use to hype companies they were trading.

My friend, whose father teaches philosophy at a university, was shocked by what he discovered—from both a moral and a legal standpoint. He had two choices. He could leave the firm, or he could try to make it better from the inside. He chose the second course of action. He became the most diligent stockbroker in the company. He would read every bit of legally available information about the companies he invested in and everything he could on successful stock trading. He consulted advisers and asked lots of questions about how he could be successful without breaking the law. And it paid off. He started making large amounts of money for his clients, and pretty soon the other partners in his firm were taking notice. When he had their attention, he arranged a staff conference at which the ethics of stock trading were discussed—and, of course, the topic of insider trading came up. At this point, because of the amount of money he was making for the firm, my friend had a lot of influence. The other brokers, who sincerely respected his financial acumen, asked him for advice, and in response he described a more traditional, ethical method of trading. Eventually some of them started to follow his example. Regardless of the environment he found himself in, he never stopped serving the higher truth—honesty.

We've all been in situations where we were torn between fitting in and "getting away with it" or doing the right thing because it is right. When you find yourself in a poisonous environment, or confronted with a choice between right and wrong, go back to that obituary I asked you to write at the beginning of this book. How would you like to be remembered? We all make a choice: either we allow our environment to influence us or we influence our environment. Goodness isn't something that can be practiced only under optimum conditions. As biblical heroes, we can find it, in some measure, wherever we go.

21

❦

DARE TO LET IT GO

Egotism is nature's compensation for mediocrity.

—L. A. Safian

We're culturally accustomed to thinking of heroism as a matter of action. Heroes go out, kill the bad guy, rescue the girl, save the world. Biblical heroism inverts that model: where the Public Adam exerts dominion over the world, the Private Adam simply wants to redeem his own little corner of the world. If providence should decide that he attain global influence, so be it. But he does not go searching for it. If we are going to follow in the footsteps of the biblical hero, we must recognize that heroism can have as much to do with the actions you don't take as with those you do take. The biblical hero is fully developed both in his active as well as passive side.

The first direction God gave Adam and Eve was a commandment *not* to act—to refrain from action, to summon their courage to gain control over their persons. It was a commandment *not* to eat from the Tree of Knowledge. Passivity and self-restraint are essential to the concept of biblical heroism.

Sigmund Freud spoke of his humiliation at seeing an anti-Semite knock off his father's hat. His father refused to assault the man in return. "This struck me," Freud wrote, "as unheroic conduct on the part of the big, strong man who was holding the little boy by the hand. I contrasted this situation with another which fitted my feelings better; the scene in which Hannibal's father, Hamilcar Barca, made his boy swear before the household altar to take vengeance on the Romans. Ever since that time Hannibal has had a place in my fantasies."

Freud felt ashamed of his father's biblical heroism and wished for him to swing a large sword. But the biblical model teaches us that a hero does not have to be active (the masculine virtue) but instead can be passive (the feminine virtue). Passivity may sound like a cop-out, but in practice it can be far harder to achieve than the opposite. Consider: in the face of temptation, it is the passive, biblical hero who will choose not to sin. It is the passive hero who chooses to avoid a battle, especially with a vastly morally inferior enemy. Freud's father picked up his hat because he would not permit a lowly anti-Semite to degrade him. He wouldn't let himself be forced into the other man's gutter. Becoming a hooligan, taking revenge, would have been the shameful thing to do, though even so keen a mind as Freud could not see it.

Passivity is more difficult than going out to conquer the world, because it requires that you wrestle with your inner demons. Moreover, there is no public reward for choosing *not* to do something, so passivity requires tremendous inner strength.

Biblical heroism requires us to have the courage to subordinate ourselves to the rule of morals and the application of ethics. It therefore first involves restraint, the exercise of self-control. Moving forward to advance the ego, always promoting the interests of the self, runs counter to the idea of the biblical hero. Without an adequate check on the power of the ego, there can be no heroism.

Even today we witness certain public figures whose inability to restrain the forward advance of their ego impedes their heroic action. Take former President Clinton as an example. Amid the scandals of his time in office, he was still acknowledged to have served the people of the United States faithfully. Yet when he left office, he encountered ferocious derision, even from many of his staunchest supporters. He just wouldn't go away. No departing president has ever held a rally on the day of his departure, for fear of upstaging the incoming president. But Clinton held *two*—one in Washington, the other in New York. Now, whatever heroic action he undertakes—even visiting victims of the September 11 tragedy in lower Manhattan—is questioned by a suspicious public.

The same is true of the man with whom I shared a solidarity mission to Israel, the Reverend Al Sharpton. There can be no question that Sharpton has, at times, undertaken heroic action by standing up to the establishment, serving as a voice for the voiceless and an advocate for the disenfranchised. And yet his disapproval rating is considerable. Even when he is fighting like a lion for those who have experienced injustice, many in the public believe that he is doing it at least as much for his own ego as for the cause. It is a shame not to confront this perception directly because it neutralizes one's efforts.

We respond most strongly to the reluctant hero, the hero who distinguishes himself or herself either by moving out of the spotlight and allowing others to shine or by undertaking heroic acts with no thought of self. The only reward is the knowledge that he or she did the right thing because it was right.

I am convinced that reluctant heroism is the reason for the meteoric rise to fame of the actor Russell Crowe. Before *Gladiator*, he was known primarily as a talented actor who won an Oscar for playing a disheveled scientist who takes on big tobacco. But he was hardly someone who made women swoon. In *Gladiator* he plays the perfect reluctant hero, the great Roman general who, while achieving great victories in battle, simply wants to return home to his wife and son and get back to farming. When he finally defeats the evil emperor in front of a huge crowd in the Coliseum, he cannot even enjoy his victory, for he bleeds to death after the fight. This theme persists in his next movie, *Proof of Life*, in which he helps Meg Ryan rescue her husband from kidnappers. Inevitably, she falls in love with the dashing young ex-commando. But after rescuing her husband in a stunning act of military heroism, he restores Meg to her husband, even though she would clearly prefer to remain with him. He doesn't even get to keep the girl! Crowe plays the ultimate reluctant hero, passive and retiring to the end, putting himself forward only when it's absolutely necessary. And the public loves him for it.

The biblical hero doesn't need to prove to us how special he is by constantly trumpeting his own virtues. He is as comfortable with passivity as he is with activity, and he does whatever best suits the situation. The soldier in the trenches who must scramble out from safety and attack the enemy lines is surely being called upon to perform a heroic act. But refraining from making someone else look bad is no less heroic.

Here is another hero: the woman having tea with a friend. There is a lull in the conversation, and she thinks of offering a tidbit of information, garnered that day, that will hurt the reputation of another friend but provide a few minutes' worth of cheap entertainment and perhaps even make her seem like the kind of bubbly storyteller who ought to be invited to her friend's next dinner party. As tempting as it is to spill, though, she chooses to be silent. Suppressing her desire for popularity in favor of a deeper desire for goodness, she neutralizes her tongue and becomes a hero.

Here is the deeper meaning of the famous story of Solomon and the sword. You're probably familiar with the story. Two women have babies at the same time. One of the babies dies, and the other lives. The woman with the dead baby goes in the middle of the night and exchanges hers for the live baby. A huge dispute erupts in the morning, and both women are taken before the adolescent king for adjudication. Solomon commands that a sword be brought and the child be sliced in two. The real mother cries out and asks that her son be turned over to the charlatan rather than put to death. Here again we see all the elements of the passive hero. The agony of the real mother as she gives up her child forever must be enormous. But she is prepared to retreat, to draw back from the stage permanently, in order to witness the apple of her eye live and flourish. This is real love—the gesture that comes with no reward.

A lawyer friend in Oxford told me this story. One of his clients was a landlord with a few residential properties. He contacted the law firm to write to a recalcitrant tenant who refused to pay his rent. My friend sent numerous letters to the tenant to try to get him to pay the money owed, to no avail. Finally he told his client that he would be writing a letter of eviction to the tenant. But the client objected. "You cannot do that. I am a Christian. I would never put someone out on the street." My friend persisted. "You're a Christian, and I am a lawyer. You pay me for my counsel, and I'm telling you: this guy has been given ample warning and he has paid absolutely no attention. He has to be evicted." But his client was unmoved. "I believe in a just God who will compensate me for the financial loss. I could never put a family out on the street."

There are two things about this story that surprise me. The first is that we find the landlord's actions surprising in the first place, rather than just ordinary and run of the mill. The second is that we would normally characterize this man as a good man, or even a good Christian, rather than a man of greatness. We call this Christian charity rather than identifying it for what it really is: an unbridled act of heroism. This man had conquered the inner beast that wishes to destroy and consume and sees others as enemies who must be stopped.

Once I was sitting on an airplane next to a large woman. She could barely fit into her seat, so the metal flap that separated our seats was open. I had to rest my arm on the metal edge for the five-hour duration of the flight. I could have said something, but not without robbing her of her dignity. Her size was her size. There's no fifteen-minute miracle diet that would have allowed her to fit comfortably into her seat without spilling over into mine. It fell to me to restrain myself so that she wouldn't feel that there was something wrong with her. By holding my tongue, I believe I was acting in the tradition of the biblical hero—even if my arm was sore.

There is also the story of Rabbi Boruch, one of the great sages of Galicia in eighteenth-century Poland. Once he was invited with his wife to the home of a newlywed couple for Sabbath lunch. The husband began to set the table by removing the candelabra where the Sabbath candles had burned the night before. His young wife rebuked him. "Don't you know you are not allowed to touch the candelabra on the Sabbath, since its use is forbidden?" The husband shook his head. "You're wrong, my dear. You're only forbidden to touch the candelabra when the candles are actually burning. But since they're out, I'm allowed to move it." The wife was flabbergasted. "I can't believe this. Everyone knows the candelabra can't be touched the whole of the Sabbath, whether or not the candles are burning."

She then turned to the great rabbi for support. "Rabbi Boruch, please educate my ignorant husband. I can't believe he doesn't know this." And with that Rabbi Boruch knitted his eyebrows and said, "Actually, the law is much more complicated than one might imagine; it involves various disputes among important legal scholars. I'm afraid I can't give you a definitive opinion." After the lunch, it was Rabbi Boruch's wife's turn to be flabbergasted. "Boruch, any schoolchild knows the woman was correct: the candelabra is off-limits. Why did you allow yourself to appear an ignoramus?" To which her famous husband replied, "Better that I appear an ignoramus than allow a husband to appear a fool in front of his young wife, before whom he seeks to make a favorable impression."

The story goes that in ancient Israel the single women would dress down and not put on makeup so as not to upstage the married women. They wanted husbands to find their wives beautiful in comparison to the more plain single women. This is the act of a passive hero, prepared to withdraw from the spotlight and experience humiliation rather than cast others in a negative light.

An analogy story appears in Oscar Wilde's classic play *Lady Windermere's Fan*. A young bride, born of a scandalous mother, marries a rich and respected young lord. Feeling that her husband doesn't love her sufficiently, she runs off one night to be comforted by an old flame, leaving her fan behind. When the fan is found, it is her mother who immediately claims the fan, although the scandal is sure to ruin her reputation for good. She protects her daughter and never reveals the fan's true owner—and in so doing becomes a hero.

Where are the opportunities for passive, reluctant heroism in your own life? Are you shoving people aside to grab the glory, or are you able to step aside and allow glory to pass you by?

The passivity of the biblical hero allows other people to make an impression on them. I did a live chat on the *USA Today* website, and a woman wrote in with this sad story. She'd lived with her husband for thirty years, raised their children, and followed him around the world, wherever his career took him. He went to his high school reunion, reintroduced himself to his high school sweetheart, and divorced his long-suffering wife to marry her instead. "How could he have done this to me after all I've done for him over the years?"

The answer is that none of the things his wife did made an impression on him. He refused to let her make an impression on him. Like waxy paper, which isn't porous enough to take ink, this man wasn't soft enough to learn anything from his wife or to feel gratitude for her sacrifices and love. It takes a secure person to let other people's kindnesses make a mark on them. This man's selfishness kept him hard.

Passivity allows us to just *be*. The classical hero must proceed, must move forward. It's the only thing he knows how to do. He has to keep crossing things off the checklist: women, cars, awards, money. If he stops swimming, he'll drown. He has no confidence in his own innate buoyancy, his God-given ability to float. The spoils of his success are his life preserver.

This all makes sense to a generation that has replaced *being* with *doing*. In *being*, what concerns you most is the journey, the process. Life itself is the goal. *Being* is profoundly means-oriented. In *doing*, on the other hand, there is no goal other than the goal itself. The only thing that concerns you is getting the thing done. The means are utterly unimportant.

Where has this goal-orientation gotten us? Instead of loving our children, we're concerned with the finished product. As long as they become the kind of mature adults who can get into Ivy League colleges, we're happy. We give them skills—tennis lessons, piano camp—rather than ensuring that they have enough love and attention. We're prouder of their careers than their characters. We focus on doing things for each other in marriage rather than on sharing time and experiences. A husband buys his wife things and takes her places rather than giving himself to her as a gift. In religion we focus on rituals and attendance rather than on always being in loving proximity to God. It's the ends of "being religious" that are important to us, when what we should be doing is walking the godly path so that the Creator is never distant.

All I suggest that you do is the hardest thing of all: just *stop*. Just for a minute, stop collecting notches on your belt, dollars in the bank, accolades for your work, skills for the future—the "stuff" of life. Focus, for that moment, on the intangibles: the love of your parents, your spouse, your children, your friends; the pride you feel in a job well done; the knowledge that God loves you just because you exist. Just *be* with yourself for a minute. Doesn't that feel amazing?

22

❦

FIGHT EVIL

For everything there is a season, and a time for every matter under heaven . . . a time to love, and a time to hate; a time for war, and a time for peace.

—Ecclesiastes 3:1, 8

The only purpose for which power can be rightfully exercised over any member of a civilized community, against his will, is to prevent harm to others. His own good, either physical or moral, is not a sufficient warrant.

—John Stuart Mill, *On Liberty* (1859)

One of the most frequent themes of my books and lectures is that Americans, with our higher than 50 percent divorce rate and our professional singles scene, have forgotten how to love. It may surprise you to learn that I'm also concerned that we have forgotten how to hate, which can be just as damaging. In other words, I do believe that there are times when it is *not* appropriate—not heroic—to forgive.

The mandate to promote and uphold dignity has a flip side: the hero must stand up against those who would rob others of their dignity. We must oppose and be ready to fight those who trample on holiness, those who seek to erase the divine imprint from the human personality by harming and murdering people. Just as we are commanded to uphold goodness, we are also commanded to resist the opposite of goodness; evil. Indeed, exhortations to hate all manner of evil abound in the Bible. Hatred is a valid emotion and an appropriate response when directed at the truly evil: those who have gone beyond the pale of human decency by committing acts that unweave the basic fabric of civilized living. The New Testament exhortation to turn the other cheek has its place, as Freud's father recognized. But there are times when Judaism obliges us to act otherwise—to resist the wicked at all costs.

About two years ago I was on the BBC discussing the tragic bombing of a gay pub that had left three dead. I referred to the bomber as an abomination. I was told that Pastor Tony Campolo, President Clinton's spiritual adviser, had said that we had to love the bomber in the spirit of compassion and forgiveness. Similarly, during my years in Britain I was used to hearing victims of IRA terrorist attacks, after losing fathers or brothers or sons, immediately announce on the air their forgiveness and love for the murderers in the spirit of Christian love.

I disagree vehemently. The individual who, motivated by irrational hatred, chooses to murder innocent victims is irretrievably wicked. He has cast off the image of God that entitles him to love and forfeited his place in the human community. To love the terrorist who flies a civilian plane into a civilian building or a white supremacist who drags a black man three miles while tied to the back of a truck is not just inane, it is deeply sinful. To love evil is itself evil; its passive nature, in this case, constitutes a form of complicity.

Contrary to those religious figures who deny Solomon's proverb and preach that religion is about unconditional love and forgiveness for all, I believe there is a point of no return for the mass murderers of this world. The Talmud certainly teaches that the true object of proper hatred is the sin, not the sinner, whose life must be respected and whose repentance should be effected. The Talmud also teaches that it is forbidden to rejoice at the downfall of even those sinners whom it is proper to hate: "Rejoice not when thine enemy falleth." However, this attitude does not apply to impenitent and hardened

monsters who pay no heed to correction. For us to extend forgiveness and compassion to them in the name of religion is not just
insidious, it is an act of mocking God, who has mercy for all yet
demands justice for the innocent.

Pacifism is the belief that goodness means never hurting another
person and never resorting to violence. This explanation of goodness
takes the traditional understanding of the Ten Commandments one
step further, making nonviolence the very essence of goodness. Pacifism interprets the Sixth Commandment to mean: *Thou shalt not kill
under any circumstances whatsoever, notwithstanding the provocation.*
In short, pacifists maintain that pure goodness means never causing
harm to another person, no matter what the provocation or what
harm could be caused by refraining. Pacifism may also take the
extreme ethical position that none of God's creatures should be
harmed, from animals down to worms.

One of the great frustrations of parenting is our inability to
guarantee the safety and well-being of our children with complete
certainty—to protect them everywhere, and all the time, from all
evil things. We have a responsibility to try, though, and certainly to
educate our children, to the best of our abilities, about the difference
between right and wrong. Parenting is more than bedtime stories
and starting a college fund and going out for ice cream. A parent
who slaps a child's hand before she touches a hot stove or punishes
her for running into the street without looking for cars is a good
parent. A good part of the responsibility of parenting is serving as a
bulwark against evil until our children are old enough to take care of
themselves. We have that same responsibility to act as a bulwark
against evil for the world at large.

Pacifist nonviolence reached its apogee and gained the most
attention during the nonviolent campaigns of Mohandas Gandhi
and Martin Luther King Jr. I have the highest respect for both of
these men, and Martin Luther King Jr. in particular has had a significant and highly inspirational effect on me. Still, I believe that of
all the interpretations of goodness, pacifism can be among the most
dangerous. Furthermore, I believe that the changes that King and
Gandhi brought about through passive nonviolence could be

achieved only within the framework of liberal democracies with a fundamental respect for the rule of law, like the United States and Britain. Pacifism is the kind of doctrine, however, that allows true evil to flourish. It facilitates evil by refusing to fight against it. Just imagine Gandhi or King trying to bring about changes in Nazi Germany. Such men would have disappeared from their homes in the dead of night, never to be heard from again. Their followers would have been mowed down in the street. There was no free press to report their struggle, and there were no sit-ins at Auschwitz.

Throughout history, those who have chosen not to fight evil have most often been destroyed by it. It was during the 1930s that the debate over pacifism reached its heights. Both America and England were unsure about entering the war. After all, the fight was going on in Europe—chances were good that it wasn't going to reach their shores. In an effort to make the best of a dubious situation, Prime Minister Neville Chamberlain went to Munich in an attempt to appease Hitler. He offered the Führer Czechoslovakia in an effort to stop his march through Europe. Chamberlain came back to England waving the peace treaty in his hand, telling his country that he had achieved "peace with honor."

Of course, he had done nothing of the sort. Hitler had made no secret of his intentions—he had never professed to be a peaceful or an honorable man, a fact that Chamberlain chose to ignore. By signing over the Sudetenland to Hitler and giving him unchecked access to that territory, Chamberlain was essentially facilitating evil. Remember the aphorism that those who are kind to the cruel end up being cruel to the kind? The tragedy of it all is that Hitler could have been easily stopped in 1936, when he first violated the Versailles treaty. He himself admitted as much. I cannot accept that it would have been a sin to kill Hitler as soon as his intentions were clear.

There is no "appeasing" people like Hitler, Stalin, Milosevic, Saddam Hussein, Yassir Arafat, or Osama bin Laden. Appeasement is no way to get peace. Those who refuse to fight them are not good people. They are neither pious nor holy. They are wicked and they are evil, just one step above the murderers themselves. If a murderer comes to your door, do you offer up your children to make his job easier? Do you undress for the rapist? Doing so does not achieve peace, or a greater good in society.

The pacifist will respond that fighting hatred with hatred also accomplishes nothing. As Bob Dylan put it: "If we take an eye for an eye, we all just end up blind." This might be true if the purpose of our hatred is revenge. But as we've noted already, revenge is a waste of time. We do not hunt Nazis in order to take revenge—we have better things to do than chase a bunch of pathetic, old, murderous thugs in order to avenge ourselves, and our Torah prevents us from taking retribution. Rather, we are pursuing justice. We are fulfilling our God-given mandate to make the world into heaven on earth. We are upholding the principles of right and wrong and protecting the dignity of the innocent. We teach our children to refrain from stealing not because they might get caught, but because theft is intrinsically wrong, whatever the chances of getting away with it. We seek out evil on behalf of all humanity so that all of the world may know that there is no apology for genocide.

In the Hebrew language there are three words for forgiveness: *selicha, mechila,* and *kapparah.* The essence of all of them is that the individual is so valuable that we allow a person the opportunity to start afresh after error. But since repentance is based on recognizing the infinite value of human life, its premise cannot be simultaneously undermined by offering it to those who have irretrievably debased human life. The bottom line is that there are some offenses for which there is no forgiveness, some borders whose transgression society cannot tolerate breaching under any circumstances. Mass murder is foremost among such offenses. Only if we accept our hatred for the truly evil will we summon the determination to fight it fervently. Odd and uncomfortable as it may seem, hatred has its place.

Furthermore, it is not enough to despise and resist evil from a passive position. We must rally our forces and engineer its destruction. I believe that the real enemy of goodness is not the evil one, but the silent one. The evil one might one day be turned to good, but the silent one is condemned by his own harmful passivity. Claiming that we're not our brother's keepers won't get us off the hook so easily. God's cry to Cain in the Book of Genesis rings down through the ages: "The blood of your brother calls out to me from the earth." Although they referred to a different era in history, the words of Martin Luther King Jr. still ring true today: "We will have to repent in this generation not merely for the vitriolic words and actions of the bad people, but for the appalling silence of the good people."

Over and over in the Bible it's said that a love of God is a hatred of evil. The classical hero is always asking, "How will this affect me?" If evil isn't going to directly touch him and his, then he's not going to get involved. We'll intervene if our vital interests are threatened, but people dying of starvation? Not our problem.

I firmly believe that we have a moral obligation to speak up and challenge those who advocate evil ideas of any kind. It is not enough simply to dismiss them as crackpots howling at the wind.

A few years ago I publicly debated Larry Flynt, the publisher of the pornographic magazine *Hustler*. I faced severe criticism for even agreeing to appear at the discussion. "How can you give that man a platform? You're legitimizing him," was the recurrent theme of the complaints I heard. A close rabbinical colleague wrote to me, "I stuck by you through the attacks you encountered when you published *Kosher Sex*. But I truly believe that you have now demeaned yourself by appearing together with that abominable man."

On Saturday after the debate I went to a synagogue in Los Angeles. At the conclusion of the service, a man walked up to me and berated me severely for participating in the debate. "How could you invite people to hear that man speak?" he asked me. So I began to tell him the reasons I felt the debate was important. He abruptly cut me off. "Sixty years ago would you have debated Adolf Hitler?" "Of course I would have," I told him. "Hitler was democratically elected. One of the reasons he was able to rise to power and prominence was that everyone refused to debate him. No one took him seriously. They all thought he would just go away. And because he was not being challenged by intelligent opponents, no one found out what he was really about until it was too late. But while the respectable crowds ignored him, dismissing him as a delusional hooligan, the rabble embraced him. It wasn't long before he gained mainstream credibility and an enormous following."

It is becoming typical for religion to recuse itself from the great debates of the age. We're afraid of unpopularity, so we opt out of the debate completely. I believe that this is a tragic error—that we are contributing to our own irrelevance. Rather than engage with the great issues of the day and demonstrate to the young that a strong, logical, and compelling case can be made for a spiritual way of life, what believers now do instead is simply denounce the nonbelievers. "They're wrong because they're sinners." Case closed.

Once upon a time religion regularly used torture and warfare to silence its dissenters. Today it uses the stern voice of moral condemnation. But there's one major problem with this tactic. It doesn't work. When people see that religion ducks the great debates of the modern age, preferring instead to engage in character assassination, the conclusion they draw is that religion is unable to make its case rationally. They see right through the moral condescension and interpret it as moral cowardice. By squirming out of taking a position, modern religion is denying one of its most important functions, which is to inject a moral counterpoint into the society at large.

We need to try to block evil at every turn, and we need to get the voice of goodness out there. There is evil in all of our lives—on a massive, geopolitical scale and on smaller, more mundane ones—and it falls to the biblical hero to make sure evil doesn't slip in through the cracks. It's not enough to abstain from participating; the true biblical hero must love the righteous and stand up courageously against evil with equal passion.

23

❧

PRIORITIZE RELATIONSHIPS

The easiest kind of relationship for me is with ten thousand people. The hardest is with one.

—Joan Baez

Moses and Aaron were brothers with two different perspectives. Moses was a judge. If a couple came to him miserable saying that he hated his wife, Moses might tell them to divorce. If they were making each other unhappy, he'd say, that was a perfectly good reason to choose to live apart. But Aaron was a priest and had an entirely different perspective. He would go to the wife and say, "Your husband loves you so much. He really wants to get back together and make this work." And he'd do the same with the husband. When he was accused of lying, he turned on his accusers, asking, "Do you really think they hate each other? Do you think that's the truth? That's not the truth. They're just angry. I'm serving a higher truth—that of love."

Aaron would say that justice isn't always the truth. He believed in preserving the relationship at almost all costs. And because he saw this higher truth, Aaron achieved a popularity among the Children of Israel that even Moses did not attain. When Moses died, the Bible says, "The *men* of Israel mourned him for thirty days." But when Aaron died, the scripture says, "They wept for him, *all* the children of Israel." Aaron was a hero to both men and women because he went beyond justice and promoted love.

Why does the Bible place such emphasis on relationships?

Someone told me about a speech that Bishop Desmond Tutu gave when speaking of his work as chairperson of South Africa's Truth and Reconciliation Committee. He explained the concept of *Ubuntu,* the African view that a person is a person through other persons. Bishop Tutu explained: "My humanity is caught up in your humanity, and when your humanity is enhanced—whether I like it or not—mine is enhanced as well. Likewise, when you are dehumanized, inexorably, I am dehumanized as well. In a way, therefore, to forgive is the best form of self-interest, because I'm also releasing myself from the bonds that hold me captive, and it is important that I do all I can to restore relationship. Without relationship, I am nothing. I will shrivel."

We are not meant to be alone in the world. We are meant to have relationships with others. In the Book of Genesis, God says, "It is not good for man to be alone." As John Milton says in *Tetrachordon,* "Loneliness was the first thing which God's eye named not good." Severe loneliness is one of the most devastating conditions that affects humankind. A baby who is not touched will not flourish. We need tactility. We all need to be loved.

In his masterful work *Naked Nomads,* George Gilder made a study of single males, and the results demonstrate why the biblical verse concerning the negative consequences of loneliness should be understood literally. It is truly not good, and certainly not healthy, for a man to be unattached and unmarried. Among the amazing statistics Gilder cites: the death rate for late-middle-aged single men is more than twice as high as that for married men; single men are six times more likely to die from accidental falls; bachelors are twenty-two times more likely to be committed for mental illness, and three times more likely to suffer from insomnia; and single men are far more likely to commit suicide than attached men. Nor does society as a whole benefit from a man's decision to remain unattached. While single men comprise only about 13 percent of the population over the age of fourteen, they commit about 90 percent of major and violent crimes.

We also need to love someone else. The truly lonely man is not the man who is unloved, but the man with no one to receive his own love. Every human being is unique. When someone needs our love, the way only we can give it, it reinforces that feeling of uniqueness. It makes us feel there is no one in the world quite like us. We possess a unique spiritual gift that only we can bestow on someone else. When our love goes unneeded, we feel ordinary, mundane, and replaceable. When our love is chosen to the exclusion of all others, as it is in a monogamous marriage, it tells us that our love is special enough that it satisfies our beloved's every urge.

The biblical hero's duty is ultimately to enhance the dignity of others, to increase the amount of love in the world. You can't do that just by loving yourself. Our gifts, whatever they might be, are enhanced when we deal with other people, in comforting them, advising them, thanking them, making them laugh, taking their opinion seriously. It's only when you rub two sticks together that you get a fire. I often think of how much of my personality lay dormant before I became a father. My children gave me the opportunity to exercise stagnant gifts, and for that I am eternally grateful to them and to my wife.

Sometimes it takes a little creativity to make relationships work, especially as our circumstances change. Look at your relationships— and if something is blocking their success, fix it! A friend of mine became very wealthy through a series of clever investments. He noticed that it was beginning to put a strain on his relationships with his old friends. He could finally afford some of the things he'd always wanted in life—to go to good restaurants, to travel—but he didn't want to experience those things alone. Nor did he want to put his less fortunate friends in the position of having to "keep up," since he was clearly in a better position than they were. He finally went to them and said, "Look, this is ridiculous. I have all this money, and I want to do things with it, and I'd like you to join me in doing those things. I don't want to sit in my box seats at Yankees games alone. I know it's too much for you, so let's just agree that I'll pay for things. And just so that you're not made to feel bad, what I ask is that once a year you give however much you can afford to a charity of my stipulation. Then our relationship is equitable. I do some things for you, and you do this one big important thing for me. It's a two-way street."

It was an awkward transition, but eventually it worked to everyone's satisfaction. My friend wasn't going to let something external like an imbalance of money interfere with his relationships. More important, he understood not only the value of his friendships but the importance of preserving the dignity of his friends. By encouraging them to give money to the charity of his choice, he ensured that they'd feel good about themselves, both for supporting the charity and for reciprocating his generosity. It was a creative solution to a problem that could otherwise have destroyed relationships he valued.

This man could have gone out and made new friends, people who could afford the same toys and treats, but he chose continuity instead. He recognized that his relationships weren't replaceable. It is said of Harry Truman that he kept the same friends throughout his presidency that he'd had as a haberdasher in Kansas City. I am always impressed by wealthy or powerful men who keep their old friends and include them in their new lives. It can be difficult, to be sure—your old friends won't be treating you the same way they used to either. Jimmy Carter talked often about how impossible it was to have a conversation with old friends visiting him in the Oval Office. Even someone he'd known his entire life would be dumbstruck, staring around the room, intimidated and bewildered.

But the biblical hero who makes authentic connections with other people's inner dignity has no difficulty understanding the importance of maintaining relationships. In contrast, classical heroism is all about imbalance. It's about seeing people as functional, as stepping-stones whose value is measured by what they can do for you. When people are reduced to their functions and nothing more, they are robbed of their dignity. Every waiter is the same until you make eye contact, share a joke, a word of gratitude—that is, until you recognize your waiter as a human being.

Michael Jackson and I went to have a conversation at Elie Wiesel's house. Before we sat down to dinner, Elie asked Michael to come with him. "There's someone I'd like you to meet," he said. It turned out that the housekeeper in the Wiesel home was an enormous Michael Jackson fan, and she was overjoyed to have the opportunity to shake his hand. What impressed me in that moment was that Elie cared as much about his housekeeper as he did about this huge celebrity—that he wanted to make her happy, maybe even more than he wanted to make Michael Jackson happy.

It is important that you treat every single encounter with another human being in your life as a social interaction. When people see their friends, they are apt to smile at them, exchange pleasantries and inquire after their welfare. We are less excited about being that friendly to the woman working behind the counter at the supermarket or the teller working at the bank. These people we see merely as facilitators, people we need to help us get things done. We might not smile at them, nor even acknowledge them beyond the task that we are giving them to do. This kind of behavior is wrong.

If you stepped on the mayor's toe in the subway, would you react the same way you did yesterday, when you stepped back onto the foot of the kid with the too-loud Walkman? It's the same phenomenon that's at play in the movie *Gosford Park:* the servants aren't even known by their own names, but by the names of the people they serve. Are we any better when we refuse to acknowledge someone else's humanity over the course of our own transactions? I think America would be a better place if manners had a higher spot on our list of priorities, but this is a matter of more than just good manners. It's about making every interaction an opportunity to confer dignity on someone else.

I know that a call for adding a kinder, more solicitous tone to such everyday transactions could be seen as motivated by self-interest—that exchanging a kind word with a sales clerk may seem to be merely a good way to get what you want and to ensure special treatment in the future. If you're nice enough to the producer of a talk show, perhaps she'll make sure you're invited back. If you're nice enough to a waiter, maybe you'll get a better table next time. I think of this kind of self-motivated gesture as an emotional tip—and I think most working people would rather have an actual tip than someone else's inauthentic interest. The key, as in so many things in life, is sincerity.

The code of biblical heroism doesn't permit us to ignore people, and it doesn't permit us to treat them less than sincerely either. An important part of human dignity is the right to sincerity in human relationships. People have a right to know where they stand in your estimation and in your affections. When a man makes love to his wife, she has the right to know if he's thinking about her or about a woman from the office. To mislead anyone in any kind of interaction—romantic or otherwise—is a moral wrong.

When people understand you to be someone who sees others as functional, then even your real relationships can be polluted by it. This is a feeling I've experienced myself, and it taught me a valuable lesson. After we founded the L'Chaim Society at Oxford, I became consumed with the important work we were doing, work that benefited many thousands of people. Like every charitable organization, Oxford L'Chaim needed money to run. So as the organization grew and branched into other cities, I found myself spending a lot of time with the wealthy, encouraging them to support our good works financially. After a couple of months of this, though, I began hearing complaints from the students. I had changed, they were saying: no longer completely available to them, I was spending too much of my time and energy on these other people, trying to cover our budget.

At first I found such complaints extremely frustrating. What I was doing, after all, I was doing for the students. They benefited from the organization and enjoyed the facilities, speakers, and services we provided. All I was trying to do was to find a way to pay for it. With a little introspection, though, I realized that the students were right. I *had* changed, and they had recognized it before I had. It wasn't so much the time I was spending with the wealthy donors, but the implication that the time I spent with the wealthy was more important to me than the time I spent with the students. I had gotten caught up in the classical hero's game, even though my initial motivation was within the biblical model, and I was grateful to them for having brought it to my attention. My behavior changed—and the organization flourished.

Sometimes we find ourselves confronted by people we genuinely don't like. How can we prioritize relationships with people we find intolerable? They might keep us on the phone for hours talking about inane subjects. They might show up at our door and hover at the most inopportune times. They might badger us about something we have no interest in. We might regret ever having met them in the first place. In such situations, how can we be expected to extend even a modicum of kindness or patience?

The answer is simple: remember your heroism. You're not an animal or a child. You can control the way you behave, and you must. And make it sincere: force yourself to find something in them that is redeeming and virtuous. Be gracious, even if it calls for restraint. Is there anyone who hasn't carped at a traffic cop when getting a ticket after being stopped for doing eighty-five? Or who hasn't freaked out at a customer service employee for a problem with our account? Is there anyone who hasn't used the dinnertime tele-marketing call as a "harmless" way to blow off steam? At best in these situations we can be dismissive, and at worst abusive. When you treat someone badly, even—or especially—someone you don't know, you're effectively saying, "I don't care about you as a person. Your feelings don't matter at all. Only *my* feelings matter. I want to exercise supremacy over you." If you don't want a speeding ticket, slow down. You have no right to take your anger out on those who are only doing their job. Do you think the telemarketer calls you because it's the only way he knows to follow his dream?

Our heroism is tested in deeply uncomfortable situations. When I went to Israel with the Reverend Al Sharpton, he accepted a meet-ing with the Palestinian leader Yasser Arafat. As you might imagine, I was very disappointed and heartbroken in his decision—the point of the trip was supposed to offer comfort to the thousands of inno-cent Israeli victims of Palestenian terror and to strengthen and heal relations between the black and Jewish communities. I had also hoped that the trip and the media coverage would help to bolster Israeli confidence and morale during difficult times. By meeting with Arafat, Reverend Sharpton was negatively affecting all of our mutual goals. But I was his host, so I accompanied him to Gaza for his meeting, although I refused to join him with Arafat because I was not going to legitimize the murderer of my people.

I sat in the anteroom outside Arafat's office while I was waiting for Reverend Sharpton. As you might imagine, just being there was a tremendous trial for me. On the wall was a map of Israel with the Palestinian flag superimposed over Israeli cities like Haifa, Tel Aviv, and Jerusalem—evidence of plans to push the Jews into the sea! I was saddened by such glaring evidence of nefarious Palestinian intent.

During my wait, though, I was joined by one of Arafat's staff, his right-hand man. And I realized, as the disgust and anger rose in me, that I had a choice. I could treat this man coldly and with hatred, or I could struggle against my instinct and be human. Wasn't it better to show this person that a rabbi is capable of finding common ground, even with a sworn enemy? And so I did. He had attended Oxford, it turned out, so we talked about our experiences there; eventually he even asked me if they could send out for some lunch for me. I told him I was kosher, and he apologized that there were no kosher restaurants in the Gaza strip. We both laughed. Restraining myself that afternoon was one of the hardest things I have ever done, but it may also have been one of my proudest moments. I chose to fight my own ego and sanctify God's name with kindness while making a point of my revulsion for the Arab terrorist Yassir Arafat.

The Public Adam sees everything in terms of conflict and out-come—winning and losing. The Private Adam can find, even in a moment of conflict, an opportunity to build relationships. The ancient rabbis said, "Who is a hero? He who makes his enemies into friends and his detractors into associates."

My great spiritual mentor, the Lubavitcher Rebbe, once had a private audience with a leading secular Jewish scientist who worked for NASA's Life Science Research Institute. The conversation turned to a paper the Rebbe had authored critiquing Darwinian evolution. The professor was scathing about the article. Although the Rebbe had trained as an engineer at two of the world's most prestigious universities, the professor told the Rebbe that he had no knowledge of science. For an hour he disparaged the foremost Jewish spiritual authority in the world. All the while, the Rebbe was silent and accepted the abuse.

Years went by, and the professor, through his friendship with the Rebbe and other rabbis, became an observant Jew. The Rebbe met with him on many occasions, yet never mentioned the earlier, unpleasant episode. After eleven years had elapsed and their friendship had been strongly solidified, the Rebbe suddenly sent a letter to the professor, responding point by point to the arguments he had made so many years before. The professor was most impressed with the Rebbe's counterarguments and said so. "First of all, I'm amazed that you still remember what I said. Second, your points are completely valid. So why didn't you do this years ago?"

The Rebbe responded calmly. "Had I refuted your arguments all those years ago, I would have won the argument and lost the relationship. And I'm in the business of losing arguments and winning relationships." He was able to subjugate his own ego to the bigger picture. That's heroism.

24

⊷

CHOOSE LOVE OVER JUSTICE

Great services are not canceled by one act or by one single error.
—Benjamin Disraeli

Have you noticed that in this age of lawsuits, we spend a lot of time worrying about who's "right"? If you were driving and someone jaywalked across the road in front of you, you would put on the brakes, even though the right of way was technically yours. Being "right" means nothing if it means killing someone. So why are relationships different?

I once watched the marriage of friends of mine disintegrate before my eyes. Married for twenty-four years, they had allowed their marriage to degenerate to the level of the functional. They started as lovers but ended as parents and mortgage partners. Not having a lot of money, they went years without going away together. Saturday nights, their one night alone together, descended into the predictable routine of going to a movie with scarcely a word exchanged between them. Slowly the spark was lost, and they drifted apart.

Eventually the husband informed his wife that after the wedding of their daughter, set to take place in a few months, he would be moving out of the house. I went to talk to him. "I work hard to support the family. I have certain rights. I deserve to come home and eat, I deserve to have basic domestic support. I want a wife who

180

doesn't mind being a wife. But my wife feels that housework degrades her. She's always going out with her girlfriends. Nothing will stop me from moving out."

I went to speak to the wife as well. "I did everything for him all these years," she said. "We had a traditional marriage. He worked. I raised the kids. And do you think he appreciated anything I did? He never showed me affection or thanked me for any of it. He took it all for granted. The kids got all his love, and I got nothing. I'm sick of being treated like a doormat. If he wants to move out, then let him move out."

As the daughter's wedding day approached, the situation escalated. Every day the husband would remind his wife of his impending plans to leave. "I hope you have someone to shovel the snow this winter because I'm not going to be around." "You better ask the next-door neighbor who they use to do the gardening because once I go, all the hedges are going to grow over and you'll be fined by the city." She listened with indifference.

All he wanted was for her to say—just once—that she wanted him to stay. I pleaded with her to ask him. "Divorce is final," I said. "Wouldn't it be better if you asked him to stay, and the two of you tried to work your problems out? I'm not telling you to be a doormat, and I understand the pain of neglect. You're right—he was wrong. But whose purpose will be served if this marriage is dissolved because two stubborn people simply couldn't admit that they still need each other?" But she wouldn't do it, *couldn't* do it; her pride got the better of her.

So I ran back to him. "She's not going to ask you to stay. But that doesn't mean that you have to go. Would you rather be proud or be married? You've got to change your attitude. You've got to be more loving. You have to show your wife that you need her, you value her, you appreciate her. Is that the message you're sending by leaving the house? She hasn't behaved all that well recently, but can't you find it in your heart to forgive her? Look back at your past together. Can't you find at least one incredible thing she did for you that will remind you of your promise to love her forever? In fact, can't you find a whole slew of those things? Get off your high horse and show her some humility. Show her you're prepared to humble yourself in order to win her back. Show her that her love is more important to you than your own sense of honor."

But he wouldn't do it either. And so these two classical heroes who weren't prepared to swallow their pride, who weren't prepared to forgive a slight, who weren't prepared to lay down their arms and embrace each other with love, ended up divorcing after a quarter-century of marriage. They each wanted to "win." Being "right" was more important to them than being loved. And they've both been alone to this very day.

A truly heroic husband or wife would have behaved otherwise. Sometimes love and justice are in conflict, and when this happens, the biblical hero always chooses love. He sets aside his pride to win back love. He forgives slights to win back the relationship; he says he's sorry when he's wrong, and even sometimes when he's right. Being in love is more important to him than being right. To him, harmony is more important than some abstract scorecard of honor or respect. So remembering a wife's past devotion is more important than the unwarranted snappish comment she made in a moment of stress and fatigue.

We all have a self-destructive streak: we overindulge in food and wine, we shop 'til we drop, we have sex too early in a relationship. We indulge our desires, our egos, our tempers. But that's the Public Adam in us, always in the thrall of his appetites and his yen for spectacle and self-indulgence. The classical hero is a ticking time bomb, one that always goes off. Only biblical heroism can help us to overcome such self-destructiveness.

We rarely look at our relationships in their entirety. Humans have what can be called incident-sensitive memory, rather than context-sensitive memory. Our memories are only as good as the last interaction. We have to learn to contextualize behavior. People do dumb things. That's life. Is it really wise to throw out an entire relationship because of one mistake?

I knew a woman who was incredibly pious and religious. She had a terrific husband, a man who thought she'd hung the moon. One weekend his wife's best friend came to town, and in a moment of incredible stupidity and weakness the husband peeked through the bathroom keyhole at the showering female friend. His wife caught him and left him that same day. I tried to stop the divorce— I couldn't believe she could throw away a rich history of love and commitment because of a ridiculous, stupid, sinful mistake. It was all of those things, to be sure, but to throw an otherwise good marriage away because of it?

I have often said that if I were walking along a beach and found a genie in a bottle, I would rub it and wish to be Bill Gates ... er, just kidding. No, I would wish to eliminate judgment from the world. I honestly believe the world would be immediately and infinitely improved if we could remove our trigger-happy instinct to judge our fellow humans. It would create so much peace and openness in the world if we could stop sizing people up as soon as we meet them, trying to figure out what kind of person they are, which stereotype we can apply to them, which pigeonhole might suit them best.

Justice and goodness are different things altogether. Justice dictates that all people must be treated fairly. Goodness dictates that sometimes people must be treated more than fairly—that the flawed among us should also benefit from our generosity, whether or not they deserve it.

Once I approached a philanthropist about helping a man whose business had collapsed; he couldn't afford to pay his mortgage and was in danger of losing his house. The philanthropist told me, "I'm not going to help that guy. In the good old days, he was profligate in his spending. He bought a fleet of cars instead of saving his money and always traveled first-class. He was a big shot who put on big, expensive parties to impress people. So he's blown all his money—big surprise. Now that he's bankrupt, those of us who have always conserved and led a modest life should give our hard-earned money to bail him out? Forget it." The philanthropist was confusing justice with goodness. Justice dictates that you reap what you sow. This man had spent selfishly, justice argues, so he should lose his house and live in a hovel, humiliated and abandoned. But sometimes goodness dictates that you go beyond the letter of the law and help people.

We've got to stop judging! It's not our job to judge one another.

It's not our place to determine who deserves help. The only thing we need to know is that when someone is in need, they deserve whatever help we can give them. It's our job to try to alleviate suffering through love. This applies to the world at large as well. After five thousand years of recorded history, we have still failed to bring civilization deep into the heart of man. Everywhere we turn there is war. Society as a whole seems to have improved in that more governments are tolerant of religious freedom and provide a social welfare structure that meets the majority of human needs. But as individuals, our comfort with the principles of society seems to have developed at a far more leisurely pace. The world is still plagued by lots of violent crime, hatred, conflict, and malice among people, even those living in the most stable and civilized countries.

Worse, it seems that there is more and more judgment out there in the world. Newspaper editors sell us bad news on the front pages every morning because they know how much we love to read of other people's misfortunes and calamities. News programs lead with the latest political, business, or social scandal because they know that nothing makes us stay tuned like the downfall of someone successful. The reason for our failure to evolve, I believe, is this: our society.

Each of us has a deep-seated indignation against injustice. It shakes us to our very foundation when we witness the wicked prospering or the good suffering. But is this the only proper way to feel under such circumstances? Perhaps it is far more important to help those who suffer than to cry out against injustice. In today's society we hate injustice more than we love people. We hate the wicked more than we love the righteous. Even our pursuit of goodness follows this outlook: we look to right wrongs rather than increase love. We enjoy watching the evening news and firing off our contempt against everyone who has hurt innocent victims—but we stay focused on the bad guys rather than the good guys.

When I was working at Oxford, it was common to hear the news that another of the many cyclists who used the Oxford streets (mainly students on their way to tutorials) had been struck down by a careless motorist. Suppose you witnessed a drunken motorist hit a bike. Would you run to catch the motorist's license plate? Or run to the aid of the injured cyclist? Justice dictates that the motorist be held accountable for his wickedness—but goodness dictates that the welfare of the stricken cyclist comes before anything else. And which is more important at the end of the day? Leave the motorist to his own conscience, and make sure you get the cyclist off to the hospital. Justice may suffer in the wake of such a choice, but goodness will prevail.

The Talmud tells us that the principal calling of humanity is to become candles, or "workers producing light." Every single one of us has a responsibility to help heal the world in some way. Our first prerogative in this world is to advance the cause of goodness, and as an adjunct to that we engage in the promotion of justice. Justice is the business of God, the one supreme judge. Our task is not to question how and why good people suffer, but rather to alleviate suffering to the best of our ability. Neither is it our task to seek to punish the perpetrators of injustice before we first assist those who suffer. Our first purpose is to help the light shine out, not to attack the darkness.

The Talmud, in a famous passage, asserts that he who quarrels with someone else and exclaims, "May God judge you for your iniquity," is immediately judged by God Himself. If his purpose is to invoke divine justice rather than mercy, then it shall first be visited upon him. And while earlier I spoke of the obligation to resist evil, this applies principally to murderers, racists, and other hate-mongers and perpetrators of evil.

The Arab world loves to accuse Israel of cruel treatment of Arabs, conflating Zionism with racism. But even while Arabs are accusing Israelis of atrocity, they are turning their backs on their own people. Arab-on-Arab injustice is a serious problem: hundreds of millions of Arabs can't read and can't vote; in many Arab countries, women are openly beaten in the streets for immodesty; and majority-Muslim Arab countries rate among the worst in terms of human rights violations. If Arabs would redirect their energy toward fixing the problems in the Arab world instead of attacking Israel, they might be restored to their former glory. Let's address the problems in our own backyard rather than spending all of our energy on hating those different from us. Before you throw that stone, ask yourself: Am I doing everything I can to heal the world?

Please don't think I don't know how difficult it is to choose love over justice. Recently a man came to me with a problem. He had married into a wealthy family, and his in-laws assumed that he loved money more than their daughter, so they treated him very disrespectfully, both in private and in public. There is nothing more horrifying, more soul-destroying, than being accused of inauthenticity, especially as it pertains to the people who mean the most to you, and these people were saying a truly terrible thing about this man's great love for his wife. He was justifiably upset, and when the situation became intolerable, he came to see me and told me how he planned to respond to their abuse. "I will no longer allow them to come to our home," he said. "I'm not going to let them see their grandchildren." He planned to seek justice by treating them as cruelly as they had treated him, retaliating with the tools he had at hand. "But then you will become just like them," I advised him. "You and your wife have a divine imperative, an obligation to promote goodness and loving-kindness. We humans must concern ourselves first and foremost with being good people, not with punishing the unjust or stooping to their level."

Luckily, the man found it within himself to continue treating his in-laws with respect despite their cruelty, and they grudgingly began to reciprocate as time went on. The situation still isn't really perfect: unfortunately, his in-laws love money so much that they can't imagine anyone finding it less important than something insignificant like their daughter. But the husband who came to me finds consolation in his own heroism and in the wonderful relationship he has with his wife and children.

But, Shmuley, you may be wondering, isn't there a contradiction here? If we're supposed to choose love over justice, as you suggest, how are we then to fight evil, as you've said earlier? There's no contradiction actually. We can be compassionate and still hold people to a standard. Take Dostoyevsky's *Crime and Punishment.* Your sister desperately needs money or she will be sold into white slavery, and a loan shark refuses to give the money she needs. So you kill the loan shark who is a wretched human being anyway. You have committed evil. You are a murderer and must pay a steep price. But there are mitigating circumstances and room for compassion.

When God first created the world, the ancient rabbis say he made justice its cornerstone. The wicked failed while the righteous prospered, but He saw immediately that what he'd created wouldn't work. As they say, it was subject to human error. People are fallible. They make mistakes. We have to believe in a world where people are more than their actions, a world where people can fix their mistakes and be redeemed. A world created entirely on the principles of justice doesn't allow for any kind of forgiveness, and it cannot survive. So God mixed in a healthy dose of love and compassion, and the world endured. In other words, God also chose love over justice. So must we.

25

❦

HAVE AUTHENTIC
RELATIONSHIPS

Intimate relationships cannot substitute for a life plan. But to have
any meaning or viability at all, a life plan must include intimate
relationships.

—Harriet Lerner, *The Dance of Intimacy* (1989)

The biblical hero must choose love over justice, for he knows
there's nothing more important than preserving the human relationship. Relationships are important because they provide the means by
which we see our own dignity reflected in other people. We have an
obligation to make all of our relationships authentic, from the central ones in our life to the seemingly insignificant social and business
interactions that populate our days.

In an authentic relationship, you have nothing to prove. You can
just be. Indeed, even our heroism can be recognized only in an
authentic relationship. Celebrities have so little dignity because their
self-esteem is dependent on inauthentic relationships. They are con-
tinually proving themselves to people who don't actually care about
them at all. To the classical hero, the individual doesn't matter—it's
the masses, the crowd, the throng, that commands his attention.

A central tenet of Judaism is that everyone has a right to
authentic relationships. If I get good news and pull a bottle of

champagne out of the refrigerator to celebrate, and you happen to stop by my house, I would certainly be tempted to pretend that the champagne was in honor of your visit. But Jewish law prevents me from engaging in such a pretense, because to do so would be to misrepresent our relationship. Such a charade would rob you of the truth and the opportunity to have a true opinion of me, and that's both unlawful and wrong. In fact, on the eve of Yom Kippur, Jews are obliged to tell people what they've said about them behind their backs. These phone calls are so horrible to make that they really ensure that you will stay clear of maligning people during the rest of the year.

Authenticity is very difficult to achieve, and sometimes it seems we'll do anything to avoid the exposure it entails. I've noticed that there's a trend away from giving praise because we don't want to deal with the fallout—the lawsuit, for example, that we fear will inevitably occur should we ever have to fire an assistant we've lavishly praised in writing. What a terrible situation! We've all gotten into the habit of lying to avoid confrontation. You run into someone you know casually on the street and say, "I'd love to have lunch sometime," when you both know that'll never happen. We say, "It's not you, it's me," when we're breaking up with someone, or we make love to our spouses while thinking of someone else. This amounts to lying, and lying is a sin. But how does our obligation to tell the truth jibe with our obligation to confer dignity, you might ask? Isn't it a good thing to make people feel better about themselves? How will they benefit from the truth? Who wants to hear: "I'm not interested in dating you any longer because you're overweight and have bad teeth. And by the way, I hate your dog." Isn't a lie sometimes the better alternative?

It's not. It's patronizing and disrespectful. First of all, when it comes to dating you have an obligation to make sure everyone whom you date has a fair chance. It's your responsibility, and it also works to your advantage. I can't tell you how many wonderful couples I know who aren't each other's type. "I didn't even look at him twice because he was too old/young/short/tall/shy/loud/bald/hairy —but then we got to talking, and I couldn't believe how funny and nice and attentive he was, and suddenly I couldn't even remember why I'd found him unattractive." You can't throw away the possibility of a wonderful relationship because someone's got a bad haircut. Don't write someone off at the door even if you open it to find a green ogre there. Take that ogre out, talk to him, and get to know him. Don't let superficialities obscure his inherent dignity. Use the date to uncover his unique gift, and see how you feel at the end. If you're still unattracted to him, find a way to tell him while allowing him to maintain his self-confidence and respect. One challenge of biblical heroism is to find ways to tell the truth without robbing others of their dignity.

As we have discussed, there is terrific freedom to be found in giving your unique gift to someone who wants it. Our dignity can grow only when someone else recognizes the uniqueness within us. Being loved shines a spotlight on you, and it is in that light that you can see your own heroism. I can't think of any better way to confer dignity on another person than asking that person to marry you (or saying yes when asked). It's a spectacular gesture, asking someone to share your life completely, to celebrate in your successes, to comfort you in failure, and to provide counsel through all of it. What a wonderful way to tell someone, *you matter!*

Jacob knew this. After seven years of laboring in order to win the hand of Rachel, he was tricked by his father-in-law into marrying the wrong woman, his beloved's sister. So he labored uncomplainingly for another seven years so that he could marry the woman he loved. So often people are not willing to do the work. Is it any surprise that they're unfulfilled? As a guest on a panel debate show a few years ago, I got into an argument about marriage with the host. He wanted me to admit that marriage might not be the right answer for everyone. After the show we spoke about our differences in a slightly more personal way. He said, "The relationships I see, even the good ones, look like work. I work really hard during the day to be good at what I do—I don't want to have to work at home too!"

I have no idea whether or not this man is happy in his personal life. For all I know, he might be blissful. But I personally believe he won't be truly happy until he finds himself in a relationship with an equal whom he chooses. Yes, he will have to struggle to stay faithful and attentive and loving with the same woman for a long time. It won't always be easy—the hardest battles we wage are against ourselves. As a husband, he'll have to struggle against the urge to go after every pretty young thing in a short skirt, especially given the way women fawn over TV personalities. Within his marriage, he'll have to struggle against the desire to cut to the chase in the bedroom, instead of giving his wife the foreplay she desires. Is it a struggle? Yes, sometimes it is. But I don't think too many people spend a lot of time complaining about foreplay. Like so much of biblical heroism, it's the kind of struggle whose end result is such a pleasure that it makes the "work" feel like a pleasure.

It is an act of biblical heroism to have a completely authentic, naked relationship with someone else. We keep a little something back because we're afraid of getting hurt. But if you can truly stand naked before your spouse, then you will be rewarded with an ever-deepening bond. What a liberation it is—what a revelation—to be completely known by another person! When my wife is away, I feel like I'm not completely present either. Nothing I do without her, none of my career achievements, mean much to me unless she is with me to share them. Even when I travel and we talk on the phone, I try and communicate to her that I need her. It's extremely difficult to make yourself vulnerable like that, especially for a man. And yet I don't care if being vulnerable makes me sound weak, because it's the truth, an irrepressible truth. And in our capacity to show vulnerability, we then find strength.

I'm in good company. The legendary chef André Soltner was once asked, along with a number of other panelists, to name one human being, past or present, with whom he would most like to have dinner. His colleagues all chose historical figures like Thomas Jefferson and Eleanor Roosevelt and Jesus, but Soltner said that he'd choose to eat dinner with his wife.

When Israeli Prime Minister Ariel Sharon was my guest to deliver a lecture to the students of Oxford in 1991, I was struck by how visible his relationship with his wife, Lilly, was. This was no arm-candy consort. He knew exactly where she was in the room at all times, and he was openly solicitous of her opinions and needs. When they walked, he took her hand or arm, and he made a point of thanking her when he spoke. He was completely unashamed of his real need for her, and I was tremendously impressed by his willingness to display it so openly. After his lecture he sat down to do three hours of television interviews. I said to his wife, "Mrs. Sharon, why don't we take you on a small tour of the university while your husband does his interviews?" First she got up to follow me, but then she sat back down. "No, on second thought, I'll stay. I know that Arik will look around for me if I go, and he'll be more comfortable with me in the room." This man is considered the toughest statesman in the Middle East, and yet he was completely comfortable expressing dependence on the woman in his life.

I was always struck by Princess Diana's genuine and exuberant joy when she saw her children. She was known for it, in a culture that isn't big on public displays of affection, especially among the royals. She had no mixed feelings about whether it was more important to have an authentic relationship with her children or to avoid offending her mother-in-law. And the public loved her for it. Once, when she came to visit Oxford, I took my eldest daughter, Mushki, who was five at the time, to see her as she visited with crowds in the street. "Look, Mushki," I said as Diana took her hand, "this is a real-life princess." And Diana responded, "No, I'm not a *real* princess." Her expression was so sad that it startled me, along with two student friends who were with me. I will never forget the interest she took in my daughter, her gentleness with children, and her ability to make a real connection with the people she met, even if just for a moment.

In sharp contrast, I remember having dinner with a friend in his midthirties whose marriage had been unraveling for months. His wife's complaint was that he had become cold and distant, but the real truth was that he was having an affair with an eighteen-year-old gymnast. I spoke to him of heroism. "You think you're pretty macho, having this affair with a woman who is half your age. But a real man is someone who can keep his wife smiling. The test of masculinity lies in a man's ability to make a woman happy. Because only a woman can make a man feel like a man. A man who can't satisfy the woman he's got is incomplete." He wasn't impressed. "That might sound okay in one of your books, Shmuley, but it doesn't wash with me." Then he leaned over and looked with great seriousness into my eyes. "Do you have any idea what it's like to be with a woman who can bend her legs back behind her head?"

I looked back at him in complete disbelief. Was this guy for real? "Do you have any idea," I said, "of what great sex really is? You think it's going at it with a woman who can contort her body into a pretzel? You can't have great sex with this person—not like the sex you can have with a woman whom you can totally let go with, for whom you release your complete passion, around whom you can behave with no inhibition—a woman who isn't ashamed to reveal her deepest sexual fantasies, so that her sexual core and essence is revealed to you because she trusts you completely. You may have a gymnast in your bed, but you could have had a tigress. You could have brought out your wife's deepest fire, the kind of fire that a woman reveals only when she's sure that she'll never be hurt by the man she's with. That's when women get so excited that they completely let go and lose all control. When you're having really great sex, your *mind* bends into a pretzel, not your body. You're alive with every erotic sentiment. Your mind gives your body not just three erogenous zones but makes your whole body a giant erogenous zone. That's impressive sex, and I know that you have never had it."

As I wound up my tirade, though, my anger was replaced with sadness as a new thought struck me. I was in the presence of a man who thought he was alive, but really he was dead. He thought this postpubescent teenager brought him to life, and yet his sensitivities and sensibilities were wasting away in the morgue. He had killed his own heart, and unfortunately he had taken his wife's heart with him. They ended up divorcing in the most acrimonious way, fighting over every last penny, as their two young daughters suffered in between them. But he still had his pretzel!

It's devastating to me when such men can't rally and be their own best selves in the relationships they've chosen. Once I received a call from a distraught woman, the wife of a world-famous musician. She told me that her sixty-year-old husband had run off with his twenty-five-year-old apprentice. I went to see him. "Why should I give up this young woman?" he asked me. "She makes me feel young and alive." I responded immediately: "Why should you give her up? Because you've already conquered the whole world. The easy part is over. Now the hard part begins. Now you must conquer yourself. Go home and become a hero. Only a mediocrity succumbs to a fleeting passion. A hero honors his commitments."

To have authentic relationships, we have to be completely faithful to the people in our lives—and I'm not just talking about avoiding adultery. I'm talking about faithfulness in thought, word, and action, and faithfulness to our friends as well as our spouses. Consider true fidelity. Are you faithful in a friendship if you talk about someone behind their back? Are you really faithful to your spouse if you're doing something you know would break her heart, whether it's lusting after a film star or talking late into the night with an unattached woman?

Creating and maintaining authentic relationships in our lives gives us a sense of dignity because we feel like we're making a contribution. Relationships give us people who really care about us, and places where we really belong, and it does the same thing for the people with whom we share those places. What better way to increase the amount of goodness in the world than to increase the number of authentic connections between people? The people you know become "your" people, and your interest in doing right by them naturally increases. If it's my country, my city, my family, I care. Relationships make everything personal.

26

⟨⟡⟩

SHOW GRATITUDE

A man's indebtedness . . . is not virtue; his repayment is. Virtue
begins when he dedicates himself actively to the job of gratitude.
—Ruth Benedict

I have watched many couples fall in love and marry. At first everything generally goes beautifully. But when the pressures of everyday
living begin to encroach upon the couple, sometimes they forget to
take the time to show each other gratitude and appreciation. The
result is two people who live together in resentment. Soon they are
at each other's throats instead of in each other's arms.

Katie and Peter were married two years and had a baby girl. One
night my wife and I were guests with them at a dinner party hosted
by a mutual friend, Janine. Throughout the dinner we watched in
amazement as Katie disparaged Peter unrelentingly in front of all of
us. Her verbal abuse was so vituperative that it soured the dinner for
all present.

After dinner a despondent Peter came over to me and said,
"Look, the truth is, we didn't just come for dinner tonight. Janine
told us that you counsel couples, and I thought you might be able to
help us. You can probably see from Katie's invective what the problem is." In Peter's mind, their marital troubles were entirely due to
Katie's mean-spiritedness and abuse. To be sure, she was handling

her frustration in the worst possible way. But Peter gave absolutely no thought to what could have so turned his wife against him. I offered to speak to Katie the following afternoon.

Katie immediately admitted that her mouth was out of control. "I know I'm wrong for what I say. I really am very mean to Peter. I cut him down all the time. I can't help it. Doesn't he understand that this is a cry to get his attention? When we dated, I used to love him so much. He was the most caring and attentive man. But after we married, I gave up my job and career to be at home and look after our daughter. Since then he has become completely neglectful. He comes home, and the TV goes straight on. I call him at the office, and he never has time to speak to me. But if some attractive client comes to his office, he has all the time in the world for her. I need someone to talk to, too. I'm going crazy at home, just watching *Sesame Street* and thinking of him."

"Does he ever thank you for all the sacrifices you've made?" I asked.

"Thank me?" she responded incredulously. "He barely acknowledges that I'm alive. And to make it worse, he's a huge flirt—and seems blind to how much it hurts me." While her hurt feelings didn't justify Katie's behavior, it was Peter who was responsible for taking a loving partner and turning her against him. As the old saying goes, "Hell hath no fury like a woman scorned." In my opinion, it should be amended to, "Even hell is a pleasant place compared to a woman ignored."

Peter didn't realize that he wasn't the only one in the household who wanted to feel like a hero. Every morning when he went off to his law practice, he was setting out to be a hero, to his family, to his fellow law partners, and most of all to his clients. But his wife had the very same need. She needed to have her own actions recognized as no less grand, even if they were on the home front. While she didn't need an equestrian statue of her erected in the kitchen, she did need to feel that, at least to her husband, she was a hero. Had he only thought to write her the occasional poem or e-mail of gratitude, she would have received it as the equivalent of a government proclamation. Instead, she was like a soldier who had served her government for a lifetime and never gotten so much as a promotion.

I took Peter out to dinner. "The situation is salvageable," I told him. "You have to show your wife extravagant love over the next few months. Go to the opposite extreme. Give her *too much* attention. Make her the center of your world, and you'll win her back. It won't even be hard to do. Speak from the heart. Call her up during the day and thank her for being such a great wife and mother. Bring her flowers at night. Take her out to dinner and the theater. Three times a year, go away for weekends and leave the baby with your parents. Above all else, show gratitude for everything she does for you and take nothing for granted."

At first Peter listened to my advice, and for a few months the relationship improved. But then he reverted to his old ways and rekindled his affair with the television. Fed up with his pixilated mistress, his wife left him and after being alone for a few years fell in love with a dentist, and they were now planning on getting married. Peter, of course, did not live happily ever after. But he's okay—whenever he feels down, he just changes the channel.

The lesson here is clear: don't forget to thank your spouse, and your friends, and anyone you come into contact with along the way. Say it with words, with little presents, with compliments, with your own thoughtfulness in return. The Private Adam is as generous with gratitude as he is with his other gifts. He recognizes it as his responsibility to appreciate gestures made on his behalf. When Mikhail Gorbachev came to speak to our organization at Oxford in 1992, I was impressed by many things about him, but one thing stood out above the rest. He thanked everyone, no matter how modest, for their efforts on his behalf. He thanked the man who drove his car. He thanked each and every motorcycle cop in his security detail. After the luncheon we hosted in his honor, he went back to the kitchen and thanked the prep cooks and the busboys. And he gave me a big hug as I bid him good-bye outside Oxford's beautiful Bodleian Library. These simple gestures spoke volumes: here was someone dedicated to conferring dignity upon others.

When you show gratitude to people, you're telling them that they matter. Powerful people and celebrities can do this almost without thinking, because whenever someone who gets a lot of attention gives you attention, you feel that much more important. People are happy when I thank them, but they're happier when they're thanked by a head of state. In that respect, celebrities have a tremendous opportunity. It's a tragedy that so many of them are too self-involved to take the opportunity that their prominence presents to them. If they could divert some of the energy that's always directed at them toward someone who needs it, it could be very powerful indeed.

There's a story about the Beatles learning this very lesson. At first John Lennon and Paul McCartney were uncomfortable with the custom of giving front-row seats at their concerts to disabled children. To be confronted with so many suffering children was discomfiting, and they felt ridiculous and frivolous to be rock stars in the face of so much pain. But they learned that when they gave those children attention, they were able, in a way, to contribute to their healing. The children had so much awe and reverence for the Beatles and their music that when they shared their joy and music with them, the Beatles actually helped make some of the pain go away. And you don't have to be a Beatle to shed that kind of light. Haven't you ever noticed how you can make someone's face light up just by taking the time to say thanks? There are so many people who deserve our thanks! We must thank our assistants for doing a good job, our spouses for remembering to pick up the dry cleaning, our children for a drawing, the person who puts the groceries in the bag.

The ability to show gratitude is a heroic quality. Cicero, the great Roman man of letters, said that "gratitude is not only the greatest of virtues, but the parent of all others." It would seem that the Bible would agree. The most derisive term in the Jewish religion is *kafuy tov*, the term for an ingrate. He is not large enough to attribute credit to another party. His world is too small, his ego too brittle. He is imprisoned by a deprivation mentality. For the ingrate, the whole world is a small pie, and his only objective is to get the largest possible piece. To give another person even a small crumb is to infringe upon the already inadequate piece the ingrate has grabbed for himself. The ingrate sees all men and women not as brothers and sisters but as belligerents, not as companions but as competitors. He can't give others their due because he isn't convinced that the world is big enough for the two of them. He feels weakened whenever he attributes his success to someone else's influence. His heart is too undersized, his ego too brittle, to thank others for what they have contributed to his life. He is a small man, who acts like a pygmy. A man of greatness, a large man, would have no problem giving credit where credit is due.

Of all the virtues, I believe that true gratitude is in the shortest supply. The deficiency mentality that is so pervasive in the world today has bred a generation of ingrates. Sure, we know how to offer a token thank-you. But when the going gets really rough, we have all learned to abandon those to whom we are greatly in debt.

Take politics as an example. Al Gore was a somewhat obscure southern senator before Bill Clinton made him his running mate. In years gone by, this act of recognition would have engendered an unending sense of loyalty on the beneficiary's part. Instead, when Gore's turn came to run for the presidency, he almost didn't mention Clinton's name at all. The reason, as we all know, was an impulse to distance himself from the Monica Lewinsky scandal. But that should have had nothing to do with it. If someone is good to you, you stick by him. You can, of course, criticize his behavior even in the context of overall loyalty, and there would have been nothing wrong with it if Gore had done so. But abandoning someone who has helped you is the hallmark of an ingrate. And in Gore's case, I believe it cost him the election. If he had run on Clinton's economic record, he might have been victorious.

In sharp contrast, Joseph Lieberman said that he would not run in the next election if Al Gore decided to run. He was grateful to Gore for selecting him to serve as the Democratic vice-presidential candidate during the last election and would not stand in opposition to him. There is a man with gratitude.

I will share a story that caused me a tremendous amount of personal pain. There was a woman who came to me because her marriage was a total disaster. Her husband had started an information database company and become wealthy, but he had no idea how to be a husband. He yelled at her in public and criticized her incessantly in private until she was ready to walk out the door. Through many counseling sessions, I was able to help them find common ground; their marriage was saved, they were reconciled, and in time they even had a baby.

But then I was devastated to learn, by chance, that I wasn't invited to the baby's bris, the ritual circumcision performed when a male infant is eight days old. I'm generally pretty good at putting petty slights behind me, but I was so shocked and hurt by this that I called the man's brother for an explanation. It so happened that the event occurred at the time of the publication of *Kosher Sex*, which had attracted a measure of controversy and even public attack, especially in England. The brother explained that the couple was very invested in their respectability and had become concerned that my presence at the bris would be a social liability. I was even more shocked to discover that the person blocking my attendance wasn't the husband—it was the wife.

I will admit that this incident gave me pause; the old feelings of resentment and questions about being good in a cruel world raised their ugly heads. But I help people with their marriages because I have the opportunity to do so, not because I expect anything in return—not even gratitude. I won't lie. I would like people to be grateful when I have helped them, but I can't make it so. We all have stories like this. Sometimes it seems that if people can get some mileage out of you, they will. But we have an obligation to stay true to our course and to our gifts, no matter how ungratefully they are received.

Gratitude is a strange animal. First of all, it is one of those emotions that begins strong and then slowly weakens. When someone does a favor for us, we initially feel immensely grateful. It would seem logical, then, that if that person did us the favor fifteen times over, we would be grateful fifteen times more. But the truth is that the more times someone does the same favor for us, the more we come to expect it. So rather than strengthen with time, the unexpected quality of gratitude is that it diminishes.

When my wife gave birth to our first child, I was so grateful to her for the blessing she had brought into our life that I went to the florist and bought a huge and expensive bouquet of flowers. It was so big that it barely fit into her hospital room. I spent all my time in the hospital with her, and when she came home, I did the vast majority of the housework. The same was basically true for the second child, another daughter. But by the time our third was born, I was much busier with work and went to the hospital only in the evenings. Moreover, when my wife came home, I wasn't as helpful as with the first two children and hired a helper to fill in for my absence. By the fourth child, I had my secretary call her a cab home from the hospital (just kidding, but only just). It was only when my mother came to visit from Miami to see her new granddaughter that she told me how warped my behavior had became. "If you showed appreciation for Debbie when she had one child, do you realize how much more appreciation you have to show when she's given you three more?" I thought to myself, "Easy for you to say. You don't have a kid vomiting on your tie." But her point was well taken.

If we're indebted to someone, then we must have the courtesy both to recognize it and to show it. The onus of responsibility is on the recipient of the favor. It is our job as beneficiaries to do the right thing—to show gratitude when someone has shown us kindness. Remarkably, the Bible teaches that this even applies to the gratitude we owe to animals and inanimate objects that help us in some way.

I have my own experience of gratitude for an inanimate object. Because my parents quarreled a lot when I was a kid, every day in my morning prayers I would ask God to help them get along better. One time my father called home in the late afternoon to tell my mother that the worn-out jalopy of a truck he drove to deliver fabrics to customers had broken down. He needed my mother to drive to where he was and use her car to push his truck back home. My parents certainly couldn't afford the expense of a tow truck to get the car home. I was afraid that if my mother's car couldn't do it, my parents would have another huge fight. I prayed to God that her car, half the size of my father's truck, would be strong enough for the task. My siblings and I piled into the car to accompany my mother, and little by little her small car pushed the big car all the way home. Peace prevailed in our household, and I was ecstatic.

What did I do? That night, after everyone had gone inside to eat dinner, I went outside to that car and thanked it from the bottom of my heart. I even kissed its chrome bumper. Of course, you can dismiss this action as the naive behavior of a six-year-old, or the crazed behavior of a major loon. You might also wonder how I'd look in a rubber room accessorized with a straitjacket. Or you can view my action as the innocent gesture of someone uncorrupted by life who was simply offering thanks to the inanimate object that had saved the day.

Take a moment in your own life to reflect on gratitude. Is there anyone who deserves your thanks? Try an experiment: over the course of an entire day, thank everyone who does something for you, from sending you a contact name you requested to giving you back the correct change. Thank the man who is the father of your children, and your parents for having and raising you. Aren't the rewards immediate? Gratitude is so easy—and it makes such a tremendous difference.

27

❧

ESTABLISH TRUST

You may be deceived if you trust too much, but you will live in torment if you do not trust enough.

—Frank Crane

When we show gratitude, we increase the amount of trust in the world, and that is one of the foremost charges of the biblical hero.

I spend much of my time giving lectures to groups and audiences around the world. Very often I'll be invited to speak to four old men and a goat in Armpit, Nowheresville. I'll agree to go, chiding myself for my reluctance: "Stop being arrogant, worrying about how you should be getting more prestigious gigs." Then, as the day approaches, I start regretting my decision and think of a million ways to cancel. "I can call them and tell them I died. No, no, that won't work. Better get my assistant to make the call." Or, "I'll tell them I was abducted by space aliens and the current me is only a double. If they want the real me to speak, they'll have to pay round-trip airfare from the Alpha Centauri star cluster."

Unable to come up with a credible excuse, though, I generally admit defeat and drag my bones all the way to Armpit. Sure enough, I'm greeted by an audience consisting of four guys and a goat. But I am not dissuaded. I will make no compromises in my delivery. I will speak for forty minutes, as if I were speaking to a crowd of at least ten. At the end of the lecture, those four guys inevitably humble me with their gratitude and go on for fifty minutes about how honored and touched they are that I made the trip all the way just for them. They fuss over who's going to make me a cup of coffee, and they crowd into a picture for their grandchildren. It never ceases to amaze me how this all works. The gratitude makes me feel amazing—ashamed as I am of my churlishness—and I always return genuinely glad I made the trip.

Hearing the words "thank you," or receiving a simple letter of thanks, reinforces our natural goodness, encouraging us to continue performing acts of kindness. Gratitude is the necessary pause that must come in between every heroic act in order to further our desire to continue with such acts. Indeed, just as being taken advantage of makes us hard, being shown gratitude makes us gentler, more tender. A little gratitude can transform a heart of stone into a heart of flesh. Indeed, no human emotion is capable of transforming us as quickly and radically as gratitude. It can literally turn an enemy into a friend overnight.

When we thank someone graciously for a favor they have done us, they feel good about themselves and their good deed. By thanking them, we greatly increase the chances that they will do good again for someone else. The opposite of a *kafuy tov*, an ingrate, is a *makir tov*, a grateful person. When a *makir tov* shows gratitude, she increases acts of goodness in the world. When people see how much their sacrifices are appreciated, they yearn to do even more. This establishes a firm bond of trust between the benefactor and the world.

This may sound reductive, but imagine the alternative. If we forget to show gratitude to someone who has bestowed a favor on us— or even worse, if we take advantage of someone who has shown us love—any trust between us will be threatened. When friends expose themselves to us and we rip out their hearts in return, they will never trust us again. More important, their very ability to trust will have changed, and they will be less likely to trust everyone in the future. In other words, it's not just our relationships that we're safeguarding when we show gratitude—it's all relationships. We all have a moral obligation to ensure that a benefactor does not become cynical by feeling taken advantage of or used.

Nietzsche objected to goodness because it makes us weak and vulnerable. Love makes us put down our defenses. And when we get hurt specifically through loving, we swear to ourselves, "I will never let my guard down again." Slowly but surely, we harden our hearts into stone in order to protect ourselves. Women who have been in abusive relationships find it very difficult to trust men again. I have seen terrible experiences turn women who were once gentle and sensitive into warriors, protecting themselves against the opposite sex. Ultimately their inability to trust prevents them from conducting a successful relationship. Instead, they learn to do something highly unnatural: they reconcile themselves to living on their own. It is not that they enjoy loneliness; it is that to them the pain of loneliness seems not as bad as the hurt and betrayal they're likely to experience if they allow themselves to trust someone again.

Showing gratitude upholds trust in human relationships and society at large. Remember the movie *The First Wives' Club?* We can all identify with the scorn of a woman who has been dumped by a husband who can show no gratitude. The saying goes, "He owed his success to his first wife, and his second wife to his success." How many men make it to the top, only to trade in the wife who stood by them when they had little money or prestige? Such abandonment, in turn, leads otherwise benevolent women to be less giving in relationships.

Yet too often the men who conduct their lives this way remain our heroes. Their wives develop a chin or two, and out they go with the garbage. Donald Trump trades in one bejeweled model for another, and we chuckle at his behavior. Are Paul Newman and Joanne Woodard the only two people in Hollywood capable of a long and faithful marriage? It's epidemic—every year, someone we thought was a good guy (Harrison Ford, are you listening?) leaves his wife for someone younger.

Ingratitude always causes a ripple effect, leading to diminished acts of kindness in the world. After all, most people's natural reaction to dealing with an ingrate is to swear that they will never practice another act of kindness again. Once we're convinced that no good deed goes unpunished, we stop extending ourselves to others. Indeed, nothing undoes our desire to help people more than when we feel taken advantage of and unappreciated. Thus, one person's ingratitude is dangerous for the entire community, since it lessens our natural desire to assist one another.

Charlie and Helen were a middle-aged couple in Oxford who attended my services. After their kids moved out, they rented out several rooms of their home to lodgers. One of the lodgers was a young widower named Helmut, whose wife had been killed in a rock-climbing accident. Helmut had a young daughter named Julia, but at first he moved in without her because Charlie and Helen would not allow children. Later, however, when Helmut asked if he could bring Julia to stay with him, Charlie and Helen did not have the heart to say no. Everyone warned them that the landlord-tenant law strongly favored a father with kids and that they were putting themselves at a significant disadvantage if they ever wanted to sell the house. Still, they thought it was the right thing to do, and so they agreed to see the family reunited under their roof. They didn't even increase the rent, although Helmut offered. Thanking them profusely, Helmut promised that he'd move out with a month's notice if they ever wanted to sell the house.

The father and daughter lived in the house comfortably for two years. But when Charlie and Helen informed Helmut that they wanted to move closer to their recently married daughter, Helmut refused to move out. They gave him three months' notice, but still he protested to the local housing council that he and his daughter were being left with no place to live. The council sided with him, and Helmut remained there for months on end. Because of Helmut's intransigence, Charlie and Helen were unable to sell their home. After they lost three prospective buyers, the price of their house plummeted. It took them two years of legal wrangling and high legal fees to get Helmut to move out. Exhausted with the entire ordeal, Charlie and Helen swore to themselves they would never help another person again.

Ingratitude serves to deflate the hero. Charlie and Helen had every right to feel good about what they were doing. They had every right to be proud, to walk tall. But Helmut's ingratitude punished rather than rewarded them for their heroism. The ingrate is the antihero, reducing heroic action to regret.

In the Bible there is a curious fact: long life is promised for the simple act of sending away a mother bird who is sitting atop her young in her nest before taking her eggs. One is allowed to take the eggs, but only after the mother has been removed from the scene. Why so great a reward for so seemingly inconsequential an act? The explanation is that every mother possesses a powerful maternal instinct, and in order to protect her young she renders herself vulnerable. Capturing her while she sits atop her chicks is relatively easy, because she will not abandon them even at the expense of her own destruction. God tells us that we must not capture her eggs while she is caring for her young because we must not take advantage of her weakness—the vulnerability she endures because of her devotion.

The motherly instinct, the part of us that risks our life to defend our young, is a part of our heroic instinct. It's the ability to stand up against something harmful and to protect that which is precious. What the Bible is saying is that harming someone in normal circumstances is bad enough, but what is infinitely worse, and what one must never do, is become the antihero. Never destroy someone while they are demonstrating heroic action.

This injunction not to steal the eggs while the mother is present is one of only two instances in the Bible that promise long life to those who comply. The other is honoring your parents. The two injunctions are related. Our parents are the people whom we can abuse the most: we can yell and scream and take their money, but they'll still love us. We are therefore entrusted with an incredible responsibility not to take advantage of them, not to use their special feelings for us against them.

To grasp the dramatic import of these two prohibitions, consider two contemporary scenarios. A man walks down a dark alley and gets mugged. He's upset about it and swears never to walk down a dark alley again. Another man walks down a dark alley and sees an old man in front of him keel over from a heart attack. He rushes to the old man's aid, bends over, and starts to give him mouth-to-mouth resuscitation, but just as he undertakes the heroic action of trying to save a life, the old man pulls out a knife, puts it to his rescuer's throat, and demands that he hand over his wallet. This is truly sinful. In that moment of betrayal, the would-be rescuer foreswears not merely dark alleys but heroism itself: he vows never again to take the chance of helping some-one in need.

Sometimes our heroism is reflected in what we choose *not* to do. We have an obligation to show gratitude, for when we do, we establish trust in the world. Our obligation to maintain that trust is as strong as our obligation to establish it in the first place. Don't ever betray someone's trust in you, or use someone's generous nature against them. It's the mark of an ingrate—and an antihero.

28

❦

TELL THE TRUTH

He who walks blamelessly, and does what is right, and speaks truth from his heart.

—Psalm 15:2

I don't want any yes-men around me. I want everybody to tell the truth even if it costs them their jobs.

—Samuel Goldwyn

As we have seen in the last two chapters, gratitude involves both a moral imperative to show thanks and an ethical responsibility to foster trust. But gratitude is more than just a moral and ethical obligation. Gratitude is truth itself. When we thank someone, it turns the spotlight away from us and illuminates the truth.

Human beings love to be original. We absolutely hate having to copy or borrow ideas from somebody else. We delight in ingenuity and covet the credit that comes with great achievement. We don't naturally share our glory with others. In fact, showing gratitude can feel as challenging as being monogamous. In both instances, we sacrifice cheap gratification for the richer rewards of a relationship based in authenticity. The imperative to show gratitude, therefore, is one that compels us always to tell the truth, no matter the consequences.

This issue has been raised in the Jewish faith in very specific ways. The Talmud teaches that we must publicly attribute a source not only when quoting someone else's material in a speech or essay but even in everyday conversation: "He who learns from his fellow man even one chapter, one rule, one verse, one expression or even one single letter, must pay him honor." And the ancient rabbis said that "all who quote the name of the person whose material they are using brings salvation to the world." As a public speaker, I know how difficult it can be to stand up in front of five hundred people, say something really clever or witty, and then have to admit that it wasn't your line, that it really belongs to someone else. We all want to lay claim to originality; we want the world to think we're smart, and clever, and thoughtful, and like no one else.

Which is all the more reason that such an act of gratitude demonstrates true heroism. To give proper credit for ideas you have borrowed, you must have the courage to believe that greatness can come not just from originality but also from truth, not just from novelty but also from authenticity. It takes a hero's strength of character to shine the spotlight elsewhere at just the point when it's turned toward him.

Overlooking gratitude is one of the most common mistakes we can make. A sad example: Dimitri was a medical student who came to Oxford from the United States with his wife, Esther. While Dimitri was doing advanced medical research at the university, he was entirely supported by Esther, who was a lawyer. She worked exhaustingly long hours on behalf of American firms operating in the United Kingdom, but she was happy to do it because she loved her husband and knew that he would become an outstanding doctor.

During Esther's endless time away at work, Dimitri became close to Penelope, another young doctor. What started with innocent lunches quickly escalated into a full-blown affair; Dimitri and Penelope fell in love, and one day Dimitri broke the news to his wife that he was leaving her for another woman. Devastated, Esther promptly flew back to be with her parents in New York. I told Dimitri that he had to get on the first plane to try to win back his wife. "You owe her everything," I told him, "and this is a pretty pathetic way of showing your gratitude." But Dimitri just didn't get it. "Hey, I did plenty for her too. I taught her all kinds of things, and she took plenty out of the relationship. It was her coldness that drove me away. She should have appreciated me more."

The problem was that Dimitri had only the shallowest understanding of gratitude. In his mind, gratitude was merely a matter of parity, of quid pro quo. His wife did things for him, and he for her; in his mind, they were "even," and with his emotional checkbook thus balanced, he felt free to fall in love with someone else. The truth, however, was that Dimitri was nothing without Esther. What he owed his wife wasn't just a simple thanks or a debt of gratitude repaid in kind. His success was *her* success. Without her, he would have been teaching at the local public school to make his rent. Paying homage to his wife, showing her love and fidelity—in other words, establishing the truth—is how he should have been spending his time. Sadly, there are those individuals whose hearts become so desensitized to the goodness of others that they lose their aptitude for gratitude. Even the mutual joys of sharing a life with someone else no longer leave an impression. These people simply move on callously, without so much as a regret.

Like so many selfish people in our time, Dimitri wasn't a hero. He was a cowardly figure with a short memory and a brittle ego. Not only could he not rise above temptation, but he couldn't even rise above his own lies and weak rationalizations.

This is what I mean about an incident-based (as opposed to a context-based) memory. Let's say there's someone who's done a lot of favors for you. It could be a sister who showed you endless encouragement and warmth during a difficult time. Maybe it's an office assistant who always stays late to help you get all your work done. Maybe it's a car mechanic who did a lot of extra work on your car and out of friendship never billed you for all of it. Or maybe it's your doctor, who time and again went out of his way not just to cure you but to alleviate your anxieties about your health.

Then this person does one thing wrong, and you forget all the good things they did for you. The sister gives you bad advice about a boyfriend. The secretary accidentally deletes an important file. The car mechanic accidentally causes you thousands of dollars in engine damage. The doctor makes a mistake during an operation and replaces your heart with a chicken. Instead of demonstrating forgiveness out of respect and gratitude for all the things they've done for you over the years, you terminate the relationship (a neat trick, of course, for the chicken-hearted). It's a weakest-link mentality—one simple mistake can negate thousands of small, important kindnesses along the way.

I've seen this happen a thousand times. Justin and Webb were best friends who started a restaurant together. After a big fight over whether to feature live entertainment, the two refused to speak to each other—first for months, then for years. When their friends tried to reconcile them, each referred back to the animosity that had been generated over this last incident. "But don't you think that one incident pales in comparison to all the good things your friend has done for you?" No way, they said. For these two, gratitude was entirely dependent on their last interaction, even if it was only a speck of trivia in the greater context of the relationship. Of course, their recalcitrant ingratitude would deprive them of their closest friendship, quite possibly for the rest of their lives.

To let a single incident disrupt an entire friendship is to misrepresent the relationship. This kind of ingratitude is a type of dishonesty—it paints a false portrait of the relationship that preceded the breach. You may have to swallow your pride and apologize for something you didn't do, but it's less of a lie than allowing the relationship to dissolve. Is there a relationship in your life that fractured as a result of a single, stupid argument? Is there a break that you'd be able to mend just by apologizing? Go ahead: pick up the phone. Any relationship is worth more than an angry grudge.

29

꧁

BE HUMBLE

I think it's very unheroic to point out your own heroism. That's a question best left to the thousands of people whose lives I've saved.

—Andy Richter

When I was the rabbi at Oxford, a few times a year I would bring a small group of Jewish Rhodes scholars to meet with Sir Isaiah Berlin at his office in All Souls College. Sir Isaiah loved talking with them about all kinds of issues, especially topics that pertained to Jewishness, and the discussions tended to be friendly rather than intellectual.

One of the students felt cheated by this approach; he had come to talk philosophy with the great thinker, and that was what he was going to do. He started barraging Sir Isaiah with all kinds of questions, and the philosopher patiently responded to every one. In response to one of his answers, the student shot back, "Well, I think Heidegger would dispute you on that." Sir Isaiah said, "Oh, well, I wouldn't know. I have not really read much Heidegger." The student was in shock. Here was one of the world's foremost intellectuals admitting cavalierly to a student a quarter of his age that he wasn't very familiar with one of history's most influential modern philosophers. "You haven't read any Heidegger?" the student said in disbelief. "No," responded Sir Isaiah, in complete sincerity, "but I'd be very grateful if you would come some time and teach me." It was a lesson for all of us who were watching: here was an arrogant young man, riddled with insecurities and desperate to make an impression, eclipsed by the generosity of a frail old man, one of the most respected in the world, who had nothing to prove and knew he had nothing to lose by telling the truth.

Humility and gratitude are inextricably linked in the world of the biblical hero. As we shall see, humility is in itself a form of gratitude, an extension of the idea that gratitude is an important way to attribute the truth. Humility isn't just a matter of looking embarrassed when you're praised, or halfheartedly saying you couldn't have succeeded without the support of your parents. Humility involves acting with genuine honesty, whether that means admitting to ignorance on a subject or attempting to turn the spotlight away from yourself onto the people who have made your success possible.

All the great men and women of history were first in line to attribute their successes to others. Small people—even those whom history remembers as classic "heroes"—do the exact opposite. Not only do they fail to thank others for their contributions, but they go so far as to claim the successes of others. They spend as much time arguing with others for recognition as they do trying to get things done.

My Rebbe, Rabbi Menachem Mendel Schneersohn, built the largest Jewish educational network the world had ever seen. He had become the head of a small and impoverished Hassidic community in 1950 that had been decimated by the Holocaust. In the space of four decades, he opened more than two thousand Jewish communal centers in more than one hundred countries. Today Chabad-Lubavitch outlets run an annual budget of more than two billion dollars and are largely responsible for the Jewish renaissance of flourishing synagogues and Jewish day schools the world over. And yet, in every public speech he ever delivered, the Rebbe always attributed all of the movement's success to his predecessor and father-in-law, Rabbi Joseph Isaac Schneersohn. He never even formally acknowledged that he had succeeded his father-in-law. Whenever he referred to the leader of the movement, he was talking about his father-in-law—and said so by name. That kind of magnanimity is true heroism, and it was a great inspiration to me every time I heard him speak.

This brand of heroism follows in a long rabbinical tradition first established by Moses, who was referred to in the Bible as "the most humble man who walked the earth." Unlike other founders of a great religion, Moses never took any credit for his miracles and teachings. His sole purpose as shepherd of the Jewish people was to maintain their connection with God as the source of his power and prophecy.

We know that humans hate to give credit—not only for our best lines but also for our successes. Many students who come to Oxford are from wealthy and accomplished families. Naturally, this gives them a head start on the other students, but they hate it when people point that out. Getting into Oxford, they want everyone to believe, was something they accomplished on their own merit. Getting a great job was entirely their own doing; the strings their father pulled had nothing to do with it. If you insinuate anything to the contrary, they become deeply offended. Because we all want to be our own person, we are prepared to compromise truth in the name of originality.

A case in point is President George W. Bush. To be sure, there is little doubt in anybody's mind that he is president today partially, if not largely, because his father was president before him. Without his father's financial and political connections and counsel, he might not have become governor of Texas so quickly. And I don't say this to criticize him; I am a fervent admirer of President Bush. Indeed, there is something moving in the modern world about a father and a son being so close that a father will exert every effort to assist his son, and a son loving his father so much that he will do everything to repair his father's legacy. And yet Bush's advisers all tell him to deny this. They don't allow him to acknowledge that he consults his father on any important matters of state. I personally would much rather have a president who has no problem telling the world he is grateful for his father's counsel and support. And I want a president who has no problem leaning on former presidents for guidance and advice, especially when he has such a close connection. But President Bush knows that the American public would clobber him if he admitted that Daddy played a major role in his election. That's because our model of heroism is so flawed. We would rather have a self-made man who has to deny his origins than a grateful man who is humble and confident enough in himself to pay homage where homage is due.

When I was a boy of ten, I was taken under the wing of a very special sixteen-year-old rabbinical student who was in charge of communal programming for boys in our Miami neighborhood. He became an older brother to me, and it was largely due to his inspiration that I became a rabbi. After he got married, rather than getting a congregation, he decided to go into his father's business. Although he became a successful businessman, he always regretted his decision not to enter the rabbinate. His wife would always tell me that this was the great regret of his life. He hated receiving phone calls from his former classmates about how their congregations were growing and all the books they were writing on Jewish ideas because it reinforced his feeling that he had missed out on something special.

When I published my book *Judaism for Everyone,* although we were not as close as we had once been, I decided to dedicate the book to him. Without his influence, I would never have become a rabbi, and I wanted to recognize his contribution. When the book came out, his wife called me to thank me and told me that he had been showing the dedication to his friends around town. "You made him feel like a hero," she said. "It's like someone gave him a medal for past service."

Showing humility can do more than make you a hero—it can make someone else feel like one too. I can't honestly take credit for becoming a rabbi without sharing some of it with him; he was instrumental in guiding me at a very crucial time, and I owe him much. It's important to note that this kind of gratitude and humility makes for a win-win situation. My mentor feels good about himself, and yet giving him credit doesn't detract from my own accomplishments. Whatever scholarship I possess and whatever good I've done are my own, and I can take full pride in them even as I pay homage to the figure who inspired me. What a discovery! The pie isn't finite—by giving him credit for his contribution to my life, I lose nothing and gain everything.

We see this idea at play in every area of life. Those who aren't threatened by people who help them and who share the wealth, whatever form that might take, are rewarded. One of the most fascinating things about Microsoft is that Bill Gates isn't the only rich man at that company. He's not even the only billionaire. He has made a lot of people very, very wealthy by sharing his success with those who helped to build it. And when he acknowledges that the pie isn't finite, he is richly rewarded. His staff is loyal to him, and his reputation as someone who makes other people rich means that the best and the brightest will fall all over themselves to work for him.

These stories illuminate once again why, as we've seen, to call someone an ingrate—a *kafuy tov*—is one of the greatest insults in the Jewish religion. Judaism spurns the ungrateful person who refuses to acknowledge that he is the beneficiary of someone else's largesse. In fact, there is a direct correlation between a lack of humility and idolatry. Judaism's principal goal from its inception has been to uproot idolatry and establish God as Lord of the earth. Of course, people don't exactly worship idols these days the way their pagan ancestors did. People today don't prostrate themselves before lead or marble. Yet idolatry is still alive and kicking today in the great secular religion of the ego: worshiping idols has been replaced with worshiping the self. Few are the men and women today whom, amid their phenomenal prosperity, feel the need to give thanks to God. Rather, they pat themselves on the back and say, "My power and the might of my own hand have gotten me this wealth" (Deuteronomy 8:17).

The Public Adam, conscious that he was made in the image of God, can't admit that he's number two to anyone—his mentor, his parents, his God. To do so would be to deny his own godlike power, he thinks. The essence of humility, however, is to establish the truth by acknowledging that our success is not the result of our own effort but rather of the collaboration of so many others, beginning with the Almighty Himself and including the family, friends, and others who have showered us with love and given us the confidence to go forward. Humility reminds us of our place in the world and of the fact that many have preceded us and contributed to the canvas.

The ability to show humility is also a sign of our ability to be touched by someone else and thereby build a relationship. When we are humble, we show our understanding that whatever gifts we have in life are really loans. We repay these loans by showing gratitude, by giving thanks, by establishing trust. Every person wants to be recognized. And when they do something good, they have every right to feel good about it. To rob someone of the satisfaction of goodness is a great crime, and when we take sole credit for our accomplishments, that's precisely what we're doing.

If we don't create the expectation that gratitude and recognition will come through shining the spotlight on others and facilitating their success, how can we expect people to put themselves out to mentor others?

If there is one trait that defines the classical hero it is arrogance. Humility is the recognition of the role others play in our success, but arrogance is the opposite—the contention that we alone are responsible for the success we enjoy. The classical hero is a tin soldier—hollow on the inside, brittle on the outside. Arrogance is the most egocentric of all the emotions, as well as one of the most unhealthy; indeed, in the extreme it can lead to mental illness, even breakdown, as the mind begins to crumble under the weight of its own perceived self-importance.

Arrogant people always think of themselves through the eyes of the audience they live for. Born performers at heart, they wonder constantly what it must be like for other people to meet them. Celebrity is corrosive because so many celebrities think of themselves in this highly self-conscious, detached way. If they don't get the right table at the restaurant, they tell the maitre d', "Do you know who I *am?*" Indeed, the celebrities who remain healthy—and there are precious few—are those who try to negate that sense of self-importance at every turn. I once had a meeting with Katie Couric. We sat and had tea in the lobby of the Four Seasons in New York while we waited for our third party. The waiter took a long time delivering it. Katie, whom I consider one of the most wholesome (not to mention sweetest) celebrities in America, just laughed and said, "Doesn't that waiter know who we *think* we are?" Most celebrities fail at the "don't take yourself too seriously" game. They have an external and internal self—the alternative persona of the "star." This kind of fragmented personality is the mark of a true disconnect between the self and the surrounding world, and egomania is the terrible result.

The Bible's grave insistence on honoring our parents at all times and under all circumstances is ultimately predicated on the idea of humility. Because our parents have endowed us with the incomparable blessing of life, our existence must always stand humbled by that gift. Unfortunately, as noted earlier, children today will catalog a thousand and one ways their parents ruined their lives. These childish complaints, however, overlook the simple fact that without their parents there would be no "them" to hurt. In its commandment to honor your parents, the Bible establishes the fact that one of the ten most important rules of civilization and holy living is to show unwavering gratitude and humility for your own existence.

As a Jew, I have to say that one of the most inspiring things about our faith is the way we mourn our parents. Our religion obliges us to spend eleven months mourning our parents and saying the Kaddish, the Jewish mourner's prayer (which is actually a hymn praising God), three times a day in the company of at least ten other Jews in a synagogue. I have watched hundreds of nonobservant Jewish acquaintances suddenly start going to synagogue the prescribed three times a day out of respect for a lost father or mother. Indeed, the recitation of Kaddish remains until this day one of the most steadfastly observed rituals in all of Judaism. And that's a real mark of humility, for when we mourn someone we are turning our attention away from our own state of being and toward the departed souls who have had such a profound effect upon us.

When I was on a book tour for *Kosher Sex* in 1999, I was a guest on the comedian Howie Mandel's television show. Howie, who is Jewish, met with me in his dressing room after the show and told me that a few years earlier his father had died. He was in the midst of doing a national stand-up comedy tour at all the big venues, but he inserted a clause in his contract that there had to be a quorum of ten Jewish men backstage at every theater so that he could recite Kaddish for his father. He recognized how important it was for him to show gratitude through devotion to his dead father. It is an act of humility to acknowledge that someone else is responsible for you and your successes, and this is an honorable display of heroism.

The rabbis teach that our feelings of gratitude and humility toward our parents are the means by which we come to experience similar feelings, at an even greater level of intensity, toward God, our ultimate parent. We thank God daily with blessings, psalms, and prayers to remind us of the bounty God has given us. The first words a Jew is supposed to utter upon awakening, for instance, is a prayer of gratitude for having his soul restored: "I gratefully thank You, O living and eternal King, for You have returned my soul within me with compassion." Upon hearing exceptionally bad news, we praise God for being the true judge of the world. We even thank God after going to the bathroom for properly furnishing us with the plumbing necessary to rid ourselves of waste.

Such gratitude is often mistaken for weakness, and it's no accident that ever since the European enlightenment of the early eighteenth century, it has become commonplace to think of religious people as weak and close-minded. Secular people don't need a God to lean on, the argument goes; only weak religious people do. That's exactly the point Karl Marx was trying to make when he famously referred to religion as the opiate of the masses. Think of it: he was equating religious people with drug addicts. They find reality too hard to deal with, so they turn to spiritual narcotics. Just a few years ago, one of America's classical heroes made the same point. Former professional wrestler and Minnesota governor Jesse Ventura—and if I were to spend the rest of my life trying to come up with a perfect parody of classical heroism, I could never come up with anything as good as professional wrestling—created headlines when he told *Playboy* magazine, "Organized religion is a sham and a crutch for weak-minded people who need strength in numbers."

What if the opposite is true? What if the governor is the weak one, as demonstrated by his inability to acknowledge the truth by showing gratitude and giving credit where credit is due? Did he create himself? Does he know any scientist who ever created life in a laboratory? And the intelligence he brings to bear in commenting on society (if intelligence is the proper word here)—where did that come from? The governor's claims strike me as nothing more than empty arrogance. He has spent his entire life playing to the crowd (or the mob, in his wrestling days). Needing constant and external corroboration of your internal validity is the greatest crutch, isn't it?

On the other hand, this isn't an argument I'm really interested in winning. I have no problem with being a "weak" religious person. Guilty as charged. I don't want to be Stone Cold, or a Rock. (Ventura, as you may know, wrestled under the name "The Body." See what I mean? You couldn't make this stuff up.) I need God and other people in my life. I'm very happy being dependent on the love of my relatives and friends. I rely on my wife's advice and continued good opinion of me. I have no problem admitting that I need my children to hug me a couple of times a day, and I certainly have no problem acknowledging my complete and total dependence on God. I can't honestly take full credit for any of the happy blessings of my life, my work, or my family. In my weakness, I hope to celebrate my humanity, as opposed to my arrogance.

Just as we are obliged to attribute the sources of our ideas in books or lectures, we are equally obliged to attribute the source of our very existence. The religious individual has the humility and the courage to point to the heavens as the source of his blessings. He knows that a guy who works as hard as Bill Gates, or who is as savvy as Warren Buffet, still won't make one dime if God isn't on his side. After all, how many brilliant and hard-working geniuses are there who are totally broke? How many Bill Gates wannabes are on welfare today? And how often do we see the most successful people in the world have their whole life turned upside down in the blink of an eye because of one mistake? Look at Martha Stewart, who is in the news as I write this. Her amazing success story has crashed and burned because of a single mistake—she sold a stock to make a little over $200,000, which may be a lot of money to most of us but was a mere drop in her financial ocean. Now her whole world has been shaken. She risked all her success for that drop.

We're all familiar with the expression "There but for the grace of God go I." Well, I mean it literally. God's grace is certainly the thing that stands between me and disaster, and I'm not afraid to give credit where it's surely due. To take credit for our achievements and not offer thanks to God is not only arrogant but cowardly. Only a weak-minded person, fearful of being overlooked and living a life of obscurity, needs to hog all the spotlight and push God out. The classical hero cannot share the glory, even with God Himself. He believes that he alone is responsible for his achievements.

Maybe this is why, in the very same interview, Ventura compared being governor with being king, adding, "The best thing is that there's no one in this state who can tell me what to do." (I guess he discovered otherwise when he chose not to run again because he was certain to lose.) Of course, a king can never share his crown. But that's one of the reasons Americans got rid of monarchs, replacing them with democracy. Look at all those centuries of European kings, often mediocre tyrants who stole the wealth of their people and built themselves grand castles while their subjects starved. Where are the great monarchs of Europe now?

Acts of humility before God are woven into the fabric of Judaism. We need reminders that we're not the ultimate architects of our lives. The holiest day of the Jewish calendar is Yom Kippur, the Day of Atonement. On this very serious day all material pleasure is prohibited—things like food, drink, showering, and sex. It is a day on which man emulates an angelic existence by refraining from material indulgence. So what do Jews do over this twenty-four-hour period? We pray. We go to the synagogue and pray all day long. Why do we do this? To teach us an important lesson. Throughout the course of the year, we can easily be led to believe that what sustains us in life is the physical: food, money, possessions. Yom Kippur, however, humbles us by serving as the supreme reminder that we are ultimately dependent on God alone. By depriving ourselves one day a year of that which nourishes our existence, we tacitly acknowledge that in truth all sustenance comes from God and it is to Him that our devotion must be directed.

Likewise, Maimonides argued that the rationale behind the commandment to pray was for man to always acknowledge his dependency on God, even for the provision of his most basic material needs. As the Bible teaches us: "He humbled you by letting you

hunger, then by feeding you with manna, with which neither you
nor your ancestors were acquainted, in order to make you understand that one does not live by bread alone but by every word that
comes from the mouth of the Lord" (Deuteronomy 8:3). Of course,
we should give thanks every day for the bounty that God has
bestowed upon us, but Yom Kippur is the ultimate opportunity to
show gratitude and humility by acknowledging our complete
dependence on God—and if that means recognizing our own relative weakness, surely there is no harm in that.

Ultimately arrogance is another way of denying God. Indeed,
the opposite of theism is not atheism, but a lack of humility. The
opposite of heroism is not cowardice but a kind of shrinkage of the
spirit: without humility, you become so small that you're forced to
puff yourself up in other people's eyes. Avoid the impulse to take
credit for your accomplishments—there are many people who supported and helped you who deserve the credit long before you do.
Remember that the more someone inflates himself, the more he
denies God.

30

❧

STEP OUT OF THE SPOTLIGHT

A hero is someone who has given his or her life to something bigger than oneself.

—Joseph Campbell, *The Power of Myth* (1988)

Biblical heroism is entirely about the realization that you were put on this earth to use your unique gift to shine light on something other than yourself. The classical hero, on the other hand, is a dark planet, desperate to grab as much of the light for himself as possible. But too much light is as bad for us as not enough. In jealously, grabbing at the light, the classical hero burns himself up. What a great gift it is to know that you have light to bestow on someone else! You're not a dark moon, you're the sun itself—an endless source of warmth and energy and light.

When a good person has light to spare, the only thing to do is to share it. It's not a tortuous obligation, or a duty to be fulfilled, but a natural outcome, a liberation. When a cow has milk, she must give it or she'll be in terrible pain. She must do it. When she shares her gifts, she experiences tremendous relief and discovers that her gifts are inexhaustible and self-renewing. What is your gift? And what are you doing to share it with other people and the world?

The classical hero seeks to subdue and triumph over his fellow man, to be a champion in whatever field of battle he chooses. But the biblical hero seeks to raise up his fellow human and live together in harmony. The classical hero puts his face on a cause; the biblical hero effaces himself for it. Whereas the classical hero receives the adulation of the adoring masses, the biblical hero is unconcerned with popular opinion and often remains unappreciated throughout his or her life. Biblical heroes aren't concerned with the effect of their actions on themselves. They want to make an impact on the outside world.

This distinction is important. Someone who practices loving-kindness and charity out of heroism would continue to do so even if a magical poverty-solving law were passed tomorrow. The biblical hero experiences the need to help others as a necessity, not a burden to be negotiated. If such a law were passed, the biblical hero would put his charity fund in a special account, against the day when it might once again be needed. Let the classical hero receive his rewards in the form of riches or beautiful women; the biblical hero finds his satisfaction in pleasing God and serving humanity. It is the journey that is the reward.

Biblical heroism requires us to step out of the limelight. Influence and example are the real means of exercising power in the world, not force or strength. The true heroic act is one that may take centuries to bear fruit—not the temporal victory that is overturned as easily as it is realized. True heroism depends on what we call principle-centered leadership—when men and women allow their cause to be in the spotlight while they themselves remain on the sidelines, taking greater pride in seeing their legacy realized than in looking at themselves in a mirror.

Consider the life of Varian Fry, a young, Harvard-educated, American journalist who left New York in 1940 with a list of some two hundred prominent European artists and intellectuals known to be living in parts of Nazi-occupied Europe. His mission was to help those at risk of Nazi persecution to escape their would-be tormentors. Fry went to Marseilles and set up a front organization, the Centre American de Secours, which masqueraded as a charity working for the relief of poverty.

Behind this facade, Fry was running a high-risk, illegal escape program that helped vulnerable artists, writers, scientists, political activists, and academics get out of France and escape to the relative safety of Portugal, North Africa, and the United States. The people he helped save included some of the most famous cultural figures of our age: Max Ernst, Marc Chagall, Hannah Arendt, André Breton, and Marcel Duchamp, among others. In total, Fry and his collaborators helped to snatch around four thousand people from the clutches of the Gestapo, including trade unionists, British soldiers, and a number of prominent scientists, including the Nobel Prize—winning chemist Otto Meyerhoff.

In 1942 Fry was arrested by the police and eventually deported. After the war he wrote *Assignment Rescue,* a memoir of his days in Marseilles, but he never received the acclaim that his remarkable courage merited. He died alone, in obscurity, in 1967. It wasn't until recently that Fry's contribution received the recognition it deserved, when the Israeli Yad Vashem Memorial Museum, which investigates the history of the Holocaust, accorded him its highest accolade: he was named posthumously as one of the Righteous Among the Nations, making him the first American to receive the tribute. Varian Fry wasn't motivated by the impulse to secure a place in history. In fact, his success depended in large part on making sure that no one found out what was going on at the Centre American de Secours.

Please don't think that I fail to appreciate how very difficult it is to resign yourself to what seems like a life of obscurity. For many, this may feel like one of the hardest things about deciding to live a life of biblical heroism. We all have to struggle to free ourselves from the need for recognition. We have to work very hard to overcome the ego-driven show-off in our natures. Our culture tells us we're nothing unless we can recognize ourselves in a blind item on Page Six and be recognized by others when we walk down the street. It tells us that our opinions mean nothing unless they're beamed into millions of homes every night, and that we can't be involved in the public debate unless we're household names.

Like the proverbial tree falling in the forest, we're convinced that we cease to exist when nobody's looking, that only the attention of

the masses can bestow importance upon us. It's terrifying to mortgage our self-worth that way. I know from personal experience how
very difficult and painful it can be to withdraw from the public
stage, especially after getting hooked on the drug of recognition. We
feel irrelevant, and that can be very painful.

It can be excruciating, it's true: ego effacement is like recovering
from the bends after rising from the heady waters of public attention
too quickly. You have to purge yourself of internalized pressure—the
pressure to be a somebody, to be noticed. Rising into the light from
the deep, deep darkness, your eyes are naturally going to hurt as they
adjust. Like all acts of heroism, such a journey is an act of courage,
and it requires tremendous bravery and inner strength. When I turn
down an invitation to appear on television show because doing so
would be undignified, or because the producers want me to spill the
beans on a high-profile friend, you can bet I gnash my teeth when I
see the guest they chose instead of me. Or at least I used to. Now I
rarely even think about it. It's become so easy. I have made the decision to only do media appearances that relate to substantive issues
on which I have something important to say. And I have stuck to
that resolution. It was difficult at first, but now this chosen way of
life gives me infinite peace.

Our need for recognition is fed by our insecurities. When we
understand the root cause, we understand that seeing ourselves in
the spotlight won't make it better. When I first arrived at the Rabbinical College in Jerusalem as a student, I found that I was very far
behind my classmates. Most of them had grown up in extremely
religious, ultra-orthodox families, and they had years of study on
me. They could read Aramaic, the language of the Talmud, like it
was English and were equally conversant in Yiddish, while for me
every step was slow, hard work. Our schedules were grueling—we
were all expected to study fourteen hours a day—but I had to put in
eighteen just to keep up. Saturday afternoons were a time of relaxation and contemplation for most of my classmates, but I never
lifted my head from my books. I worked through lunch hours during the week, and late into the night.

I didn't mind that I had to work when the study hall was empty: I was working hard because I wanted to succeed. But often I chose a prominent place in the library to study, secretly hoping that someone would walk through and see me working while my colleagues were reading and taking walks and eating and otherwise enjoying themselves. Because I was so behind, I was horribly insecure. So I was desperate for people to know that at least I worked twice as hard as anyone else. Of course, as my studies paid off and I began to measure up to my better-prepared classmates, my insecurity abated, and it was less important to me that everyone know how much I worked.

I tell this story to emphasize that I understand how weak insecurity can make us. I don't think that our desire to be recognized stems entirely from megalomania. Perhaps I would have been less worried about who saw me in that library if there had been someone in my life to offer a little encouragement and love for the effort I was making. My family was not as religious as I was and not very supportive of my decision to be a rabbi; moreover, at the still impressionable age of sixteen I was already living in Israel, seven thousand miles away from my parents and siblings. I know personally that our efforts to be recognized can have their origins in nothing worse than a simple desire to be recognized for success or a job well done.

Other people's approval will always be important to us, and I don't think that's always a bad thing. I want my wife, for instance, to expect a high standard of behavior of me, and it is an honor to dedicate my life to living up to that standard. The difference is that living a life of biblical heroism means operating not out of insecurity but out of the confidence that comes with following the right road. When we're living in the moment, our potential flows out of us naturally, like the river flowing from a spring. Our deeds become an organic expression of our authentic selves. What we're doing is no longer detached from who we are, and we're not doing it to impress anyone else.

We need to succeed in the world, and in the eyes of those who love us, because it is the right thing to do, not because it's the only way we know to confirm that we have value. Only when we are able to leave our insecurities behind are we truly able to efface ourselves to something greater than ourselves. What freedom there is in overcoming the fear of nothingness! If you truly believe you have value—simply because you are human—then you no longer need the approval of the masses to tell you you're worth something. If you know your cause is noble, as Varian Fry did, then you don't need crowds of screaming fans to reassure you that you matter.

Walking away from the possibility of personal glory requires a tremendous leap of faith. But it is the only way to break the shackles of ego that motivate our every action and enslave us to the opinions of others. Look at your own life and ask yourself: Are you more worried about getting love and respect from the people who really matter, or from everyone else? In the same way that I'll choose happily to be weak and dependent—on my family, my friends, and my God—I'll gladly choose the obscurity of real relationships and an authentic, meaningful, purposeful life. As long as my children are happy to see me when I walk through the door at night, I'm not obscure. As long as the people I've helped joyfully join us at our dinner table, I'm famous. As long as my assistant greets me with friendship and respect, I'm fulfilled. It may seem like obscurity, but it's just a more authentic existence.

31

⁓

FACILITATE OTHERS

Oh, that I were as in the months of old, as in the days when God watched over me; when his lamp shone upon my head, and by his light I walked through darkness.

—Job 29:2–3

Light itself has no substance, and it cannot be captured. It lacks the strong qualities of the desk, the intricate and complex nature of the computer, or the beauty and splendid color of the painting on the wall. *But it makes them all possible.*

Perhaps we were put on this earth not just to be happy ourselves but to make others happy. Not just to succeed ourselves, but to encourage and applaud the success of others. Not just to feed ourselves, but to feed the stranger. One of the most beautiful teachings I have ever heard was said in the name of the Baal Shem Tov: "When you have a problem which seeks resolution, find someone who has the same problem. Pray for him and help him first. And God will then shower upon you abundant blessing and you will thrash your way out of the darkness and into the light."

We're raised to believe that the spotlight in our lives should be squarely on us. Having lost the ability to look outside ourselves, we search for "personal growth" through gurus, self-help programs, even travel. We enter relationships looking to have our needs met and our desires fulfilled instead of asking ourselves how we can be of service to the other person. If things don't work out in the most gratifying way possible, we're happy to wash our hands of that person. We choose not to have children, or postpone having them, because we don't want to lose any of our disposable income or freedom.

We're always looking out for number one. All of us want to be "the man," or "the woman," as opposed to the honorable man or woman who helped create "the man."

Rose Kennedy, who died at the age of 104, was never really seen as a role model for American women, although she was the matriarch of the fabled Kennedy dynasty. She gave up her career to raise nine children, and although her family spent much of its time in the public eye, she was content to remain in the background. Once an interviewer asked her why she had dedicated her life to her husband and children rather than herself. She said that if she'd made something of her own life she would have given only one great person to the world, but as a mother she was able to give nine. She was like an artist, crafting treasures to be appreciated by all. No one ever asked Rembrandt or Picasso why they didn't devote their lives exclusively to self-portraits. Why, then, do we ask mothers why they don't focus exclusively on self-promotion?

Children never used to be considered such a chore. People saw children as an embodiment of their love for one another, the natural outcome of marriage. Having children didn't necessarily interfere with their ability to function in the outside world either. Queen Victoria had nine children and still managed the world's largest empire, spanning 25 percent of the world's land mass. We can do so much, but we limit ourselves. Husbands and wives are concerned that having children will interfere with their love for each other. We have so much to give, and yet we insist on making our love exclusive rather than inclusive.

We need to make peace with this aspect of biblical heroism by turning our primary focus to making other people matter. We know there's no dignity without autonomy. America is based on freedom: the Jews were born as a nation when they were freed from Egypt. Shining light on others is the only way for us to preserve that freedom and protect this way of life. We are free to say what we want, to start a successful business, and to educate our children, but more important is the freedom of mind and spirit to do what we really want to do without worrying if we're making an impression. The true test of whether we've lived or not isn't to ask whether we've affected our environment, but whether we've had a *positive* affect on those around us.

The biblical hero has no use for games of one-upmanship and no need to remain constantly at the center of attention. His life is devoted to making others feel important. He lives by the dictum of Hillel: "That thing which you hate, don't do unto others." It is interesting to note that Hillel does not use the plural—he doesn't say "those things" but "that thing." In his commentary on Hillel's pronouncement, Rabbi Manis Friedman has said that "that thing" is to rob others of their dignity. Broadly speaking, there is one thing in life we all hate most, and that is rejection, or dismissal. Being robbed of our dignity, being made to feel that we amount to nothing. We may be able to handle not feeling like number one in a given context, but who wants to feel like a zero? The dictum of Hillel is clear: if you hate feeling like a zero, never make others feel like a zero.

Since the biblical hero knows he would be robbing people of their dignity if he treated them as if they didn't matter, he directs his life to making others feel special. The ancient rabbis said, "Who is wise? He who learns from every single person." To the biblical hero, other people matter. Their opinions matter, their life experiences are important, their love makes all the difference in the world. As we've seen, he is the first to greet people when he meets them on the street or sees them at a communal function. He exchanges pleasantries with people in an elevator instead of feeling too intimidated to open his mouth. He knows that the warmth he shows others will be reciprocated. And if it isn't, he doesn't give up in despair. He tries again with the next person.

The biblical hero has no need to subdue other people, or dominate them, to feel like he has value. When he hears of other people's good fortune, he is happy for their success. And if he doesn't feel happy for them naturally, he wrestles with his nature. For he won't accept mediocrity in himself—and being jealous of another's success is a mediocre emotion, the emotion of a small man. He reaches out instead of doing battle. For him, maintaining the connection, winning friendships, and being in a position to grant others dignity is the only hallmark of success. He feels good when he makes others feel good. He feels accomplished when he makes others feel accomplished, and he spends his life bringing others light.

Just as the moon deflects the sun's light onto the earth, the biblical hero is always searching for a way to deflect light onto others. When he graduates from college, he thanks his professors and his parents for facilitating his education. While other students go on drunken binges in their fraternities, he brings small tokens of appreciation to faculty members who made an impression on him. Halle Berry took a lot of flack for her acceptance speech at the Academy Awards. She was the first African-American woman to win Best Actress, and while that is certainly an achievement worth celebrating, you would have thought from the tone of her speech that she'd found a cure for cancer. People responded badly because she seemed so eager to claim all the glory for herself. In contrast, when Denzel Washington accepted his award the same night, he paid tribute to all the great black actors who paved the way for his success—and restored a measure of dignity to the night.

The biblical hero thinks, "I was placed on this earth to use my gifts to help you develop yours." We need to get some of this spirit back into our modern lives. We need to examine our lives and think about the ways in which we can dedicate ourselves more fully to facilitating the success of others. When we're successful, we have to be sure to share the credit with our teachers, our parents, our husbands and wives, our coaches, and our friends.

32

❧

BE A HERO TO YOUR CHILDREN INSTEAD OF A HERO TO THE WORLD

He who joyfully marches to music rank and file, has already earned my contempt. He has been given a large brain by mistake, since for him the spinal cord would surely suffice. This disgrace to civilization should be done away with at once. Heroism at command, how violently I hate all this, how despicable and ignoble war is; I would rather be torn to shreds than be a part of so base an action. It is my conviction that killing under the cloak of war is nothing but an act of murder.

—Albert Einstein, "The World as I See It,"
Living Philosophies (1931)

It's Friday night, and the rest and serenity of the Sabbath has just been ushered into my busy life. After the traditional hymns are sung, our guests are eager to partake of the meal, as am I. But there is one ritual left. Just before I recite the blessing on the wine, I summon my seven children, in descending order, to stand beside me as I place my hands on their heads and give them their weekly Sabbath blessing.

Although I grew up in a traditional Jewish home, this was not a blessing I received weekly in my home when I was a boy. The first time

I witnessed it was in my wife's home in Australia, just after we married. My father-in-law called my wife to his side just before the blessing on the wine, and she bowed her head dutifully as she received his blessing.

There followed an awkward moment when my father-in-law asked me if I wanted a blessing as well. At first I felt as if I were betraying my own father whom I had wished to honor and feared that I was supplanting in some way. There was something almost too intimate in receiving a blessing from my father-in-law, and I wasn't used to that kind of intimacy between father and son. My own father suffered much in life and survived by being tough, even around his own children, and since my parents divorced, I had grown up largely in his absence. Although he tried always to remain close, it was difficult with three thousand miles between us. But I was moved by my wife's example and by my own desire to make her happy, and so I bowed my head to receive the blessing as well. It appealed to me, and I've carried it on with the children whom God has blessed me with since.

In life, everyone is confronted with a simple dilemma. Each of us wishes to distinguish ourselves, to achieve a level of recognition to compensate for the insecurities we carry around with us. But we also recognize the need for relationships and a family life. And there are times when these two interests seem to present a distinct choice: you can concentrate on a successful personal life, perhaps to the detriment of your professional life, or you can focus on advancing your career, whatever the repercussions might be on your wife and children. You can either be a hero to your kids or be a hero to the world.

In our culture the preferred choice is sadly apparent. The Western world suffers from an epidemic, not of sickness and poverty, but of too few happy marriages and too many insecure children. The CEO of a multinational corporation is automatically labeled a success even if he's on his fourth marriage and his children don't speak to him.

As a rabbi, I have counseled hundreds of men and women who regretted making the wrong choice in this matter. But I'm also speaking from personal experience. I married at the tender age of twenty-one and promised myself that I would be a different kind of father. I would not put my work before my children. I really wanted to make my kids feel like they were of infinite significance.

Then, when I received an appointment to work as the rabbi to the students of Oxford University, I refocused my life, working as hard as I possibly could to service the spiritual and emotional needs of the students. During the day I gave the students classes and advice and raised the money necessary to bring in world-famous speakers to lecture for our organization. I came home late, usually well after my children were asleep, and after eating dinner with my wife, I marched straight to the computer to write my essays and books.

For several years I was a machine, and in certain worldly ways my work paid off. I quickly became one of Britain's better-known rabbis and the author of a number of noted books. I hosted world leaders as my guests at Oxford—everyone from Mikhail Gorbachev and Shimon Peres to Professor Stephen Hawkings and Benjamin Netanyahu. Although the weekends were reserved for my children, in fact we hosted about a hundred students weekly at the Friday night and Saturday afternoon Sabbath meals. I was sitting with my kids, but schmoozing with the students.

I was doing fulfilling spiritual work and was well on my way to feeling distinguished, climbing the ladder of success and gaining the respect of my peers, when suddenly I got a startling wake-up call. Our eldest child began exhibiting problems at school. She couldn't pay attention, and her grades quickly slipped. My wife insisted on taking her to a family therapist. In the course of one of the sessions my daughter said, "I dislike my friends. They always tease me. I don't like going to school. I even hate coming home because my sisters and brother bother me." The therapist then asked her, "So is there anything that makes you happy?" And she answered, "When my daddy comes home and plays with me, I'm so happy. Nothing bothers me." My daughter was becoming like me. Feeling neglected and valueless, she was becoming cynical and unhappy. And I was to blame.

When my wife told me this, I listened in stony silence. It was virtually the same thing I had told my teachers after I exhibited problems in school as well. I felt an abyss open beneath me. Was I going to transmit my insecurities to my children? Would I be responsible for their destruction? Was I destined to be a success outside the home and a failure inside it?

Those insecurities were still driving me, though. The insecurities of one generation are passed on to the next. For those of us who fear that our parents never offered us sufficient love, our almost incurable feeling of insignificance often leads to a manic devotion to professional success at any price. We're hell-bent on showing the world that we're special and deserve to be taken seriously. Unfortunately, external achievement only incites those demons, which feed off our weakness and pursue our destruction. The feeling of worthlessness is never assuaged, no matter how much money or how many awards we pour down its cavernous chops.

About a year later I was on the American book tour for *Kosher Sex*. I was away from home longer than ever before, but I justified my absence by convincing myself that I was earning money and a reputation that would benefit my family. About three weeks into the tour I made a routine call home. All my girls came running, but my six-year-old son refused to come to the phone. He was playing on his computer and couldn't be bothered to speak with me. "Tell him I'll talk to him when he gets home," he told my wife. My son was learning how to occupy himself in the absence of a father whose career was proving more important than his family. He was learning to live without me. His computer was supplanting my affections as his principal companion.

I was gripped by a pain that I have rarely felt in my entire life. I had an interview booked immediately thereafter, but I could barely concentrate. My professional success was turning from a blessing into a curse.

I was being a poor father—one who loved his children deeply, but not enough to make them a priority in his life. From this dark moment sprang two saving revelations. First, I was finally able to forgive my own father for his apparent neglect. Confronted with evidence of my own weakness, I saw at once how harshly I had judged him. He came to the United States as an impoverished immigrant and wanted to prove that he was as good as anyone else. All he wanted was what I wanted—a bit of recognition, a bit of attention, the feeling that he was significant—and he went after it the way he knew how. He thought that if the outside world said he was important, he was. I was no different and had no right to judge him.

The second realization was that I wasn't the success I had imagined myself to be. A father's first obligation is to make his children feel like the most special people in the world, and I had made my children feel ordinary. If they didn't feel loved, then I had failed. Again, I was in the very same position that my own father had been in. I was a hero to the rest of the world and a stranger to my kids. I grew up hearing from our entire community about what an amazing father I had, and how much charity he gave and how much he contributed to the community but his own wife and kids felt neglected. Simple logic dictates that you can't really call yourself a success when those who matter most to you think the least of you. So was I a success?

I credit my children with my own decision to strive for biblical heroism. I am now significantly closer to my father, and infinitely closer to my children. I try to give them at least three hours of my time each day, which is what the renowned child psychologist Dr. Stanley Greenspan maintains that children need in order to be properly nurtured. And I am a much better man as a result. I am their hero again, the way a father should be. Nowadays, when I travel, they complain about how much they're going to miss me, rather than accepting it as part of an ordinary routine.

We have to save our children before we can save the world. Who is the classical hero trying to impress? Strangers, who will abandon him the moment he suffers his first major defeat. Is it logical to assume that strangers will continue to love us even when our family members have long since given up? Is it so hard to see that when we impress the world with our money or our power, it's just the money and the power that they love? Can't we see that only our children want *us*, not just what we have to offer? Our children want the greatest gift of all—the gift of ourselves. We give our children objects in lieu of real affection, and then wonder why our children call only when they need some cash.

When I was a fundraiser, I watched an interesting pattern of success and wealth: one generation makes the money, the next generation squanders it. One of the main ways I raised money for our organization at Oxford was by helping successful parents with their problem children. Why do so many highly successful fathers raise troubled sons? Look at how they spend their time! Their share prices rise as they invest more and more resources into their business, but their kids' share prices sink. Their children feel devalued and deflated. I remember one big businessman who asked me to talk to his son and help counsel him through a difficult divorce. When I did, it became clear that the son really just wanted his father to show some hint of interest in his life. When I told the father this, he responded, "It's been so many years since he and I have really spoken, I wouldn't know where to begin." This was a man who had given a fortune to charity—who had all the time in the world for everyone except his own kids.

Isn't your family supposed to love you already, though? Presidential candidates aren't supposed to have to work hard to win the vote of their own family, whose loyalty is taken for granted. Winning over those who are already playing for your team doesn't always feel like a big victory. The same is true of parenting your children. We so often take it for granted that they're already won over to our cause that we make no effort to treat them as well as we do perfect strangers. And too often they end up as either bitter adversaries or lonely mediocrities whom no one has ever made feel valuable.

It seems incredible that throughout history so many men have made the same mistake. They think they'll find glory by conquering the world, only to discover that in the course of expanding the frontiers of their own empire, barbarians have come and sacked their capital cities. They find glory by conquering the world and lose honor by desecrating their homes. Long numbed by their husbands' neglect, wives take their frustrations out on his credit cards or sit alone at night fantasizing about other men. Their children, pacified by TV and Nintendo, go to school and look longingly to male teachers or more confident students as possible father substitutes.

There is precious little communication going on between parents and children these days. Too many American kids eat dinner with their families only on special occasions like Christmas and Thanksgiving. Most children find it difficult to talk to their parents about things that are bothering them in school and at home. In fact, statistics show that the most popular topic of conversation in homes is what television shows people watch. Imagine—people have real problems that they want to discuss with their families, and all they can talk about is whether *Dawson's Creek* is better than *Friends!*

This failure to communicate is widespread enough to qualify as an epic tragedy. Children grow up feeling their parents have somehow wronged them, then reach adulthood filled with resentment. They spend a lifetime trying to impress authority figures—first their professors, later their employers—all in the hope that finally they will be loved. Alas, when our children discover that it is only the productivity of their hands rather than the quality of their hearts that is appreciated by their employers, they sink deeper into the nether reaches of insecurity and fear. Often they spend years in therapy trying to work out these childhood dissatisfactions.

Having witnessed the oblivion that awaited me if I continued on my father's neglectful path, I vowed to try to change. I took it upon myself to come home every night and help my children with their homework. Even if I had to go out again that night, I would first come home for a while and help them do their assignments. At first it was great: despite the humiliation of having forgotten everything about multiplication, division, and geography (am I really expected to know where the Zambezi River is?), I loved it.

But after a few nights the jitters set in. I would walk into a Barnes & Noble and see all the new books coming out. I was being overtaken by everyone. Here were all these authors churning out acclaimed new books; what was I doing helping the kids with their homework when I could pay some high school student a few bucks to do it for me? I started yearning to pass the responsibility to someone else. Surely life is about the pursuit of excellence and maximizing my own potential, right? Wasn't I really wasting valuable writing time by adding 3 + 5 with my six-year-old? I had two outstanding book contracts waiting to be fulfilled. They tugged away at me. Without being productive at all times, I felt a pit of nothingness opening beneath me, and I began to fear that I would fall into it and disappear into eternal insignificance.

But that was the classical Shmuley talking—from the insecure perspective of the Public Adam. I wasn't really falling into insignificance. No one lost when I started spending more time with my children—everyone won. My relationship with my children started to change. My children started to change, becoming stronger and more confident. And I felt needed—a wonderful feeling! After years of chasing ephemeral glory, I finally felt like a hero, one of those rare men who had his priorities right.

We need to get creative about parenting. Humans are ingenious when it comes to solving problems, but first we need to have the will to find a solution. It took a little reorganizing to bring my children back into my life. I travel a lot, speaking and doing publicity for my books, lecturing in order to bring in income for my family, and doing my two daily radio shows. Whenever it's possible, I try to bring them along. When it's not, I ask the people doing the scheduling to make every attempt to have me home for Shabbat and the weekend. I sometimes even take a book we're reading together with me on overnight trips, and I read them their bedtime stories over the phone. If I'm on a big trip without them, I make videotapes of the places I'm visiting. It makes me feel connected, so it's a joyful thing for me to do, the next best thing to having them all along. When I get home, we all watch together. They might learn a little something about Italy, but more importantly the videotapes let them know I was thinking about them the whole time.

Now, every week when I offer my children the weekly Sabbath blessing, I place my hands on their heads and I wonder whether in the previous week I have earned the right to call myself a father. Have I earned the right to place my hands on their heads by virtue of being their biological origin, or am I the gardener who really nourishes his saplings with great care and love, ensuring their healthy development?

Of course I pray that my own children will be successful in their chosen professions. But even more than that, I pray that even if they never achieve success according to the traditional, tangible criteria that our world uses to measure such things, they will still feel infinitely significant. There's no need for every one of us to act like Joe Kennedy, making our kids feel that they have to be senators or presidents to get our attention. Far better to let them step off that insecurity treadmill and help them feel loved just for who they are. Take the time to show your children that their unique gifts are recognized. Show them how to be means-oriented—to learn for the love of learning, to do good for the joy of doing good—rather than goal-oriented. This is how I try to parent, in the hope that my children may one day look back on their daddy as a hero—not necessarily to the world but first and foremost in their own hearts.

33

❧

MENTOR SOMEONE

Few things are harder to put up with than the annoyance of a good example.

—Mark Twain, *Pudd'nhead Wilson* (1894)

The Talmud says that man is jealous of every other man in the world, with the exception of his son and his student. In both cases, he takes pride in having facilitated their successes and achievement.

Our children aren't the only ones who need our attention. Mentoring is one of the vanished arts of today's world. In days gone by, a man learned his trade by being apprenticed to someone else. Today you've got to learn it all by yourself, largely because those with the know-how do their best to hoard their knowledge. There's not enough glory to go around.

Real leaders create other leaders. They create opportunity for others, instead of destroying it. In the Book of Numbers, when the Jews rebel in the desert and God threatens them with destruction, Moses is at his wit's end about how to save them. He is concerned that his merit alone will not suffice. So he tells God he needs other leaders to shoulder the responsibility. God tells him to gather seventy elders; he will come and give them some of the spirit that Moses has and allow them to share the burden of leadership with him.

The first thing we see in this story is a leader who isn't threatened by the prospect of sharing authority. He is the exact opposite of a Stalin, who murdered his officer corps to ensure that his supremacy was never challenged, or a Mao Tse-tung or a Castro, both of whom refused to designate a successor. The classical hero dominates through fear. Moses knows that his own personal glory is immaterial in the face of the greater cause, and he welcomes the sharing of responsibility for the good of the people. The second thing we see is that God's command that Moses choose elders to share his prophetic spirit in no way diminishes Moses' spiritual greatness. He gives light without being depleted of light. The ancient rabbis compared Moses at this time to a candle whose flame can light thousands of other candles without ever growing weaker.

Parenting and teaching are glorious ways to mentor—to light young candles with our own flame. But we can afford to expand the definition as well. It would be wonderful, for instance, if every person on this earth had four or five people who came to him or her for advice. Wouldn't we all benefit? Wouldn't the advice seekers gain by having access to someone else's experience? And wouldn't that person feel needed and appreciated in return?

Facilitating others is a form of service and also a way to confer dignity upon someone else. When you mentor, or facilitate someone else's success, you're tacitly acknowledging that this person has more than a functional role in your life. It's the personal version of John F. Kennedy's famous exhortation to ask what you can do for your country, not what your country can do for you. You're saying, "What can I do for you?" instead of, "What can you do for me?" When we behave like biblical heroes, we are exercising our choice to be the best person we can be, and a natural outcome of behaving like a hero is that we make sure other people realize that they also have choices. When we feed a homeless person, we are expanding his range of choices. When we mentor someone, we are empowering her to realize that she has control over her life.

When I was trying to come up with some of the essential qualities of a mentor, I spent a great deal of time thinking about those who mentored me when I was young.

I was fortunate enough to have a meeting with the great Rebbe of Lubavitch at the time of my Bar Mitzvah. This meeting changed my life forever. I told the Rebbe that my parents' divorce had made me a cynic. I believed that every star would one day cease to shine. The world was made of incongruent pieces of a puzzle that could never fit together. His beautiful blue eyes welled up with a sea of compassion. "You have an obligation to ensure that no child utters such despairing words again. I bless you today to become a light and inspiration to the Jewish people and the world." Here was the leading rabbi in the world, at three o'clock in the morning, helping a child with a broken heart believe that his life could make a difference. He made me feel special and inspired greatness in me.

Another influence in my decision to become a rabbi, as I have mentioned, was the boyhood friend to whom I dedicated my book *Judaism for Everyone*. This man spent an enormous amount of time with me at a crucial time in my life. He had a phenomenal capacity for empathy, and he wanted to broaden my horizons, so he took me places and showed me things. He listened—really listened—to me, to all my hopes and fears and insecurities and dreams. He created a bond of trust between us by preserving my confidences; he never made light of anything I told him, no matter how trivial or silly it appeared in retrospect. He inspired me when I was inclined to give up. He raised the standards by which I judged myself. He encouraged me to make a great deal more of my life than I would have made of it otherwise.

Most of all, he was unquestionably authentic—he taught by example. Yes, we visited the elderly, but he would have made the trip even if I hadn't been tagging along. And in this way, he introduced me to a whole world of service and the spirit—a world I had no idea existed. A hero (and what is a mentor if not a hero?) should be a model of our own greatness. Gandhi knew this. There is a story about a mother who came to Gandhi to ask him to tell her son to stop eating sugar. "He's ruining his teeth. If you ask him to stop, he will." Gandhi said no. The mother came back a month later and asked him again. This time he agreed to speak to the son. The mother said, "Why didn't you agree last month when I asked you?" And Gandhi said, "Because last month *I* was still eating sugar." When we dedicate our lives to biblical heroism, we are finally in a position to be a real example to others.

Each one of us has been blessed with a spark of intelligence that can be nurtured. When we educate others, we are honoring this part of them, raising their unique human qualities to the light. Nurturing young minds, giving young people the tools with which to use their intelligence, is another way to confer dignity. Mentoring means more than teaching someone how to do something, although that can certainly be part of it. A master teaches you how to do; a mentor teaches you how to be. A master teaches you how to become a blacksmith; a mentor teaches you how to become a person. A master gives you a title, while a mentor gives you a name. Mentoring must include love. You can teach people a trade without loving them, but you can't transform them. I felt, at a very fundamental level, that my mentor loved me, and it was his love that opened my heart to the lessons he was providing.

It has been my very real pleasure to repay the favor that he did for me by doing it for others. At Oxford I was surrounded by students looking for meaning in their lives, and I tried to provide some kind of guidance for them when it was possible. If they were disconnected from their Judaism, I tried to reintroduce them to their faith. If they were estranged from their parents, I encouraged them to go back to them with love and forgiveness. If they were unhappy in their relationships, I made efforts to help them understand what an authentic relationship really is. If they were adrift professionally, I attempted to help them to isolate their interests and strengths, and where possible I made introductions that helped give them a foot in the door. In other words, I tried to use whatever gifts I had to illuminate theirs. And instead of depleting my energy stores, I have found these relationships to be among some of the most rewarding of my life.

Please note that there's a fundamental difference between a mentor and a savior. I'm not suggesting that you completely disrupt your own life to help someone else, or that you take their problems on yourself. And you must know that there are some people you just can't help. You can't help someone, for example, who's looking for a guru. You're there to shape and to guide, not to play God by telling someone else what to do. Your primary relationships must always come first. You can't mentor someone if doing so will upset your wife or your husband, or take you away from spending time with your children. Mentoring shouldn't be a full-time job, nor should it go on forever. An essential part of mentoring someone else is planning your own obsolescence, teaching that person how to live independently of you.

Contrary to popular belief, mentoring doesn't even necessarily have to mean enriching someone less fortunate or younger than yourself. It simply means putting aside competition and selfishness to share an experience with someone else. I recently read an article about the three big network news anchors. Their industry is completely beleaguered—their ratings drop daily, the networks are slashing their news budgets, and the three of them are on the edge of their seats every day, waiting to be replaced by younger and more attractive talking heads. These three men are literally the only people in the country who can understand one another's experience. And yet the article said that they very rarely get together to compare notes, commiserate, or brainstorm. Can you imagine this? These three men have everything in common but remain separated by one thing: the fact that they're competing with one another. That one thing prevents them from having a relationship. Maybe together they could come up with some way to build all of their businesses, to make more for all of them—there are a lot of television sets in this country. As it is, the article implies that they're busy hoarding their share of the shrinking pie.

When will we learn that there's more than enough to go around? When will we learn that when another succeeds, we also succeed? The faulty model of the Public Adam calls upon man to dominate others; the Private Adam, on the other hand, nurtures the world around him. We must learn to quell the inevitable envy that rises up in us when we hear that someone else has received something good. When a young artist earns a million dollars for painting a portrait, his older teacher—and all portrait painters—benefit, even those who traditionally command much less. The rising tide lifts all boats.

The mentoring relationship can be a challenge, but it has very real rewards. Primary among them is the satisfaction of knowing that we have done our best to step out of the spotlight, that we've used our light to illuminate another. And in the mentoring relationship, as with all other relationships, we exercise our gifts—an important consideration, since even our unique gifts can atrophy like muscles that haven't been used.

When we mentor, we achieve influence, and that is far greater than power. I am often asked by friends if I have ever harbored political ambitions. I respond by telling them that I am much too ambitious for politics. You see, I have never wanted to be the president. Rather, I would like to be the individual to whom the president comes when he needs answers, when he seeks advice, when he has problems, when he needs to find his way. I want influence, not power, and so I wish to be a facilitator. I would rather be the light rather than the object upon which the light is shown.

34

❧

FIND JOY IN THE EVERYDAY

The happiest is the person who suffers the least pain; the most miserable who enjoys the least pleasure.

—Jean Jacques Rousseau, *Emile* (1762)

A friend of mine was going through a period of depression. She had an extremely devoted husband who doted on her and took her for romantic getaways; she also had four children and a public relations job she loved. But her unhappiness got the better of her. She started going out nearly every night, leaving her teenage children with their father, until their grades began to sink. Her husband complained to me that the children didn't feel loved. When I asked her what was the matter, she didn't beat around the bush. "I do love my kids, but I admit that I'm not happy in a mothering role. It's too limiting. I feel confined at home. Three of my girlfriends are divorced, and one is single. They go out a lot, and I like joining them. It makes me feel free."

Why was this woman prepared to throw away this wonderful life for a few cheap thrills? What would cause her to be so shortsighted? I would answer that she had succumbed to the illusion that life is about fireworks celebrations rather than brightly shining candles that never go out. She didn't recognize the very real significance of her own life. She had allowed HBO's concept of a life worth living to supersede her own valuable existence. She had allowed herself to become bored with the everyday. Watching her children battle acne or snuggling up with her husband in front of a fireplace had lost its charm. These activities were too ordinary. Going out to a nightclub and feeling the glances of strangers upon her and her friends—that was exciting.

As far as I'm concerned, staying home with your children instead of going out with your single friends isn't even a matter of abstaining from something you really want to do. A club-hopping life may have its attractions, but in the long run what most people truly want is to strengthen their primary relationships and watch their children grow up. How does this woman want to feel when she looks back on her evening flings in a couple of years? Does she want to remember the joy of a first tooth lost, a first step taken, a first word read—or the martini flavor of the month at the trendy bar she frequented with her friends? How many regret-filled golden years do people need to have before we all get the message?

I'm not saying that this woman doesn't need, or deserve, excitement in her life. She and her husband should have thrilling sex. They should take fabulous trips and have wonderful dinners out. These activities shouldn't be escapes from her "real" life, though. They should be incorporated into it. All these things should augment her mothering role, not detract from it. When we speak of "the good life," what we mean by that is a life where the ordinary becomes extraordinary, the natural becomes miraculous, and the everyday becomes unique.

I'm sorry if this news bursts any bubbles, but life isn't about adventure. It's about service and authenticity. We assume that some things are boring and unsatisfying, that to sign on to a life of everyday heroism is to commit ourselves to endless drudgery and personal stagnation. I don't believe in having a stultifying marriage. Nor do I believe that unvarying routine is healthy. Rather, I believe in raising the ordinary to the extraordinary, making the natural miraculous and the commonplace unique. Instead of escaping from the everyday, we can, and must, elevate it to the heavenly.

A wife who sees her husband doing the dishes can surprise him from behind and passionately kiss his neck. A husband and wife who are about to go through the nightly ritual of fifteen minutes of sex followed by yawns can choose instead to have a sinful affair with each other (see my *Kosher Adultery* book for details). A father who feels that his kids aren't as exciting as his job needs to take the time to really quiz his young kids about their day at school. Chances are good that he'll discover that his kids are far more entertaining and insightful than his golf buddies. Why is an appreciation of the setting sun something that we reserve for our vacations? The sun sets every day.

If your own tendency is to ignore the little things in favor of the big ones, how can you change your addiction? How can you get to a place where you appreciate the depth and subtleties of the fabric of everyday life? First of all, I believe we have to wean ourselves off of the attractions of commercially sponsored fantasy. We have gotten to the point where we care more about the furniture on a sitcom set than the person at the other end of our very own couch, and we have to turn this around. We have to reinvest our time and energy in our relationships instead of in a culture machinery that devalues those relationships. Turn the television off and ask your spouse a specific question about his or her workday instead. Take a walk together, go out for a drink, instead of buying a movie ticket.

I've written a great deal about ways to keep a long, monogamous relationship charged, but some of the same tactics can work in our workplaces. You are responsible for your own life, and your job is exactly as boring as you make it. An acquaintance of mine is a world-famous fertility expert. Although he acknowledges that he's doing important work, he admits that he often gets bored doing the same procedures every day. To raise himself out of that rut, he took to putting a picture of every child that he has brought into the world on his office wall. Now, when you walk into his office, you can't even see the paint on the walls, which are covered with pictures of hundreds of babies. Some are laughing, others are crying, but they're all alive and kicking. "In these pictures, I find new life in my work every day. If I ever feel myself losing passion, I look at the wall and I know there is nothing higher that I can be doing."

We must replace commercial fantasy with authentic relationships, and the very real sense of value that comes from doing something inherently worthwhile. I also believe that we need to continue the process of edifying ourselves long after we leave school. Educating ourselves is a way to dignify ourselves. Americans have traded knowledge for entertainment. We want to turn off instead of engage. And as a result, we are losing our love of knowledge and the dignity inherent in being discerning and informed. After all, how much information can people have when they endlessly watch TV and listen to music? One of the most popular skits on *The Tonight Show with Jay Leno* is "Jaywalking": Leno walks around with the camera crew and asks people on the street very simple questions like, "Who commanded the Confederate troops in the Civil War?" Not only are most people ignorant of the name of the general in question, but most barely know that there was a civil war in this country at all. When he asked someone who killed Abraham Lincoln, the response was, "You mean he's dead?" Americans have lost their love of knowledge and now choose instead to be entertained by the ignorance of others.

Amid the considerable pain of being from a broken family, there were many things I gained from having had such a fractured childhood. It certainly helped prevent me from underestimating the little things in life. When I was a child, I would stare, transfixed, at fathers walking down the street with their sons. It was such a normal thing for them, and such an impossibly miraculous thing for me, since my own father was far away. Even as a teenager, I couldn't stop staring at husbands and wives as they sat on airplanes together. I couldn't believe how lucky these men were. Their wives weren't doing anything particularly extraordinary, but as they passed each other blankets or a bag of shared M&Ms, all I could think was, "Does he know how fortunate he is that his home travels with him?" To me, married life was a truly amazing spectacle.

The biblical hero also notices such couples, but his admiration for them is more authentic than mine. I was coming from a deficiency mentality: those people had the love and caretaking that I craved. The biblical hero recognizes the simple act of giving your loved one a blanket as an act of godliness. The natural response to experiencing the divinity that surrounds us is to be overcome with awe and reverence.

When Moses encounters the burning bush, he removes his shoes. Most of us, inured to the grandeur of nature, would have kept walking, much as we thoughtlessly ignore the loving gesture of a wife waiting for a flight with her husband. But Moses, who had worked his whole life to recognize his inner godly spirit, walked by a regular bush and saw something awe-inspiring. He saw something incredible within this bush, something that stopped him in his tracks.

When Rabbi Dovber of Lubavitch lay on his deathbed after a long and godly life, he told his young grandson, who was at his bedside, "Touch me and you will see that in these last moments of life I am no longer a body. I have already become one with that all-encompassing divine energy that permeates creation." The grandson put out his hand and held his grandfather's hand. "You are mistaken, Grandfather. I can feel your hand." His grandfather looked back at him and said, "You touch me with a hand, therefore you only feel a hand. Had you touched me with your soul, you would only have felt a soul."

The more we come in touch with our own godly nature, the more deeply we experience our own spirituality, and the more sensitive we become in turn to the divinity that surrounds us. Stated more simply, practicing goodness conditions us to see everything around us as special and worthy of nurturing. This vision is the secret weapon of the biblical hero. Bring intention and love to everything you do, and you enrich everyone around you, yourself not least of all.

When we experience the divinity in the world around us, we are no longer so desperate to escape from it. We can take joy in engaging with our environment instead of fleeing it. In the same way, when we connect with the dignity inside ourselves, we don't need to be terrified to look inside. There's no chance that we'll discover that no one's there. If you live by the strength of your convictions, then you're not afraid of introspection. You're not afraid to examine your deeds and your morality closely.

The everyday may seem to be made up only of small things, but the biblical hero really believes in the details. Every time we choose to embrace an everyday act of heroism, we are putting our best and truest face forward.

35

⁂

DEDICATE YOUR LIFE TO SERVICE

The service you do for others is the rent you pay for the time you spend on earth.

—Muhammad Ali

The stereotypical religious figure is someone sitting at the top of a mountain, isolated from family and community by his pursuit of a better relationship with God. Young people often take years to travel to far-off, exotic destinations, trying to "find themselves." I don't believe in this. As far as I'm concerned, it's no less a form of escapism than going to the movies. We're not supposed to drop out. The greatest figures of the twentieth century weren't monks living in the hills. They were nothing if not fully engaged in the world around them.

Whatever you need to know about yourself is there to be learned through service to your family, friends, and community. One friend of mine was born into an extremely wealthy family. She struggled her whole life against insecurity and fell into a downward spiral. She experimented with drugs to dull the pain of her life, and when that stopped working, she joined a radical cult that cut all ties between her and her family and friends. Whatever she claimed, she wasn't running toward something, she was running *away* from her life; instead of opting for the struggle, she opted out completely. If we don't participate in society in a meaningful way, we might as well be in a cult in the desert. As we've said, life is meant to be more than just adventure.

The concept of service has fallen out of favor, a problem that can be traced directly back to the classical hero's deficiency mentality: "If I help this person, then I will be deprived of something, so I'm going to need some kind of compensation to make up for it." We're only interested in helping those who will be able to help us later. We run a tally and wait for repayment, appreciation, recognition, a reward. Real altruism is a rare thing indeed. Service isn't reciprocal. It's not quid pro quo. Asking about the reward is the wrong question indeed. "How can I help to heal the world?" is a better one.

When you choose to see your life as one of service, you're released from the shackles of the ego and your own paltry agenda. Deciding to take three seconds out of your day to hold the door open for someone coming down the hallway carrying grocery bags feels like a small thing. But it's not a small thing at all. It's a dedication of your life, at that moment, to service. First of all, when you make the decision to stand there and hold the door instead of rushing on to the next important task of your day, you're saying, "How can I help you? How can I be of service?" instead of, "What can you do for me? How will this improve my life?" That's a major shift in perspective. And as everyone who's ever been the recipient of a good deed can attest, even the smallest gesture of goodwill increases love in the world. A bad day can be lightened just because someone was thoughtful enough to hold open a door!

Holding a door is a good thing to do, but it's most important that we rededicate ourselves to service especially when it's not convenient. I was waiting to board a plane from Miami to Washington one afternoon when I learned that the flight was being canceled. My appointments in Washington were tremendously important to me— I was meeting with two senators on a matter that could not be rescheduled—and I got on my cell phone immediately, scrambling to get on another flight. The woman next to me had no phone, and she was hysterical because her boyfriend was to meet her at the other end. She had no way of getting in touch with him unless she could catch him before he left to make the long trip to the airport. The woman at the ticket counter wouldn't let her make a long distance call. So even though it was inconvenient for me, I was happy to loan her my cell phone to make the call. Again, it seems like a small thing, but of course at the moment it wasn't small to either one of us. There are so many opportunities in the course of a day, a week, a lifetime, to serve others. Explore as many of these as you can.

The rewards of service are easily reaped. Humans need to feel needed, and when we offer our lives to service, the satisfaction is immediate. When God created Adam, He made it so that Adam could converse with all the animals, and even with the angels. But the Bible says that Adam was lonely. How could he possibly be lonely with thousands of beings to interact with? The ancient rabbis answered the question this way: Adam may have had lots of possibilities for communication, but no one needed him. Angels are perfect. They never need a shoulder to cry on or a short-term loan to bail out a business. Taking pride in our ability to be of service is one of the greatest defenses against loneliness. What Adam needed was to feel needed, and so God created Eve from his rib.

It's no accident that 90 percent of parenting is about service. You change diapers, you make dinner, you clean up, you pay tuition, you comfort, you teach. Having children is unquestionably an act of servitude. It's also one of the most rewarding things an adult can do. It should be a chore, but it's a joy.

"But how can I be of service?" you may be thinking. Well, what is your unique gift, and how can you use it to heal the world? If you can't say with confidence what your gift is, you probably have a pretty good idea what your best friend or spouse would say, so start there. Ask yourself: How can I use what I've been given to help alleviate pain? As for me, I believe that my own strength is passion, and spreading passion. I'm passionate about Judaism, passionate about relationships and marriage, passionate about children, passionate about America, passionate about Israel, and I try to use my passions to spread love in the world. Maybe you're a comforter, or a good listener, or a motivator. Maybe you're good at making cold people feel, or getting tight people to open up and talk. Maybe you're good at organizing big projects, or enlisting talent, or showing up when you say you're going to show up. Whatever your gift, you can use it to make the world a better place.

And the world is where your gift starts to blossom. All of our gifts are works-in-progress. Unless we utilize them, they never bloom from the potential to the actual. This is the real gift that service gives us—the opportunity to use our gifts the way we were intended to use them: to repair the world.

You may find that you can do good in unexpected places and that service takes forms you might not have anticipated. Loneliness is responsible for some of the most terrible pain in the world. So it is by definition a good thing to do when you help to ease that pain by introducing two people to each other. Matchmaking is a form of service and one that I find particularly rewarding. Listening to someone, carefully and seriously, is a service. It confers dignity upon the other person by making him feel like he matters.

A friend of mine was on a crowded train from New York to Washington when a young man took the seat to her left. A young woman seated in front of them leaned over the seats and said hello to him—they had attended the same college and had some friends and classes in common and had met once or twice before. Although he was shy and a little gruff, they struck up a conversation. When the young woman went off to the dining car to get some dinner, my friend quietly asked the young man if he'd like her to switch seats with his new friend. At first he declined her offer, but sure enough, when his friend returned with her sandwich, he decided to take her up on it. The two of them chatted merrily all the way to D.C. My friend was overjoyed. She never found out what, if anything, happened between the two of them, but she felt like she'd done a really good thing in facilitating their conversation.

And indeed she *had*. It didn't take much, this act of service, but it took something. So often the thing that makes a hero is just *doing* something instead of not doing it. All she had to do was put herself out there—such a little thing! But it's not a little thing to put yourself out there—it's easier not to, to stay out of it, to not get involved. The moment passes, and life moves on. If she hadn't said anything, maybe the two friends would have found seats together elsewhere, or maybe the conversation would have petered out. Perhaps it did anyway. But my friend held (or opened) a door for them.

One of the great (and surprising, to some people) acts of service you can perform is to need someone. Some of the loneliest people in the world are married. Maybe you don't confide in your spouse because you don't want to worry her, or because you don't want to admit that there are issues that make you anxious, or because you are so bored with her that you don't want to depend on her. If so, you've got it all wrong. When someone confides in you, rather than feeling burdened, you feel needed and respected. You feel like your opinion and your contributions matter, and you're flattered that you've been chosen to provide solace and comfort. Instead of worrying that your spouse will feel dumped on, the next time you're worried, take the time to confide in him or her.

It's an old cliché that idle hands do the devil's work, but it's not wrong. Humans don't handle idleness particularly well—they have a tendency to get into trouble. We have an obligation to celebrate our blessings, to live joyfully. It's no secret: miserable people treat people miserably, and happy people treat people well. I'm sure that we'd all feel a lot better if we dumped our MAO inhibitor prescriptions and got out there and helped someone else. Service might be the miracle cure for depression! Feeling needed is the perfect antidote to feeling worthless.

Charity and philanthropy, of course, constitute a widely neglected form of service. The average American family gives only 1.3 percent of its income to charity—this in an age of unrivaled wealth. It's not a question of need either: according to *Time* magazine, the richest 1 percent of Americans still give only 2 percent of their annual gross income to charity. Surely, we all find this disappointing.

Put simply, there is nothing more important than helping a fellow human to meet basic needs. People cannot have dignified lives if they are poor, or exposed to the elements, or having to watch their children go barefoot and hungry. How dignified can a life be that is wracked with pain and hunger or consumed by filth and disease? The essence of dignity is recognizing that every human being is magnificent. As humans, there are a few basic things that are necessary for our survival. It is important to honor the spirit of man, but it is also important to respect the body of man, and the body of man needs these things to survive. A child living in a box is not living a dignified existence, and no amount of eye contact and authentic conversation will get that child there until she's had a bath, a hug, a change of clothing, and a hot meal.

As a young rabbinical student, I remember how inspiring I found it to discover that the founder of Hassidic Judaism, Rabbi Israel Baal Shem Tov, first taught the peasant Jews of Russia how to farm before he taught them anything about God. His first interest was in their basic well-being. How could he enlighten them about the divine spark that existed within them when they were living in wretchedness and misery? So first he gave them hope and inspiration by showing them how to bring dignity to their bodies and provide for their families.

The Hebrew word for charity actually translates as "justice." If I asked you to hold twenty dollars for me and then came back to claim it, you wouldn't expect to be congratulated for returning my money. You're giving me back something that never belonged to you. In Judaism, it's understood that 10 percent of what you earn isn't yours. You have been entrusted by God as a guardian for the less privileged. You owe it to those less fortunate than yourself, and you can't expect congratulations for giving it back.

I believe that a good deed is a good deed, regardless of source or context. A successful Jewish investor friend of mine named Joseph, who had led a secular life totally outside the Jewish community, just recently started getting more involved with the Jewish community and paid half the cost of a new synagogue. His friend Marty, another secular Jew, called him on this. "Come on, Joseph," he said, "who are you kidding? You couldn't tell a synagogue from a mosque or an ashram. You're not doing any of this stuff because you're interested. You're doing it because you feel bad that you haven't continued the tradition, and you're trying to make up for it. This isn't tradition, it's guilt and superstition."

Joseph called me and told me what Marty had said. "Do you think he could be right?" he asked me.

"I think Marty is a thief," I told him. "Helping to build a synagogue is a good thing. Marty has robbed you of the feeling of meaning and goodness that comes from doing the right thing, which is your legitimate right." When a person gives charity, whatever the motivation, he has every right to feel a deep sense of satisfaction. Robbing people of that satisfaction by questioning their motivation is criminal. It's as much a theft as if you'd stolen their wallet.

Unlike Christianity, which stresses redemption in heaven, Judaism places its emphasis on redemption in the world. The best definition of service, then, is the use of one's individual gift to heal this broken world. But whether you believe that goodness is about personal redemption or public service, motivation or action, biblical heroism builds a bridge between the two. The biblical hero's own personal struggle against his baser nature enriches the world. His struggle to become a better person makes the world a better place.

Guilt, on the other hand, is a completely useless emotion, a poor substitute for actual goodness. If a poor man asks us for money and we don't want to give it to him, we say no. But we know we've done the wrong thing, so we feel guilty about it. Feeling guilty gives us a way to feel better about ourselves without sacrificing anything to alleviate the man's pain. It's an efficient solution—we get to exercise our conscience and we get to keep our money.

Judaism has always been more interested in actions than words. Jewish sages encouraged their followers to "speak little and do much," meaning that what is important is not the sentiment but the expression of the sentiment. That's why there is precious little written in the Bible about the minds or hearts of its heroes. It's the way we behave that ultimately determines whether we are leading great or mediocre lives. I've got news for you: feeling guilty doesn't make you a humanitarian. Just the opposite in fact. Guilt is like a moral Botox injection—it paralyzes goodness. It doesn't matter how badly you feel if that emotion doesn't translate into a compassionate act.

It's hard to give to charity. There will always be something you or your children want that beckons you to use that money earmarked for charity. There will always be something you'd rather spend money on than homeless people, or Israeli victims of Arab terror, or blankets for disaster survivors. But if you look closely at those things, you'll discover that there's nothing you need more than those people need blankets.

We have an obligation to practice charity and to ensure that we educate our children to understand its importance as well. I have a friend who is a financially successful advertising executive. He travels with his wife and kids all over the world. When they go on vacation, the first thing they do is visit a local homeless shelter or home for the elderly so that his children can distribute fruits and sweets. "I want my kids to know that they can never enjoy themselves if there are still people suffering."

When we clothe the naked and feed the hungry, we do it not just because it is the right thing to do but because when we do it, we're acknowledging the innate dignity in all of God's creatures. Before I married, I spent some time in Jerusalem at a yeshiva. One winter it was particularly cold, and it started to snow—an unusual occurrence in Jerusalem. As I was walking through the streets of the Old City, I noticed that an elderly beggar woman, whom I saw every day, was shivering. She had no coat. A Chasidic man walked past, took one look at her, and took off his warm coat and put it over her shoulders. He paused for another couple of minutes to do up the buttons on the coat, and then he went on his way.

I happened to see this man a few weeks later in a synagogue. "Rabbi," I said to him, "a few weeks ago I happened to see you give your coat to a beggar woman. I was so moved by the gesture. What moved you to undertake such a sentimental act of charity?" He raised his eyebrows. "Act of charity? That was hardly an act of charity. I saw a royal princess naked of her princely robes, so I gave her one of mine."

Most of us would have passed the beggar woman and turned our heads from her suffering. Some of us might have wanted to give her our coat out of pity. Our sense of benevolence would have dictated the action. This man was able to recognize that this woman was the child of God and that she was special because of this. He gave her his coat because she was a woman of dignity suddenly placed in an undignified setting. Her intrinsic worth was determined not by the fact that she was standing there begging, but by having been created in God's image. When he put the coat over her shoulders, he didn't just make her warm. He gave her dignity. He made her valuable, and that is what love is all about.

36

❦

SAY GOOD-BYE TO GLORY

It is a mark of many famous people that they cannot part with their brightest hour: what worked once must always work.
                                    —Lillian Hellman, *Pentimento* (1973)

One of the easiest ways to tell the difference between the classical and the biblical hero is to look at the extent to which each is prepared to let go once his objectives are reached. The classical hero seeks to glorify himself—sometimes by latching on to a cause, and sometimes even at the expense of the cause. Whatever the scenario, however, the main thing is that the classical hero *becomes* the cause. He can never distinguish between himself and the cause. Make no mistake: it's never actually about the cause, it's always about him. As a result, it is next to impossible for him to let go of the reins of power.

For Mao Tse-tung, his interests were China's interests, and vice versa. The same was true of Stalin. Above all, it was true of Hitler. One of the main reasons Albert Speer, Hitler's architect and Germany's armaments minister, got off so easily with a prison sentence at Nuremberg rather than being condemned to death is that he was seen as having tried to subvert Hitler. He realized from about 1944 on that Hitler was going to die, and when he did, Nazi Germany would die with him. I believe Speer was a charlatan, but the Allies believed he helped save Germany from Hitler.

Can you imagine what would have happened in this country in

261

the past fifty years if there weren't term limits on the office of the presidency? Virtually every classical hero had to have his cold, dead hands pried from the reins of power. In the entire history of the Roman Empire, only two emperors ever voluntarily gave up the purple. Diocletian maintained that all emperors should have to give it up, then he resigned and went back to farming. He'd done his duty, and now it was time to retreat. The overwhelming majority of the others were assassinated by their rivals and their own praetorian guard. Caesar cared about Rome only to the extent that it could advance his own interests, and his people knew it. The same was true of Alexander the Great. True, he Hellenized the world. But his conquests were mostly about self-promotion and self-glorification (although he did practice kindness with the ancient Israelites, and they rewarded him by naming their children after him). And he too was assassinated by jealous generals at the height of his power.

This trend continues all the way to the present day. I lived in England in the last years of the Thatcher era. Here was a woman who rescued Britain from sinking to the nether regions of becoming a third-rate power. She had the foresight to see that the European welfare state had had its day and that it could never compete against American and Japanese capitalism. So she privatized the industries, saving many of them altogether. She also made great efforts to save Britain's crumbling infrastructure and reestablished Britain's prestige among foreign nations. Yet by the time she left she was almost universally loathed. It was one of her former confidants, Sir Geoffrey Howe, who ultimately gave the speech that pushed her out. She was replaced by a man whom everyone agreed was not her equal in charisma, experience, or prestige. How could her fortunes have fallen so low?

People were prepared to put up with Thatcher's radical reforms so long as they were for the good of the country. Toward the end, however, it began to seem that she had placed her faith in *Thatcherism,* not in Britain. Her interests and those of the country had become indistinguishable in her mind. Once she had passed her sell-by date and refused to move over for younger, more inspired leadership, she became unwelcome to the British people. She lost the support of her constituents because they felt she no longer had their well-being in mind.

Nelson Mandela, on the other hand, spent but a single term as president of South Africa, and then—remarkably—retired. True, he was already past his eightieth year. But he could have pulled a Strom Thurmond and served until he could no longer remain conscious for more than a few hours a day, as many dictators have. Mandela was content to leave the world stage because he had accomplished his purpose. Having done his duty for his people, he stepped down as his country's leader so that others could carry on in his wake.

For hundreds of years in the Ottoman Empire it was commonplace for the new sultan to mark the beginning of his reign by immediately putting to death all his own brothers and other potential rivals to power. Napoleon put members of his own family on the thrones of Europe because he could not trust anyone else. One of Adolph Hitler's first acts as chancellor of Germany was to murder his partner, Ernst Rohm, so that he would have no rival for power. And of course Stalin was famous for murdering tens of thousands of the officer corps, all of whose loyalty he suspected.

Compare this behavior with the example that Moses sets in the Book of Numbers when he is told that two young men are suddenly prophesying in the camp of Israel, presenting a direct challenge to his authority. Joshua, Moses' apprentice, runs to Moses with the news, sure that he will quickly put a stop to the competition. But Moses says to him, "Are you jealous for my sake? Would that all the Lord's people were prophets, that the Lord would put his spirit upon them!"

We see the same trends in everyday life. There are two kinds of parents. One is the parent who has children out of insecurity. Some parents wish to be immortalized in the lives of their children. With their kids around, they feel important, like kings or queens in their homes. But the children of such parents are never allowed to assert their independence. Parents who have children out of insecurity will try to make every decision in their children's lives, and they will take it as an act of disrespect, even rebellion, if their children stand up for themselves. These parents lack the security in themselves to raise and love their children and simply let go—they can't let go of their children because they're living through them.

I knew a man in Florida who fit this description to a tee. From all external signs, he seemed generous and loving to his family, but in truth he was a tyrant. Once I was invited to his home for dinner. I asked his eighteen-year-old son what he planned to do after his high school graduation. Amazingly, his father answered the question for him, saying that the son would be going to college and then to law school, just as his father had before him. When I redirected the question to the son and asked if he was happy with that decision, the father said, "Of course he's happy with that. He wants to be a lawyer." All the while, the son stared at his plate of soup.

Everything was like that for this man—even his relationship with his wife. The saddest thing about the family was that neither the wife nor the children had any idea that they were in an abusive relationship. Indeed, they looked up to this man as a heroic figure. He was a good-natured person who worked hard to support his family, achieved success as a respected lawyer, and was much admired within his community. They were right, he was a hero—but a classical one. It was all about him in his mind: his wife was born to serve him, his children to obey him, and his community to admire him.

It therefore came as no surprise to me to later learn that this man was president of his local country club and that every year he ran for reelection. He simply refused to let go. Even when other members tried to question the inappropriateness of his continued dominance of the club, he simply showed them his record of achievement. "Let's face it," he said, "none of you could do as well." And so he bullied them into submission as well.

Another father I remember from my years as a rabbinical student in Jerusalem was a hospitable man who was kind enough to invite me to his home on several occasions for the Sabbath. What I remember most from the time I spent at their family table was the contrast: on the one hand, this man was an impeccably gracious host; on the other, he was the most distant father I had ever seen. In the two years that I was an occasional guest at their table, I never once remember him referring to his children by name; instead, he called them "Boy" or "Girl." He would enthrone himself at the head of his table and bark out, "Boy, bring me tea." With his daughter he was only a little gentler: "Girl, please bring bread to the table." He never once rose from the table himself. His wife and his children ran to serve him. I always regret that I never mustered the courage to say to him, "Sir, the Bible commands children to honor their parents. It presupposes, however, that parents will also be loving enough to reciprocate and show affection to their children in return."

The imperial household is a giveaway of the classical hero. These are the men and women who will do everything for their families, as long as their families are willing to pay the price of total obedience. This pattern continues even after the children move out and marry. The number-three cause of divorce in the United States is parental intervention. There are so many parents who have never severed the umbilical cord, and so many children who have never learned to live independently, that even after their child's marriage many parents continue to rule the roost, to the chagrin of the new spouse.

The tendency of the classical hero to cling to power manifests itself in areas far removed from parenthood. It's there in the company founder who never learns how to delegate and who centralizes all the power in his own person. He is immensely distrustful, especially of the younger talent in the company. Rather than seeing the benefits of collaboration, he sees only its dangers. Handicapped by insecurity, he cannot hope to share. All the glory that his underlings win will be gained at his expense, for there is only so much glory to go around.

Ultimately the greatness of Moses is demonstrated when God tells him that he will not fulfill his lifelong dream of leading the Jews out of the wilderness and into the promised land. When Moses learns this, after years of struggle and hardship, he doesn't argue or complain. His only request is that the people not be left without a leader. "Let the Lord, the God of the spirits of all flesh, set a man over the congregation, who may go out before them, and who may come in before them, and who may lead them out, and who may bring them in; that the congregation of the Lord be not as sheep which have no shepherd" (Numbers 27:15–18). It's a remarkable demonstration of the way a true biblical hero puts the cause above and beyond any personal concerns.

The biblical hero is famous not for his ability to give up the spotlight but for mentoring others to serve the cause as ably as he did before them. The Bible repeatedly presents scenes of blessings being conferred from one generation to the next. Isaac blessing Jacob and Esau before his death. Jacob blessing all his children before he dies. Moses laying his hands upon Joshua and conferring the spirit of leadership upon him. Moses delivering his final blessing to the Jewish people before his death. What's important is not the individual but continuity.

The classical hero has a hard time letting go of his emotions too. He holds on to anger, to grudges, to fantasies of revenge, to hurt and humiliation. Maybe he's embarrassed by his parents, worried that they will reflect badly upon him, anxious about how they'll go over in other people's eyes. We're all guilty of holding on to our unhealthy emotions to some degree—and the only solution is just to let them go. Change your focus—worry about what your mother thinks rather than what people think of her. Don't feel compelled to negotiate with these emotions or to legitimize them by having them. Just let them go.

The classical hero's inability to let go extends even to death. I remember the heroism of my mentor and guide, the Lubavitcher Rebbe. I was in London on a June morning in 1994 when I heard the news that he had passed away, and I rushed to catch the next plane to New York. Arriving there only twelve hours later, I stood in the midst of a throng of fifty thousand people waiting for the coffin to arrive and the funeral to commence. There I stood with men of distinction, famous rabbis, even the mayor and the governor of New York. And then, as the wailing and the cries of the women reached an absolute crescendo, the casket came out. It was a simple pine coffin, constructed from the wood of the Rebbe's prayer lectern. They carried the body a few hundred feet, and then it was placed into an ambulance and carried off.

But wait? Where were the eulogies? This was the most famous rabbi in the entire world. Why weren't we hearing from the governor, the mayor, the chief rabbis of Israel? Because the Rebbe was a hero. He had ordered that there be no eulogies. He had worked forty-five years at the head of the greatest Jewish educational network the world had ever seen, instructing and inspiring hundreds of thousands of men and women to become communal activists and educators. He was one of the most celebrated Jewish leaders of all time, a tireless worker for the advancement of spiritual commitment and human dignity. And then, in a moment, he was gone. There was no trumpet fanfare, no twenty-one-gun salute. It was enough that God knew. He had done his duty, and then, without any ceremony, he quietly retired from the world stage.

Moses too died the way he had lived. "Then Moses, the servant of the Lord, died . . . And God buried him in the valley . . . And no one knows his burial place to this day" (Deuteronomy 34:5–6). Moses retreated from the world stage without even a wake of distraught followers trailing behind him. No equestrian statues, no troubadours or minstrels singing epic poems. He didn't want or need a great monument built to him in a public square. He didn't care if he was going to be remembered, because he never thought of himself. Rather, he served God and man because he was born for that purpose.

Mausoleums are the monuments that classical heroes erect in their own honor so that they will be recognized even from beyond the grave. The pharaohs are entombed until this day in the great pyramids of Egypt, surrounded by gold and jewels and art. Some of them even had their servants killed and buried with them. (It must have been hard to find decent help in the afterlife.) The classical hero can't think of anything beyond himself, so he can't imagine nonexistence. He can't stand the idea of disappearing without a trace, as Moses did. He would prefer to have living men spend decades preparing his coffin so that he is not forgotten. Some of the greatest artistry of the Renaissance masters—men like Leonardo da Vinci and Michelangelo—graces the tombs of powerful men, like the Medicis or the less pious Popes. The classical hero needs to leave a monument—like graffiti—so that people will always remember that he was once here.

Is this really how we want to be remembered? With a great big stone hut in a graveyard, where people can sit and contemplate our legacy of bloodthirst and ruthlessness? Or would we rather live on in the great art we've created or sponsored, or in the loving memories of our children and grandchildren, who remember us for our love and patience and generosity and humility—the qualities of a biblical hero?

37

❧

BIBLICAL HEROISM IS FREEDOM

Self-respect is the fruit of discipline; the sense of dignity grows
with the ability to say no to oneself.
— Abraham J. Heschel, *The Wisdom of Heschel* (1986)

One of the things I have noticed in my many years as a counselor
is that people do not understand that they have choices. In life there
are always at least two paths to choose from. Depression results
when people feel that they are stuck, that they have come to a brick
wall and that there is no way over, under, or around.

I hope that over the course of this book it has become clear that
we all control our destinies. Unlike an animal, which is ruled by
instinct, every human being has the choice to be good or evil. My
friend Rabbi Harold Kushner once told me that the essence of religion is to replace instinct with choice. A man can treat his wife like a
queen, or he can abuse her emotionally and physically. He can hoard
his money and buy cars he'll never drive, or he can donate money for
the vaccination of impoverished children. He can read books or
watch television—or both! His life doesn't have to be governed by an
instinctive code of behavior. He is free to make any choices he wishes.
Choice is an intrinsic component of dignity. The ability to choose
gives man a mastery over the universe that animals cannot share.

Just as God created the world, so we too are blessed with the
capacity to create our own universe. Success comes when we realize

that we have this choice and we work to make a world for ourselves that embraces the godliness within, in order to achieve a utopia around us. The rewards of striving for biblical heroism are many, but I believe that there is one central benefit—freedom.

How many of us are truly free? How many of us even understand what the word means? We spend a lot of time talking about liberation in this society, but I'm not sure we know what we're talking about. In a *Time* magazine cover story in 2000, 47 percent of American women said they didn't depend on a man for happiness. Many of these women had chosen to focus on succeeding in their careers instead of searching for a relationship. Of course I think women should pursue professional goals and seek fulfillment outside the home as well as within it—we all have talents that can best be served in the working world. We have a legitimate need for majestic recognition of our ability to impact the world. But are we really blind enough to want to be completely liberated from the shackles of love? Are our ideals truly misplaced enough to choose money and our jobs over the enriching emotional rewards of a relationship? And if women won't rescue men from their obsession with status, who will?

Our tendency is to assume that the fewer rules we have, the freer we are. But like children who are comforted by a somewhat rigid structure, we can find true freedom only when we conquer ourselves.

Here's an example. In 1998 my dreams came true with the publication of a best-selling book. I had published other books, but although they sold well, it was mostly within the Jewish community, with my mother purchasing the lion's share of copies. *Kosher Sex* took me on a book tour throughout the world—until one day I was in South Africa, delivering a lecture in Cape Town. Sitting in the front row was an attractive woman who was listening very intently to every word I said, nodding her head at every point, seeming to absorb every last syllable.

After the lecture people stood in line to get a signed copy of the book. The woman in the front row waited until the very end. By the time she came to me with her book, her eyes were red from crying. "I'm a desperate woman," she told me. "I need to speak to you privately." It was already late, and I had to wake up early the next morning to fly to Johannesburg. I asked if she could call me on the phone. "No, I really need to talk to you face to face." Since the lecture was in the ballroom of the hotel where I was staying, I agreed to meet her in the lobby for fifteen minutes before I retired to bed.

"I've been married for eight years, and we have three kids," she told me. "I have never had one erotic or passionate moment with my husband. He's a complete workaholic. I barely see him. And when I do see him, his mind is elsewhere. He has never given me even one orgasm. I had resigned myself to a passionless life and found satisfaction in my children and volunteer work, but then I bought your book. The more I read, the more I fell in love with your words, your vision for a fiery life, and I feel like I began to fall in love with you. I so badly want to experience the things you write about, but I can't even discuss this with my husband." All the while, she looked right at me with piercing eyes.

I didn't know how to react. This had never happened to me before. Sure, I'd written a successful book about sex, but I'm not exactly Robert Redford, and I'm unshaven to boot. I'm short, or in the modern vernacular "vertically challenged." I'm the father of seven children, and a rabbi, for goodness' sake. Most important, I'm married. At first I didn't know what to say, so I just sat silently. Then, after a while, I spoke. "Okay, I'm confused. Why are you telling me this?" She answered, "Don't you get it? I'm a desperate woman. I feel like I'm dead. There's nothing alive in me anymore. I need passion. I'm so desperate for it that I'm ready to go sit in a bar and get picked up by a guy. I want you to teach me about passion. I need one passionate experience. I'm so alone. I feel like I'll die without it." This situation was getting out of hand.

At that moment I thought of two things. The first was my wife, seven thousand miles away, awaiting my return, looking after our kids, loyal and faithful to me. How would she feel if she even *heard* this conversation? The second thing I thought of was myself. What kind of person did I want to be? To say that I was flattered by this woman's words is an understatement. She was very attractive—and she was practically throwing herself at me. But was this who I was? A man who could be seduced by a desperate and lonely woman who had read my book?

I rose from the couch, paused to collect my thoughts, and spoke. "You're right. You have a real problem in your marriage. What your husband is doing is cruel, and everyone has a right to happiness. You and your husband both need help and counseling, but I am not the one to provide that help. I don't want to let you down, but if my wife were here, listening to this conversation, she'd be hurt and upset by it." And with that, I quickly scribbled the name and number of a local rabbi with whom I was acquainted and who I thought could help, promised that I would call him in the morning and alert him that she would be calling, said a polite good-night, and took the elevator to my room.

And as I walked away something amazing happened. You might think I would have felt a moment of regret as I thought about the forbidden and erotic delights that I'd just passed up. But I felt something entirely different. It was pride. As I walked down that hotel lobby I felt the wings of angels buffeting my stride. I felt like a *hero*. What was it that made me feel that way? Just this: I had proven that I could reciprocate the infinite love and loyalty my wife had always shown me.

Napoleon breaking the Austrian lines at Austerlitz, or Lindbergh crossing the Atlantic—those men had conquered only a small portion of the world, a battlefield or an ocean. I had conquered an entire world: my own inner world. I had conquered time and space to become a master of myself. I had stared the beast in the eye and I had overcome.

I want to be clear about this. I didn't refrain from indulging in this woman's offer because I wasn't inclined to; almost any man would have been inclined to. Nor did I refrain purely out of consideration for my wife, for I knew that my wife loved me enough to forgive me even if I had done it. And neither did I refrain only because of God, because although my faith is the most central aspect of my life, it is not always sufficiently strong to ensure that I do absolutely everything in accordance with God's will. Rather, I refrained because I wanted to be a hero. I held back because I knew that no great man would do something so mediocre. I refrained because I knew that only a weak man would fall into that situation. And I wanted to be great.

And the amazing thing was, after it was over, I realized that I had made no sacrifice. Whatever illicit pleasure I could have had with that woman was easily overshadowed by the immense pleasure of feeling like a hero. When I went back to my hotel room alone, I had won the struggle with myself. I had made a choice—and that meant that I was free.

I immediately called my wife up in England and told her, "Did you know that you are married to an historical figure? One of the great heroes of history?" She thought I was crazy until I explained. Then she was overjoyed and proud. (Although she did make it clear that I would have been a dead man had I even thought of going ahead).

Life presents us with an endless series of challenges and decisions, and it is the choices we make, when we wrest control of ourselves, that establish us as heroes. In its vivid and timeless stories, the Bible tells us again and again that all greatness stems from mastery over self—not just achieving self-control, but rising above the material and becoming godly. Our illicit passions, selfishness, anger, materialism, defeatism, faithlessness, laziness, the part of us that would give up life for death—learning to overcome all of this is extremely liberating.

The difference between the biblical and the classical hero is as simple as the difference between being and doing. You don't *become* a lawyer or a doctor—you practice law and medicine, and when you stop doing so, you don't vanish into thin air. However, you *are* a son, or a father: no matter how cavalierly you take the responsibility, or how uneasily it sits with you, you cannot change the fact that you are a parent.

How free are we when we're chased by our insecurities? How free are we when we work eighty-five hours a week to keep up with the Joneses, or spend our lives depriving ourselves of food so we'll look more like one of the vacuous idols that have been proposed to us by Hollywood? The formula for leading a fulfilling life is to bring our internal desires for godliness, goodness, selflessness, and altruism to the fore and allow them to replace more primal inclinations: jealousy, selfishness, materialism, and self-centeredness. "Doing" is slavery. "Being" is liberation.

It is within our power to begin experiencing that liberation immediately, by recognizing our inner dignity and conferring it upon others through acts of goodness. This is heroism—the kind of heroism that gave Noah the nobility to swim against the tide of civilization when "all the earth's inhabitants had corrupted their ways." The kind of heroism that inspired Abraham to plant the seed of monotheism that would eventually destroy all the false gods of the earth. The kind of heroism that led Joseph away from judging his brothers' act of attempted fratricide to forgive them and feed them instead. These men knew true freedom, and I encourage you to begin to experience it as well.

38

❧

YOU *CAN* TAKE IT WITH YOU

I sing, not of arms and the hero, but of the philosophic man: he who seeks in contemplation to discover the inner will of the world, in invention to discover the means of fulfilling that will, and in action to do that will by the so-discovered means.
　　　　　　　—George Bernard Shaw, *Man and Superman* (1903)

There are people, such as the Dalai Lama, to whom biblical heroism comes naturally. This book was written for people, such as myself, for whom it does not. In fact, I often joke that I am destined for the role of the biblical hero—against my will. I might have preferred to be a great battlefield general, or president of the United States, but I know that God, in his infinite kindness, has better things in store for me. Even that joke comes from a classical perspective: I still can't pretend I don't care about success or the way I am perceived.

Although I struggle with such things on a daily basis, I am grateful for the struggle. I'm glad I can do more than plow thoughtlessly through life, chewing my cud. No matter how agonizing the decision, how thick the internal combat, how difficult the victory, I thank God for the ability to struggle to realize my heroism, because there's never a day when I don't feel alive. I am still ambitious. I do believe I have the potential to be a great man. I don't believe that any of us were put on this earth to live out a life of ordinariness. I recognize the need to rise to the challenge of goodness, and I feel honored to have the chance.

What God searches for in humanity is not righteousness but transformation: our gradual change from a materialistic, indulgent physical species to a spiritual people with foresight and a joyful understanding of our purpose on earth. The effort to change ourselves for the better requires a significant expenditure of energy on our part. Even true biblical heroes must struggle to become even better than they are.

Why do we do things that compromise our unique sense of self, our dignity? Because we cannot see the significance of our own lives. The spotlight of biblical heroism illuminates that significance, allowing us to see our own potential for heroism. We have all had those moments of illumination, and it is our challenge to reach for that clarity in our everyday lives, when the struggle to be good seems overwhelming.

Last summer I went up to visit some of my children at their camp on visiting day. We were all happy to be together, to be sure, but they were completely entranced with camp and their friends there, and they'd seen me two weeks before, and for the most part it didn't seem like an extraordinary day. I joked to my wife that they seemed happier to see the dog. But as I was dropping them off, my eldest daughter threw her arms around my neck, weeping. She didn't want me to leave. She wanted her father more than she wanted the fun and activity of her life with her friends at camp. At that moment, as sorry as I was to see my daughter crying, I knew that all the time I'd devoted to my children had been worth it. *This* is what's important, I thought as I dried her tears. How could I ever have thought it was anything else?

God asks Moses to ascend Mount Sinai, and when Moses reaches the top, God shows him a vision of the Menorah and tells him to replicate it in a gold, three-dimensional form. Moses goes back to earth to re-create this instrument in order to continue the divine illumination he has received on high.

Most of the time we live in the valley. We change diapers, do our jobs, eat our spaghetti, and go to sleep. We are prone to cynicism, boredom, a lack of empathy and generosity. But there are moments in every life when God takes us up the mountain. There are those moments when we seem to witness life from a higher plane. Sometimes they take place on the singular days of our lives—our wedding day, or at the birth of our first child. But they happen on less momentous occasions as well, as on a gorgeous fall morning—or on visiting day at camp.

In those moments something happens to us. Suddenly, hatred is purged from our heart and we feel an affinity with all of God's creatures. In these moments we feel inspired and moved by the beauty in our lives and the beauty of the world around us. We are lifted above the monotonous and the mundane, the alternating dullness and temptation of our daily lives. We feel a camaraderie with all human life, and for that instant we are able to rid our hearts of jealousy and hatred and feel grateful for all of our blessings and content with our place in the universe. It is a profoundly joyful feeling.

And yet interwoven with such moments of epiphany is the recognition that we cannot reside in this ethereal space all the time. Sooner or later we have to come down from the mountain and return to reality—no one lives up there. But what we can do is build our lives according to the blueprint that we saw there atop the mountain. Just as God told Moses to build the menorah-candelabra according to the vision that he witnessed atop the mountain, so too God tells us all to illuminate our lives based on the insights we garner in moments of inspiration.

Is the fact that we have to come down to the valley necessarily devastating? Immediately after the tragedy on September 11, we were treated to an extraordinary display of human love and kindness. People stood on street corners with water and food for the people streaming over the bridges into the outer boroughs of New York. The lines to donate blood were so long that the Red Cross had to turn people away. Money rushed in from all over the country and from all over the world.

Interpersonally things were different too. Estranged parents and children found each other and apologized. Couples put aside trivial arguments and bickering, happy just to have each other in good health. Strangers on the street made eye contact and greeted each other with warmth. Needless to say, this feeling of goodwill and love didn't last. New Yorkers went back to being New Yorkers, and America went back to watching sitcoms. So was it all a waste? Did September 11 make any difference at all?

I say that it did. Because even if we can't continue with the living inspiration we derived from surviving those tragic events and commemorating the innocent men and women who gave their lives, we have now been atop the mountain. We have all now seen the promised land. And we all know what it feels like to look at the world through a lens of love rather than through a cloud of hate. We all now know what it's like to carry a heart filled with compassion rather than being dragged down by everyday bitterness. So we now have no excuses. We have eaten from the king's table, and now that we've tasted something better, we'll never truly be satisfied with the nutrient-free junk they shove at us from the drive-thru window.

The Talmud says that at the wedding of your child you will dance with such abandon that you will even embrace your worst enemy. You will be so happy that you will feel grateful to everyone around you for being kind enough to partake of your joyous moment. This isn't a temporary giddiness. It's a moment of connection with a higher reality, a place where you perceive things not merely as they are but as they ought to be. The biblical text instructs us not to let it end there. When you return to business the next day, hold on to those memories and the vision of what you saw when you were dancing. Be kinder to your workers. Show more patience with your customers. Follow the harmonious vision you glimpsed atop the mountain.

The purpose of these transcendent moments is to offer us a vision of a more perfect world, a more perfect community, a more perfect self. After these times we see life from the pinnacle of existence rather than from the valley of deprivation. Despite their evanescence, such experiences are not only useful but essential. They help show us how we will be rewarded by our continuing struggle to be good, and they renew our hope. They reenergize us so that we can rededicate our lives to following in the footsteps of the biblical heroes before us.

We may not be able to have those kinds of miraculous feelings every day, but we must still go about our lives behaving as if we did. We have an obligation to reinvent our lives in the valley according to the pattern we have seen atop the mountain, the divinely inspired vision of our own heroism. We have all been up the mountain, and like Moses and Martin Luther King Jr. before us, we have seen the promised land. As we gaze upon it, we recognize it immediately. It looks surprisingly like the world we already inhabit: the city we already live in, the home we already share, the family we already love. We don't have to cross any river to obtain it or defeat any enemies to conquer it. All we need is to turn to this garden we are given and cultivate it with all the love in our hearts.

And as we stand here with our shovels, filling the earth and removing the weeds, we discover that not only are we really inhabiting paradise, but that paradise is built by everyday, ordinary heroes, just like you and me.

ACKNOWLEDGMENTS

❦

First and foremost I would like to thank my wife, Debbie, who is the personification of the biblical hero. In the fifteen years we've been married, she has taught me so much about doing the right thing simply *because* it's right. Debbie is self-effacing and always sacrificial. Ever-prepared to put the interests of others before her own, she has not only raised seven wonderful children (with my not-altogether-absent input) but has also opened up our home and offered hospitality, beginning with our eleven-year tenure at Oxford University, to thousands of visitors. Whenever we have these large gatherings such as the Friday night Sabbath supper, I take the spotlight, while Debbie contentedly moves about in the background. But her work on the sidelines is a product of an inner confidence and an inner light that ensures she never has to be in the forefront in order to shine. More than once I have heard people say that I may be the one who brings people in, but Debbie is the one who keeps them coming back. How right they are!

I also want to thank my children, Mushki, Chana, Shterny, Mendy, Shaina, Rochel Leah, and Yosef, who are my light and joy. I love writing books, especially if they sell. But what I prize most in life are my children, and I hope never to fail them as a father.

My mother is another pillar in my life who conjures images of sacrificial efforts on behalf of others, and I must express my gratitude to her as well. She has given her life to my four siblings and me, and in return she has the unparalleled devotion of each of her children. More important, however, she has always been a paragon of inspiration and kindness to all who know her. Any goodness that exists in my heart comes largely from her. In addition, my father, who always taught me about the importance of using one's blessings to help others, and who has overcome every adversity to succeed in life, has conditioned me to love and serve God for His own sake, and with no thought of any reward it might entail. The grit I have to persevere through troubling times derives from my father.

My brothers and sisters, Sara, Bar-Kochva, Chaim, and Ateret, are not only my best friends, but the noblest people I know. They have been far greater siblings to me than I have been to them. But, hey, I'm their little brother; at least they got to beat me up when I was a kid.

I especially wish to thank my good friend Laura Tucker. She edited this entire manuscript, convinced me of the validity of my ideas, and greatly enriched the final product with profound thoughts of her own. This book could not have happened without her efforts. Not only was Laura's final edit amazing, but being able to work with her every step of the way was also a privilege. I have worked with many editors, but few have so impressed me with the depth of character and kindness of heart Laura displayed. She also showed tremendous love and kindness to my children, even when they were pulling her hair while she was attempting to type. Most of all, Laura's writing is possessed of an uncanny ability to get to the heart of the matter, and she greatly simplified some of the more complex ideas in this manuscript. I remain eternally grateful to her for outstanding input.

I would also like to say "thank you" to my publisher and very close friend, the legendary Judith Regan, for always believing in me, for her friendship, and for her frequent appearances on my radio shows—both my New York morning show, which I jointly host with my dear friend and brother Peter Noel, and my nationally syndicated afternoon show. Judith is one of my favorite guests, and anything but the bland stereotype that most people have come to expect from publishers. A nationally famous talk show host in her own right, she is a supreme dynamo, super-smart, and a lot of fun. To have a publisher who is so enthusiastic about your ideas gives you the great enthusiasm to write, and I am much in Judith's debt.

Cal Morgan, my commissioning editor at Regan Books, has wrestled with me about so many of my ideas before they have been committed to writing, and they have largely been refined through his challenging insight. The outcome of our wrestling matches invariably makes for a far better book (even though I'm usually pulling my hair out as he rejects draft after draft), and I want to thank him sincerely for being such a good sparring partner. Cal is universally regarded as one of the smartest and savviest editors in all of publishing, and any author who is overseen by him has already won the lottery, whether or not his book becomes a best-seller (which I surely hope this will be). A man of natural humility and gracious character, he is a credit to the entire industry.

I also wish to thank my very dear friend and professional adviser Ron Feiner, whose wisdom guides me through all of life's vicissitudes. But what greater appreciation could I offer him than to have dedicated this book to him as a true biblical hero. I love you very much Ron, and thank you for everything.

Most of all I offer thanks to the great Creator of all existence, who gave us life so that we could be heroes. It is God's guidance, love, and infinite blessing that has provided the light that illuminated every letter in this book. May God bless us all always.

—Shmuley Boteach
Englewood, NJ
Spring 2003